Zoar, Gornal Wood

THE LIFE AND THES OF A METHODIST CHURCH

Ward Jones

ISBN 978-1-3999-9812-3

DEDICATION

For all those people who
crossed the threshold of
Zoar Methodist Church and
without whom this book
could not have been written.

Introduction

Zoar, Gornal Wood – the life and times of a Methodist Church records the history of the substantial building, Zoar Methodist Church, which dominates the centre of the Black Country village of Gornal Wood, though had it not been for the spread of Methodism across the country in the eighteenth century there would be no story to tell. Methodism began as a reform movement within the Church of England, led by two Anglican clergymen, brothers John (1703-1791) and Charles (1707-1788) Wesley. Despite the brothers' desire to remain within the Established Church, opposition and disputes led ultimately to separation and the foundation of a new Christian denomination, the Methodist Church. The story commences with an account of how Methodism reached the Black Country, the establishment of a Methodist presence in the nearby town of Dudley in the second half of the eighteenth century and the visits of Dudley-based preachers to Gornal Wood, which resulted in a small gathering in the village, meeting initially in the homes of its members. From such small beginnings, a strong Methodist presence would be established at the heart of the village.

Understanding the emergence and early history of Zoar requires an exploration of how Methodism's advance nationally was overshadowed by dispute and division especially in the early years of the nineteenth century. What happened on the national scene was soon replicated in Gornal Wood, leading to a split in the village's Methodist Society and the 'exiles' organising themselves to a point when they were able, eventually, to open a building named '*Zoar*', the first of two such named buildings on the present site. The background explained, succeeding chapters tell the story of the life and times of Zoar and its people, through to its closure as a Methodist church in 2023.

In 2012 I was granted the privilege of a three month sabbatical from my work as a Methodist Minister. I had in mind a number of possibilities, however, the one certainty was to use the first couple of weeks putting together a brief history of my home church, Zoar in Gornal Wood. My paternal forebears had been long involved with Zoar and it played a major part in the first 20 years of my life. My appetite for this 'little project' had been whetted by a visit to North Wales the previous year when friends, David and Christine Webb, showed me a picture of my home chapel as it was in the nineteenth century. I didn't recognize it. I didn't know there had been a previous building on the site. I wanted to know more and was surprised to discover that a large collection of church records had been preserved along with various pieces of printed memorabilia, penned notes and photographs. The 'little project' took on a life of its own. Having gathered a useful amount of material, I then found my interest diverted by a desire to find out something about the lives of the people who attended the chapel and the village community in which they lived, all of which lead, in 2022, to the publication of *Gornal Wood – the transformation of a Black Country village*. In 2023, I recommenced my Zoar-related research, having learned that the Methodist community had ceased to meet there and believing it to be important that the story behind the building and the people should not be lost to posterity.

Glossary

An explanation of Methodist organisation and terminology.
Within the Methodist Church nationally, a number of secessions occurred, firstly at the end of the eighteenth century and then through the first half of the nineteenth century. While this study concentrates on two in particular, *Wesleyan Methodism* and the *Methodist New Connexion* (and its successor the *United Methodist Church*), all 'branches' had the same basic organisational structures. Differences chiefly had to do with the relative power and influence of ministers and lay leaders, along with some differences of practice within the various governance bodies. The glossary identifies the common key components within the structures.

Class:	The Class was the smallest unit within Methodism. Each class consisted of small number of members of a local Society, led by a Class Leader and expected to meet weekly for Christian fellowship and reflection.
Society:	'Society' was the word used originally to describe a local gathering for worship and fellowship. An individual Society consisted of a number of classes supervised by a Leaders' Meeting. Membership of the Society was recognised by use of the Class ticket. Non-members were welcome to attend meetings, which initially met in houses or rented premises. The Wesleys, before the break with the Church of England, insisted Society meetings should not take place at the same time as services in the local parish church. Church buildings began to proliferate following the breakaway. Gradually the term fell out of usage, being replaced by 'chapel' or 'church'.
Circuit:	A Circuit consisted of a number of Societies within a particular area. Each one was served by appointed itinerant preachers/ministers. Early on they were sometimes called 'rounds' as they identified a location from which preachers travelled round, or did a circuit, of preaching engagements.

District: The District consisted of a group of Circuits within a particular locality. The District Meeting was supervised by the District Chairman and was responsible to Conference for the execution of the rules of the Connexion.

Connexion: Each branch of Methodism constituted a 'Connexion' in its own right. So, for example, the Wesleyan Connexion was the whole organisation of Wesleyan Methodism - all the circuits and chapels connected to it. The term originated among the Societies which were accepted as being 'in connexion' with John Wesley.

Conference: The Conference was the governing body of the Connexion, meeting annually. In early Wesleyan Methodism it was composed solely of preachers, whereas in the Methodist New Connexion it had a balanced representation of preachers and lay leaders.

Itinerant preacher: The itinerant preacher was a full-time regular preacher assigned to a Circuit by the annual Conference. The term was used in the eighteenth and early nineteenth century, gradually being replaced by 'Minister'.

Superintendent: The Superintendent was the senior preacher / minister in a Circuit. He usually presided at the Quarterly, Leaders' and Trustees' Meetings.

Local Preacher: The Local Preacher was a lay person approved (later, training was required) to preach and appointed to do so within a Circuit.

Stewards: 'Society' and' Circuit' Stewards were lay leaders appointed by the Leaders Meeting and Quarterly Meeting respectively. They were responsible for various administrative and financial matters.

Trustees: Until major governance changes were introduced in 1974, trustees were appointed locally, being legally responsible for the maintenance of chapels, for the servicing of their debts, and ensuring they were used for purposes in accordance with the Conference Deed (The Church's governing document).

Quarterly Meeting: The Quarterly (or later 'Circuit') Meeting exercised general oversight of a Circuit. It had an undefined composition until the mid-nineteenth century, but always consisted of the ministers and stewards in the circuit and sometimes included class leaders, local preachers and trustees.

Leaders' Meeting: The Leaders Meeting was originally instituted as a regular meeting of the class leaders to review the 'spiritual condition' of the Society and with a particular responsibility for the admission and oversight of members. Its responsibilities grew over time, taking in all matters concerning the life and activities of the Society.

Quarterage A sum of money paid to the Circuit Treasurer every three months as a share towards the total 'Assessment' to be raised to cover Circuit and national expenses.

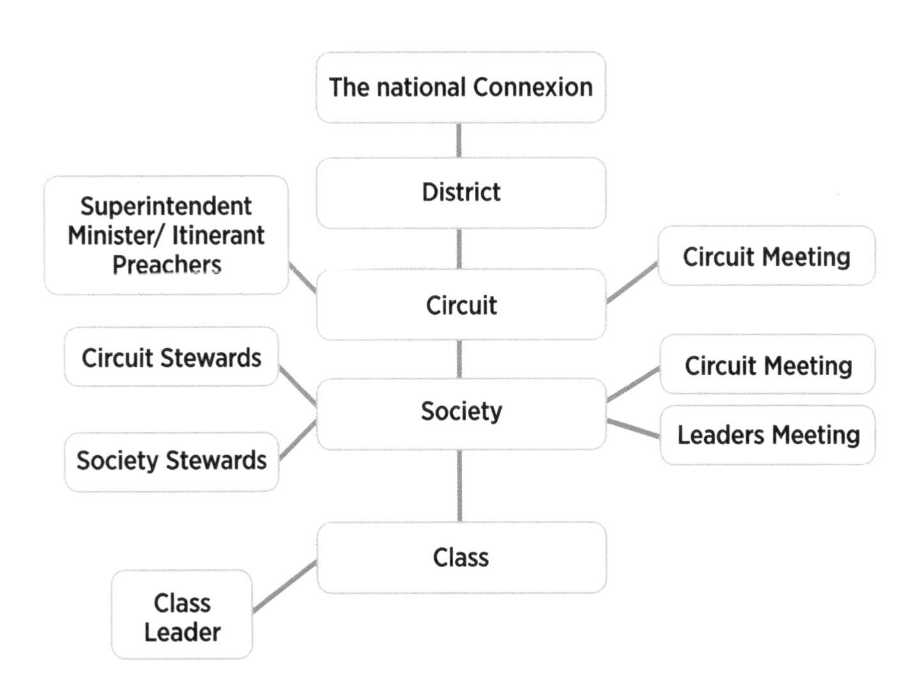

Figure 1: The structure of Methodism

Acknowledgements

This book could not have been written without the actions of those who helpfully kept minute and account records, pamphlets, service leaflets and so much more, a veritable archive, all of which was eventually placed in the church safe, installed in 1926. Most notably, the first treasurer of Zoar who, expelled from the Himley Road Society, took the account book with him and used it to record the income and expenditure of the 'exiles'. In later generations, J T Tennant, Joseph Brettle and other unidentified individuals and, in more recent days, John Jones. Despite the amount of material available to me, there are gaps in the telling of the story, because, for example, some minute and account books are missing. This means I must include words of apology to anyone who expected to be mentioned in this book but cannot find their name or that of a relative. I am more than happy to receive details, especially pictures, which could be considered for publication, if a second edition of this book is occasioned.

Thanks go to the many people who have helped me turn these resources into a story worth telling, particularly Vera Aston, Bill Caldwell, Brian Cotterill, Rose Didlick, Revd Tim Flowers, Glynne and Margaret Hale, Revd Colin Hartley, Anne-Marie Hobbs, Revd Steve Jackson, Brian Jones, Rhys Jones, Linda Morris, John Powell, Mick Toole, who has prepared the book for printing and, above all, my wife, Linda, for her editorial oversite of the text, without which this would be a more challenging read. Needless to say, any mistakes are mine, not hers.

Contents

PART ONE:
SETTING THE SCENE

CHAPTER ONE

The 'Methodys' are coming

How did Methodism arrive in Gornal Wood? The story begins in Wednesbury, the first Black Country town to be successfully missioned by the 'Methodys' as they were nicknamed locally. Methodism spread rapidly in the locality, establishing itself in other towns including Dudley and its success there subsequently led to the establishment of a Methodist Society in the nearby village of Gornal Wood.
Wednesbury was described by John Wesley as *"the mother-society of Staffordshire"* [1] and in 1746, when Circuits were first listed in the *Minutes of Conference*,[2] it was the sole Black Country name recorded. There were seven Circuits, among them Evesham which included Shrewsbury, Leominster, Hereford, Stroud and Wednesbury.[3] At the following Conference it was among ten places specifically identified from which named *Assistants* [4] were to engage in mission work. For the months of July and August 1747 James Jones and James Wheatley were to be based in Wednesbury.[5] James Jones was a local man, from nearby West Bromwich, whose name is woven into the story of early Black Country Methodism. A man of property who kept a carriage and servants, he served Methodism as a 'half itinerant',[7] a term indicating a preacher who had his own source of income.

Wednesbury: Methodist Foundations in the Black Country

Missionary activity in Wednesbury began with a visit by Charles Wesley who in September 1742, preached at 'The Hollow', a natural amphitheatre in the locality.[8] John followed on Wednesday 5 January 1743. Having set out early that morning from Leicestershire and, travelling most of the way in atrocious weather conditions, he arrived in the town at 4.00pm and preached at the Town Hall in the evening. The following Sunday he preached again in the same place at 5.00am, then attended worship led by Vicar Edward Eggleston at the local parish church. After this service, he went to preach at the Hollow accompanied by most of the congregation.[9] This visit inspired the establishment of a Methodist Society in the town with 29 members, which soon increased to around 100. In the early days meetings were held at the house of John Sheldon, who lived at Crabb's Mill.[10]

Figure 2: The Hollow and, on the left, Crabbs Mill

Four months after his initial visit, Charles underlined the rapid growth of the Society in Wednesbury, while at the same time highlighting the opposition and persecution which accompanied it,

> ***Friday, May 20.*** *Got once more to our dear colliers of Wednesbury. Here the seed has taken root and many are added to the church. A Society of above 300 are seeking full redemption in the all-cleansing blood. The enemy rages exceedingly and preaches against them.*[11]

The Methodists in Wednesbury and the surrounding area found themselves caught up in brutal rioting aimed at destroying their missionary endeavours.[12] These so-called 'Wednesbury Riots' would subsequently assume a significant place in Methodist folklore, being some of the worst opposition experienced in the whole of the country. At their height, John himself was the focus of some violent treatment on a visit in October 1743.[13] The Methodists' cause was not helped by the way in which even some Justices of the Peace encouraged and sided with the mobs[14] and it was not unknown for the local Anglican clergy to do likewise. Among this latter group were Vicar Eggleston who, having initially welcomed the Methodists, subsequently preached forcefully against them.[15] In the following February John received a report from James Jones which indicated that things were no better. Conscious of this, he went on to write about the way the Press was not averse to making life difficult for the Methodists. A report in the *Whitehall and London Evening Post* suggested that it was the Methodists who had caused the rioting.[16] In 1745 John was moved to publish '*Modern Christianity: exemplified at Wednesbury and other adjacent places in Staffordshire*'.[17] It offered a detailed account of the sufferings of the Methodist folk, along with an affirmation of their steadfastness, and as a rebuttal of the '*gross misrepresentations*' made in an attempt to generate hostility towards them.

Figure 3: John Wesley facing the mob

Charles was quite shocked by his brother's experiences, as his own Journal indicates,

> ***Friday, October 21.*** *My brother came, delivered out of the mouth of the lion! He looked like a soldier of Christ. His clothes were torn to tatters. The mob at Wednesbury, Darlaston and Walsall were permitted to take him by night out of a Society-house and carry him about several hours, with a full purpose to murder him.*[18]

The intensity of the difficulties faced by the new converts in this locality led Charles, when he experienced trials elsewhere, to describe the protagonists as being '*full of that Wednesbury devil.*'[19] He organised a collection to help the Wednesbury Methodists, sending one Thomas Butts to them with £60.[20] He also dedicated a hymn to them, "*For the Brethren at Wednesbury".*[21] Verse 4 reflects their experiences and commitment,

Smitten, we turn the other cheek,
Our ease, and name, and goods forego;
Help, or redress no longer seek
In any child of man below;
The powers Thou didst for us ordain,
For us they bear the sword in vain.

The experiences of those locals caught up in the violent opposition were exampled in the testimony of Edward Millington, whose maternal grandfather had been one of those to suffer harm. Samuel Lees who ministered in the area in the 1860s recorded Millington's memories,

I do not personally recollect much of Mr John Wesley or the early Methodists, but my mother was intimately connected with them, and her father, John Hughes, suffered in the great riots (1743-1744). He was twice carried home disabled, from injuries inflicted by the mob. My mother was a little girl at the time, and she remembers that one of the mob struck Mr Wesley on the mouth with a stone, while he was preaching in the open-air. Notwithstanding the blow, however, he continued his sermon, and quietly wiped away the blood.[22]

Methodism's Arrival in Dudley

The experiences of the Wednesbury Methodists were paralleled in nearby Dudley. Following a visit to Birmingham in 1744, Charles mentioned Dudley in his journal and what was happening there,

Wednesday, February 1. *At Dudley our preacher was cruelly abused by a mob of Papists and Dissenters (the latter stirred up by Mr Whitting, their minister). Probably he would have been murdered, but for an honest Quaker who helped him to escape disguised with his broad hat and coat.*[23]

Perhaps out of compassion, on hearing of these experiences, he chose to visit the town two days later, and noted in his Journal, '*Preached unmolested within sight of Dudley. Many Shimeis called after me, and that was all.*' [24]

John continued to pay regular visits to Wednesbury and from 1749 frequently combined them with time in Dudley,[25] where, to begin with, his reception was not exactly welcoming,

On Tuesday 24, about noon, we came to Dudley. At one I went to the market place and proclaimed the name of the Lord to an huge, unwieldy, noisy multitude, the greater part of whom seemed in no wise to know wherefore they were come together. I continued speaking about half an hour, and many grew serious and attentive, till some of Satan's servants pressed in, raging and blaspheming, and throwing whatever came to hand. I then retired to the house from which I came. The multitude poured after, and covered over with dirt many that were near me, but I had only a few specks.[26]

In 1751, John experienced a more peaceful, though not wholly positive reception,

Monday, April 1 *I rode to Dudley. The dismal screaming wherewith we were welcomed into the town gave us reason to expect the same kind of reception as I had when I was there before. I began preaching immediately in a yard not far from the main street. Some at first seemed inclined to interrupt, but when they had heard a little, they grew more attentive and stayed very quietly to the end, though it rained a great part of the time.*[27]

Charles was similarly positive on his one other recorded visit to Dudley, which took place in July 1751. This time he found that, 'the many hearers seemed to drink in every word'.[28] John was able to report another encouraging reception in 1760,

Friday, March 7. *I rode over to Dudley, formerly a den of lions. I was constrained to preach abroad. But no one opened his mouth, unless to pray or praise God. I believe the steady behaviour of the society has made an impression on most of the town.*[29]

The Revd. Alexander Mather, who, in 1760, was stationed in the Staffordshire Circuit, which included Dudley,[30] wrote subsequently of on-going success in the locality,

The next year [1760] I was in Staffordshire where it pleased God to work in a very eminent manner… In one night it was common to see five or six (and sometimes more) praising God for His pardoning mercy. And not a few in Birmingham, Dudley, and Wolverhampton, as well as in Wednesbury and Darlaston, clearly testified, that the book of Jesus Christ had cleansed them from all sin. Meantime the societies increased greatly.[31]

However, persecution continued. Mather recorded the difficulties Methodists faced, particularly in Birmingham and in Wolverhampton, where the preaching house was pulled down, no sooner than it had been built. In Dudley, he was aware that people were filled with *'terror'* at the prospect of what the mob might do and therefore it is impossible to know to what degree Wesley's conclusion, based on his March 1760 visit, was commonplace or merely temporary and exceptional.[32]

The formation of a Methodist Society in Dudley, as opposed to a Methodist preaching presence, was greatly influenced by the Southall family. William Southall (1737-1822), a lifelong stalwart of local Methodism, was a member of the first Dudley Chapel Trust (formed in 1788) and whose service to the Church was significant enough to merit an obituary in *The Wesleyan Methodist Magazine* for 1823. The obituary made use of Southall's own papers for much of its detail, recording how his parents attended Methodist meetings in nearby Tipton and going on to state, [33]

> '... *it pleased God, in his Providence, to send that extraordinary messenger of heaven, the Rev. John Wesley to Dudley, who preached in the street, and whose sermon was made a blessing to my father, who was one of his hearers.*'

The Southalls' home became the first meeting place of the Society. As well as serving as a trustee, William became a Class Leader and Local Preacher, the tribute to him concluding, '*He was for many years, the attentive and affectionate nursing-father of the Society at Dudley.*' [34]

As the local Society grew, it was able to adapt a building in 'The Mambles' as its first proper preaching house, albeit in a less than inviting part of the town.[35] It joined a growing list of Methodist properties in the Black Country which included Tipton Green (1750), Wednesbury (1760), Darlaston (1762) and Wolverhampton (1763).[36] John commended the Dudley building following a visit in March 1764,

> **Fri. 23.** *I rode to Dudley, formerly a den of lions, but now as quiet as Bristol. They had just finished their preaching house, which was thoroughly filled; and I saw no trifler, but many in tears.*[37]

In 1788 a substantial purpose-built chapel was erected in King Street,[38] described by John as '... *one of the neatest in England*'.[39] It was built with two projecting wings which were used as residences.[40]

Figure 4: King Street Chapel, Dudley

However, the town and the appointment, do not seem to have merited such a high accolade, if one early nineteenth century minister is to be believed. The Revd. Joseph Taylor, who had been President of the Wesleyan Conference in 1802, wrote to one of his colleagues, Richard Rodda, declaring,

I was only one year [1813] in Dudley, for they keep no horse, the walks are considerable, and the dirt in winter can hardly be described.[41]

Methodism takes root in Gornal Wood

King Street chapel, Dudley, was the setting for an event which led to the establishment of a Methodist presence in Gornal Wood. On one of John Wesley's later visits, possibly his final visit of Tuesday 23 March 1790, he preached in the chapel. The congregation included one Tom (surname unknown), a coal miner and barber in Gornal Wood, along with three fellow Gornal miners, Bill Turner, Joe Southall and Jack Moore.[42] The outcome was typical of so many who responded to Wesley's preaching: their lives were turned around, and they started to meet together for Christian fellowship. Preachers from Dudley began visiting Gornal Wood in 1791, meetings taking place on Sunday evenings at a cottage in Furness Row (a left hand turn off the southern end of Cinder Road, coming out from the village centre), reported to be a less than salubrious location.[43] Indeed, at that time the village itself had a poor reputation as a violent and uncouth place,

A few cottages dotted here and there; men as wild as untamed colts, without any education in the majority of cases, only a few who were able to read or write .... The one object in life is to get money, either by working in coal-mine or forge, or brutal sports.[44] *No church or chapel, school or meeting house, where selfishness and greed was rampant, their one aim, to get money and spend it in drunkenness and brutality.*[45]

While this description was written some 100 years later, contemporary accounts confirm its accuracy. As late as the 1870s one anonymous visitor to the Black Country commented that, 'most of those who go to church to be married are unable to write their names. Drunkenness abounds. A very large proportion of the miners and ironworkers neglect public worship and may be seen dawdling about on the Sabbath, gambling, pigeon flying etc,' [46]

At first, the Methodists continued to meet in various cottages on the southern edge of the village including that of Bill Turner,[47] located on what today is Chapel Walk, a lane off the main Dudley to Himley Road, alongside the site of the present-day Himley Road chapel.

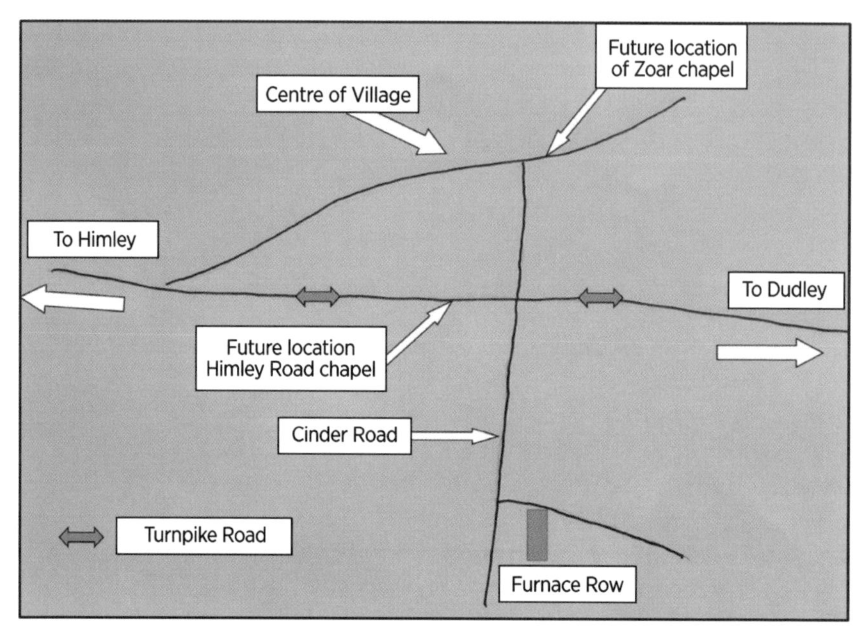

Figure 5: Furnace Row, on the southern tip of the village

Before they had a purpose-built chapel, in 1810 they acquired a *'certain building commonly called the Sow Pit situated near the Turnpike Road leading from Dudley to Himley, Gornal Wood, in the parish of Sedgley, registered for Protestant Dissenters by Jas. Shipman, Rich. Oakley, Thos. Barrs, Henry Hall and T. Theodosius'* [48] and established themselves as a constituent society in the Dudley Circuit.[49] The building was to be their home for some sixteen years. Among the first entries in the chapel account book[50] is a payment of £1/4/od in 1827 for *'one year's interest on £48'*, followed in 1829 by *'Paid to Mrs Tilley for old chapel debt £48/0/od'*, which must have been a loan to cover the cost of the Sow Pit building.

Plans were made to erect a purpose-built chapel in the 1820s but putting them into practice was delayed by a miners' strike. Many Methodists being numbered among the strikers meant money was short and so the necessary funds could not easily be raised.[51] However, during the strike the Methodists, having secured a plot of land, spent time and effort preparing the foundations. Many continued to labour on the project even after the strike had finished and on 10 December 1826 the chapel was opened. Built at a cost of £238/8/od, it was paid for initially by a loan of £240 obtained from a Mr Bayley.[52] The event was mentioned in The Wesleyan Methodist Magazine for the Year 1827,[53]

GORNAL WOOD, in the Dudley Circuit - Dec. 10th, a new Chapel was opened at Gornal-Wood, two miles from Dudley, by the Rev. Messrs. Sutcliffe, Simpson, and Hunt, on a spot of land granted by a nobleman. The collections were [£] 11.8s. It will be used for a Sunday and a Day-School, instruction being greatly wanted in that neighbourhood.[54]

Of the key figures involved in the opening services, Joseph Sutcliffe, John Simpson Jnr. and Joseph Hunt were ministers in the Dudley Circuit, while Sutcliffe was also Chairman of the Birmingham District to which Dudley belonged.[55] It was Sutcliffe who had solicited a plot of land from the *'nobleman'* mentioned in the magazine report, John William Ward, the first Earl of Dudley. Sutcliffe described how this came to be in a letter written some ten years later to the prominent Methodist, the Revd. Jabez Bunting, following a conversation with the earl after a Bible Meeting,

In about a month I ventured to send my grammar for the good of his Lordship's children, adding that we had 39 members in society at Gornal Wood, and that Sammy's house, a poor collier where they met, would not hold 30. His Lordship at once gave us land.[56]

The new church and its fledgling Society were attached to a Circuit which in 1826 recorded the largest membership in a District of 14 Circuits, reaching from Hereford in the West across to Hinckley in the East and from Wednesbury and West Bromwich in north to Evesham in the South.[57]

Birmingham District Membership in 1826

The six largest Circuits	**Membership**
Dudley	2000
Birmingham	1785
Wednesbury	1465
Wolverhampton	700
Stourport	690
Hinckley	516
NATIONAL TOTAL	**231,045**

Nationally only 11 Circuits were larger than Dudley (e.g. Bristol 2,570; Truro 3,300; Liverpool 3,000; Manchester North 2,250),[58] showing how the Circuit had developed in the time since the Wesley brothers had first visited the Black Country. Within that growth in numbers, it is possible to discern an ever-widening appeal and social mix among the membership, when comparing, for example, those serving as trustees of King Street chapel in Dudley in the 1830s compared to earlier years. The 1788 Trust consisted primarily of men from the working and lower middle classes. By the 1830s it increasingly drew in people from the more prosperous middle classes. Some of these latter, such as John and Thomas Bagnall, ironmasters of West Bromwich, and George Benjamin Thorneycroft, iron master of Wolverhampton, all of whom became trustees in 1836, would see their descendants *'classed with the county families of the kingdom.'* [59] And yet, this same Trust also included George Neath whose occupation was listed as 'miner', showing how social mix was possible in the chapel in a way in which it would not have been expected in wider society.

The confidence and growth of Methodism in this part of the Black Country was impressive. However, problems were looming which would lead to dissention and division across the Dudley Circuit and within the membership of the Gornal Wood Society. Within ten years of the Gornal Wood chapel's opening the face of Methodism locally would see substantial upheaval and change.

Chapter Two

Upheaval, Exile and Expansion 1827-1850

The calm before the storm - life in the new chapel

What was happening within the Methodist Society in Gornal Wood following the opening of the chapel in 1827? It is possible to gain some insight from entries in the first Trust Account book.[60] Money was being spent on ordinary items such as candles (13s-5½d = c.70p), a broom (1s-9d =8¾p), coal (3s-9d =17½p), a printer's bill for posters (6s-6d =32p) to publicise special services and one new bench (8s-0d =40p). To these routine items were added a number which today read as unlikely or unexpected purchases including, *'to wine for refreshment to Preachers 6s-3½d' in 1827, to ale to workmen building chapel 8s-4d' in 1830 and 'to cloth to pulpit at King's [George IV] funeral 7s-6d'* also in 1830. Funds were allocated to musical resources such as *'strings for bass viol 9d'*. Bass viols were commonly used at the time to accompany hymn singing. In 1831 *'new seats for the singers'* were purchased at a cost of £2/7s-0d. Appreciation for their contribution was evident when after the Church Anniversary of 1831 another entry indicates the princely sum of 7s-0d being spent on 'refreshments' for them.

The main sources of income were:

- 'collections for heating and lighting' for which there were seven such collections during 1835, each producing between 14 and 19 shillings.
- 'day school rent' (£4/10/6d) The chapel had both a day school and a Sunday School, something common to non-conformist chapels of the time. They provided a basic education for children who otherwise would have received very little, if any, opportunity to learn to read or write.
- 'pew rents' (approx. £14) These were monies payable by individuals to rent a seat in a particular pew in the chapel. This was then 'their' pew. 'Free' pews were available for anyone to use. The best pews merited the higher rents and were seen as underlining an individual's status in the congregation. Rented pews were indicated by a name card displayed at the aisle end of the pew.
- Anniversary Day collections of £5. 'Anniversary Day' refers to the annual celebration of the opening of the chapel building. Sometimes

the day was called 'Chapel Anniversary Sermons' (Later 'Church Anniversary'). Up until the late nineteenth century, this day marked the high point of the chapel year for Methodists nationwide.

The account book entries suggest an uneventful, routine existence. In 1835, however, this peaceful state was radically disturbed and a small group of the Gornal Methodists found themselves expelled from the chapel. They must have wondered what the future held for them. The short answer is they would become the founders of what was to become Zoar Methodist Church. Their expulsion and the future they subsequently fashioned for themselves came about as a consequence of one of several disputes which troubled much of Methodism following the death of John Wesley in 1791, leading not only to dissent, but also division.

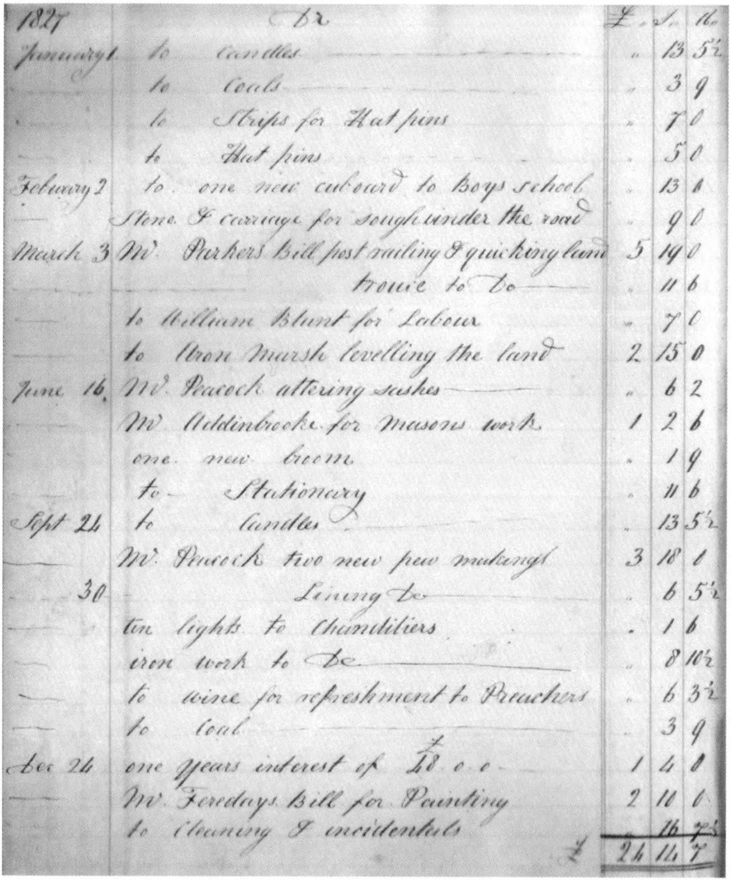

Figure 6: Account Book Excerpt for 1827

The background story to the split in the local Methodist community

To understand what happened locally requires some explanation of what had happened and was happening nationally within Methodism following John Wesley's death.

E. A. Rose explains,

John Wesley's death in 1791 left a number of unresolved problems relating to the powers of leaders, trustees and ministers, the status of the Ministry, relations with the Establishment, the administration of the sacrament etc., and the way in which the French Revolution was becoming more radical caused leaders to be afraid of reform.

In 1792 Conference decided to continue in the old way, but feeling against the Church of England grew and in 1795 Conference in the Plan of Pacification agreed to allow the administration of the sacrament at any church if a majority of the leaders and trustees agreed to it, but there was a group for whom this was not enough and they were led by Alexander Kilham. Like John Wesley, he had been born at Epworth. He was brash, opposed to the Church of England, passionately evangelical and doctrinaire. He never stopped writing pamphlets. He wanted Methodism to be much more democratic. This was at that time a dangerous word. After the 1795 Conference he produced a pamphlet, "The Progress of Liberty" and at the 1796 Conference he was expelled. He spent the next 12 months whipping up support. He wanted Conference to consist of equal numbers of laymen and ministers. The 1797 Conference rejected the admission of laymen. Three other Ministers resigned and in August 1797 the Methodist New Connexion (originally known as the Methodist New Itinerancy) was formally established.

Originally it consisted of 66 Societies with 7 Circuits and about 5,000 members. They had 20 chapels, of which 12 were formerly Wesleyan and where a majority of the members joined the New Connexion. In some cases they continued to share chapels with the Wesleyans.[61]

The emergence of the Methodist New Connexion (hereafter 'MNC') was confined primarily to the north of England. Methodists in the Black Country were not part of the initial Kilham-led breakaway. In 1799 a Birmingham Circuit was established, disappearing from the annual records between1801 and 1809, listed as the Wolverhampton Circuit in 1810 and then a Birmingham Circuit reappeared in 1811, with Societies[62] in Birmingham, Bilston, Wolverhampton and Darlaston. An MNC presence was established in Dudley following a decision taken at the 1818 MNC annual Conference, to establish a *'Home Mission Appointment'* in the already existing Birmingham Circuit[63] with the aim of missioning nearby towns.[64] In 1821 the Circuit was renamed the Dudley Circuit and included Halesowen, Birmingham, Wolverhampton and Cheslyn Hay. Total membership was 431, meeting in four chapels and with nine Societies.[65] There was a limited and fluctuating MNC presence in the first third of the nineteenth century. Its vulnerability was evidenced in the number of chapels and Societies reported each year to the MNC Conference and the way in which the name of the local Circuit regularly changed. These name changes generally came about when one Society replaced another as the strongest or most influential at a particular time.[66]

A Dudley Circuit Plan[67] for March–June 1828 records 17 preaching places. The names indicate what a large geographical area was covered by the Circuit which included Dudley, Walsall, Bilston, and a clutch of chapels in smaller Black Country communities, along with Birmingham, Wolverhampton, Lichfield and Cheslyn Hay and, further afield, Alrewas and Yoxal (sic) near Burton on Trent in the East Midlands.

The Revd. William Baggaly, one of the MNC's leading nineteenth century ministers, served a probationary year in the Circuit in 1828 and on returning there later in his ministry wrote a brief résumé of the establishment of the MNC in Dudley.

Somewhere about 1819 or 1820 the Methodist New Connexion found its way to Dudley. Its earliest friends commenced in a very humble style, holding their worship in a private house. In process of time they erected a small chapel at Caddock's End, or in what is now termed Chapel Street. The late Rev. T Batty was eminently useful in opening and fostering this new interest. He came here in the capacity of a home missionary.[68]

The chapel was named 'Ebenezer'.[69] Its first trustees were James Eldershire, Tailor; Richard Green, Schoolmaster; William Dean, Lock-maker; William Eldershire, Tailor; John Westwood, Steelyard-maker, William Smith, Edge Tool Maker (all of Wolverhampton); William Shorter, Grocer; Simeon Shorter, Edge Tool Maker (both of Cheslyn Hay); John Hemensley, Bridle Bit Maker of Darlaston; Stephen Dunn, Fender Maker; Richard Atwell, Bricklayer; James Kent, Miner; and William Dunn, Cordwainer (all of Dudley).[70] The fact that only four of the trustees were actually Dudley residents suggests that other local MNC Societies wanted to help establish the nascent Dudley cause and also that there must not have been enough suitable members locally to set up the trust body.

The members of the Dudley Society struggled, being subjected

Figure 7: Ebenezer Chapel

to persecution like many other early Methodists. Baggaly recorded one particular incident, which eventually had a good outcome. Troublemakers from the nearby 'Old Inn' hatched plans to break up a meeting at *'Brother Dunn's on Snow-hill.'* Apparently, the landlady of the public-house heard of the plans and *'being somewhat favourably disposed towards our friends, she sent to them of their danger.'* Forewarned, the Methodists packed the house, stationing Paul Elwell, *'a brother … of manly bearing'* by the door. The mob arrived, banged on the door and Elwell opened it. The leader of the mob, *'apparently unconscious of what he was doing'*, entered the house and sat down. The outcome of his time among these Methodists is clear from the words he reportedly shared when he returned to the Old Inn, *"Gentlemen, if you want to know what true religion is, go to yonder house and you will see it there."* The story did not stop there, for Baggaly's account continued, *'And now [1862] several of that man's name are both members of that society and eminently useful amongst us.'* [71]

The Dudley MNC Society struggled to make a significant impact on the town, apparently disappearing altogether in 1833/34,[72] but it served as a centre from which Societies were successfully established at Woodside, Pensnett, Bloomfield and Lower Gornal.[73] The *'Lower*

Gornal' Society is still active today, known as 'Five Ways, Lower Gornal' because it stands at what was the original centre of the Gornals, where five roadways meet.[74] This was the first MNC chapel in the Gornals,[75] being listed on the Dudley MNC Circuit Plan for March-June 1831 as *'Gornal'*.

One factor in the demise of the Dudley cause was competition from the Wesleyan Methodists. Their King Street Society was making such progress on the south side of the town, that it was decided to build a second chapel to the north of the High Street in Wolverhampton Street. The new chapel, called 'Wesley', opened in 1829 and was located very close to the MNC Caddock's End building.[76] Ironically, events which began to unfold in the mid-1830s would see 'Wesley' transfer its allegiance from Wesleyan Methodism to the Methodist New Connexion.

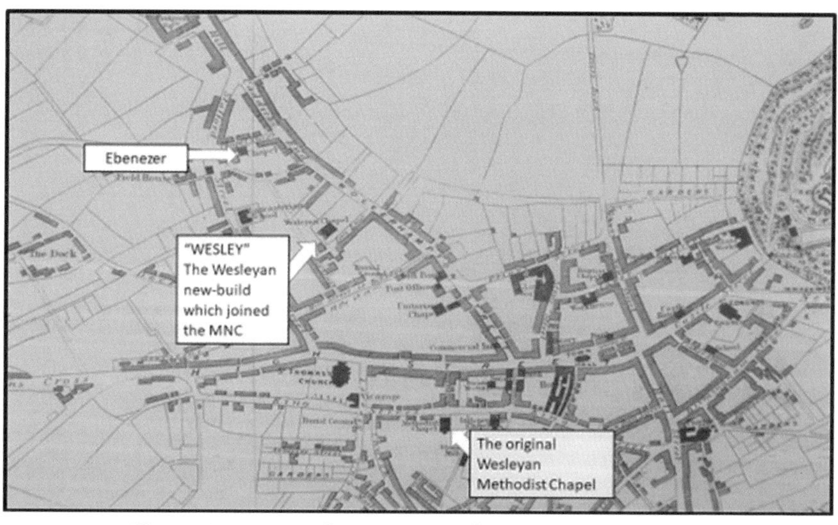

Figure 8: nineteenth century Dudley Town Plan extract

The 1830s were a period of great restlessness and upheaval across the nation,[77] reflecting the political and social ferment which was ever present across Europe. This was typified in France which, following the dramatic events of 1789, experienced a second Revolution in 1830. In Britain many groups made their voices heard, agitating for reform and championing the advancement of the lower middle and working classes. Among the more well-known and influential were the Chartists and the Anti-Corn Law League. While, in 1832, the passing of the Reform Bill under Lord Grey's Whig government (despite strong opposition, especially in the House of Lords) made for a modest extension of the franchise, it also created an expectation and agitation for further widening of the electorate. Dudley and its neighbouring towns and villages were well known at the time for their radicalism[78] and when a prevailing mood of disaffection, challenging power and influence and seeking greater democracy spilled over into Methodism nationally, it was hardly surprising that the locality was affected. The mid-1830s witnessed Wesleyan Methodism in Dudley and Gornal Wood drawn into a national dispute which, like the Kilham-led controversy of earlier years, led to further secession from Wesleyan Methodism and resulting in an upsurge in Methodist New Connexion membership.

What became known as the 'Warrenite Controversy'[79] began in the Northwest of England and came to a head at the Wesleyan Conference of 1835.[80] In the early 1830s the establishment of a ministerial training institution had emerged as a topic of serious debate within the Church. This was not the first time such an idea had been mooted, but in 1831 specific proposals were made to the Conference for the purchase of a property in Hoxton, London. Whenever raised, this topic had led to strong arguments both for and against, and on this occasion, the pro-lobby was led by the Revd. Jabez Bunting, a powerful figure within the denomination, who at the time was Secretary of the Conference (and therefore chief administrator of the Wesleyan Methodists). Samuel Warren, Superintendent of the Manchester (Oldham Street) Circuit and himself a member of the Conference committee appointed to explore the proposals, led the opposition. The controversy became complicated as those fighting for other causes joined the fray, including James Everett and James Bromley, *'two of the biggest trouble-makers in the connexion.'*[81] The Wesleyans found themselves once again engaged in heated debate concerning the limit of the annual Conference's authority over and against that of local Circuits: conservatism versus liberalism.

Warren was expelled from the Wesleyan ministry by the Conference of 1835, after which events moved rapidly leading to the establishment of the Wesleyan Methodist Association (which would have some 21,000 members within two years, more than the MNC at that time).[82] While this was happening in the Northwest, the Dudley Wesleyan Circuit and many of its chapels found themselves drawn into the controversy. The impetus and the connection came from the Revd. John Gordon.

The Wesleyan Methodist Association, which Warren set up, drew most support from Manchester, Liverpool and Rochdale but gained a vocal representative from Dudley in John Gordon. He was a former Wesleyan preacher who had returned to Dudley, his family home, after resigning in 1834 because of Wesleyan opposition to disestablishment ... In the Dudley area he led the agitation for lay representation in Conference on a democratic basis and for self-governing local societies, putting motions to the circuit quarterly meeting and gaining popular support to the extent of removing several societies from the control of the Conference and its ministers.[83]

The impact locally was substantial,

The spirit of the times is shown in Elijah Morgan's letter to Jabez Bunting in 1836 requesting a move. After describing the agitation and listing the chapels in the Stourbridge circuit lost to the Warrenites he says, "My health has suffered, my spirits greatly sunk and my character blasted far and near; we are called thieves, robbers, Conference-Devils and that which is worse than all others in the ears of the people, Tories". Wesleyan membership in the Dudley circuit fell by over a thousand and by over six hundred in Stourbridge. Gordon, however, did not stay with the Wesleyan Methodist Association and soon the whole of his Black Country following joined the Methodist New Connexion ... Its leading [Black Country] circuit was Dudley and weaker ones were based on Birmingham, Wolverhampton and Stourbridge. [84]

The speedy move from the Wesleyan Methodist Association (WMA) into the MNC was chronicled by William Baggaly in another MNC Magazine article.[85] For the year in which they were part of the WMA, Gordon served as their minister, before himself joining the MNC ministry, serving the Dudley MNC Circuit for part of 1835, then spending all of his subsequent ministry in Ireland.[86]

Following a series of meetings involving Samuel Warren for the WMA and Thomas Allin for the MNC, the Dudley WMA Circuit Quarterly Meeting met on 25 April 1836 in the New Mill Street schoolroom and voted to join the MNC from August of that year.

[Nineteen Societies were] formally united with the Methodist New Connexion. "The Wedding", as it was long called, was consummated in Wesley Chapel, Dudley, on the 29th of August, 1836. Mr Alexander Gordon, who had been a Methodist between forty and fifty years, and who had wept when he was expelled from the parent body, presided. The chapel was crowded to excess, the representatives of the various Societies sitting in the front seats of the gallery.[87]

Alexander Gordon, who had Straits House built on the edge of Gornal Wood, was the father of John Gordon. He had become a wealthy businessman, trading wines and spirits in Queen Street in Dudley.[88] He was described as a '*truly kind and benevolent old gentleman, particularly partial to his own views'*, which may help to explain the outspokenness of his son.[89]

The 19 Societies included 15 chapels, plus another 4 being built at the time, along with 1,489 members and 50 Local Preachers. The 'Wesley' chapel at which these proceedings took place was the same chapel whose building had only recently helped lead to the demise of the MNC Society at Caddock's End. Paradoxically, only seven years after its formal opening it had become the head of the new MNC Circuit.[90]

Figure 9: Wesley Chapel, Dudley

The establishment of the Dudley MNC Circuit in 1836[91] was deemed significant enough in the history of the denomination to merit a note when the MNC's 1847 national Jubilee was celebrated in print,

> *In the year 1836, a goodly number of most excellent individuals, in Dudley and its neighbourhood, who had seceded from the Old Connexion, with the parties that constitute the Wesleyan Association, but preferred becoming members of the New Connexion, were formally received at an interesting meeting, held for the purpose, into union with our Community. Subsequent events have fully justified the steps that were taken by the Wesleyan seceders on the one hand, and the New Connexion on the other. Commodious chapels have been built, many souls have been converted to God, and in the two circuits, Dudley and Stourbridge, six circuit preachers are employed, having under their pastoral care, twenty five societies, containing seventeen hundred and fifty two members.*[92]

Rose highlights the significance of this particular move in relation to the development of the MNC nationally,

During the 1830s [MNC] numbers grew more rapidly [compared to the years since its inception], largely as a consequence of Wesleyan troubles ... MNC leaders became adept at fishing in troubled waters. Their biggest catch was at Dudley and Stourbridge in the Black Country ...[93]

The strength and significance of this new Circuit can be seen from the Circuit Plan six years later. By 1842 its 22 churches, four itinerant preachers and 51 local Preachers, with 6 more 'On Trial' testified to a dominant MNC presence. This was in stark contrast to ten years earlier: 7 Societies, 6 chapels and 242 members.

Gornal Wood and the MNC

One of the local Societies brought into the MNC was in Gornal Wood. The earliest known record of what led up to this action was recorded in a 1904 Circuit magazine,

Dr Warren had a large number of sympathisers in the Dudley [Wesleyan] Circuit, who, like others elsewhere, were not wishful to leave the Church which was their spiritual home. However, the leaders of the movement in the several Societies were marked, and arbitrarily expelled from membership.

Gornal Wood Society was one that suffered in this way. Several leaders and members were expelled; notably, Joseph Fellows, Titus Fellows, John Wosdell, Alexander Turner, John Payton, George Short, Benjamin Oakley, Endor Guest, and Miss Roberts.[94] *This high handed procedure was resented by a considerable number of other members, who followed the discontinued into the "wilderness".*

On the first Sunday after the expulsion, these people, without a religious home, as many of their kind have done in every age, worshipped God in the open air. However, on the next Sunday, Mr and Mrs William Hughes, parents of the present Mayor of Dudley (Alderman John Hughes, J.P.) opened the Club room of their house, the Woodman Inn, for service. Mrs Hughes herself became a member of the new society and continued until her death. After some time, the members were offered the Barn of the Fiddler's Arms, Straits, as a meeting place, which they gladly accepted. A temporary chapel was soon built, near the Limerick Inn, and called, from the material of which it was constructed, the "Wooden Tabernacle". The Rev. John Nelson was a favourite preacher in that sanctuary. Another was Mr Alexander Gordon, a Dudley gentleman, of high character and intelligence, who built the Straits Hall, and resided in it many years. So temporary was the structure that, frequently, in the winter season preacher and hearers had to shelter under umbrellas during service.[95]

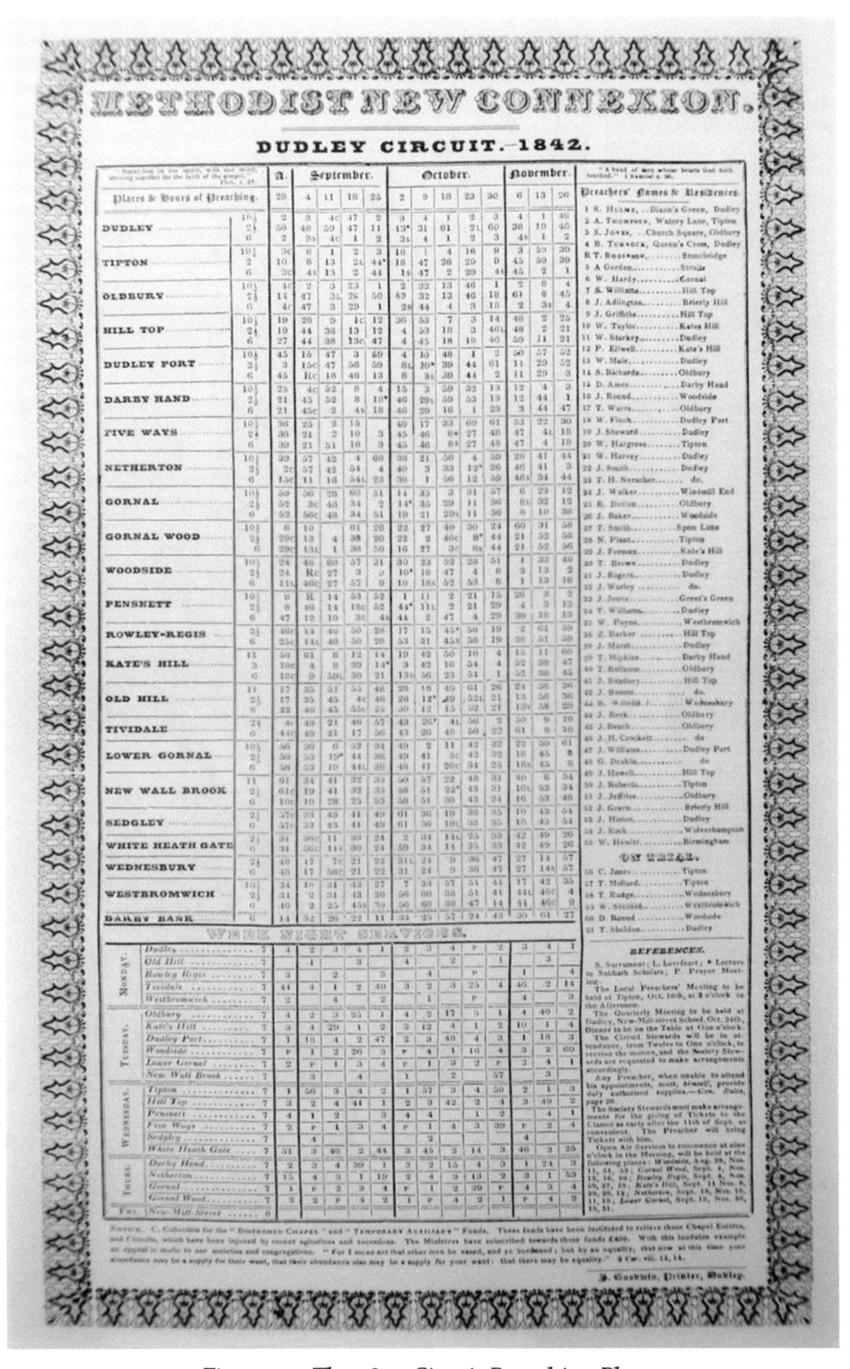

METHODIST NEW CONNEXION.

DUDLEY CIRCUIT.—1842.

"Stand fast in one spirit, with one mind, striving together for the faith of the gospel." Phil. i. 27.

"A band of men whose hearts God had touched." 1 Samuel x. 26.

Places & Hours of Preaching.		A.	September.				October.					November.		
		28	4	11	18	25	2	9	16	23	30	6	13	20
DUDLEY	10½	2	3	4c	47	2	3	4	1	2	3	4	1	40
	2½	58	48	59	47	11	13*	31	61	2L	60	38	19	46
	6	2	2s	4c	1	2	3s	4	1	2	3	4s	1	2
TIPTON	10½	3c	8	1	2	3	18	1	4	16	9	3	59	39
	2	10	8	13	2L	44*	18	47	26	29	9	45	59	39
	6	3c	4s	13	2	44	1s	47	2	29	4s	45	2	1
OLDBURY	10½	4c	2	3	23	1	2	32	13	46	1	2	8	4
	2½	14	47	3L	26	50	62	32	13	46	18	61	6	45
	6	4c	47	3	29	1	2s	44	4	3	18	2	3s	4
HILL TOP	10½	19	26	9	1c	12	36	53	7	3	14	46	2	25
	2½	19	44	38	13	12	4	53	18	3	46L	48	2	21
	6	27	44	38	13c	47	4	45	18	10	40	59	11	21
DUDLEY PORT	10½	45	15	47	3	59	4	10	48	1	2	50	57	52
	2½	3	15c	47	56	59	8L	10*	39	44	61	11	29	52
	6	45	Rc	18	46	13	8	3s	39	44	2	11	29	3
DARBY HAND	10½	25	4c	52	8	4	15	3	59	32	13	12	4	3
	2½	21	45	52	8	18*	46	29L	59	53	13	12	44	1
	6	21	45c	2	4s	18	46	29	16	1	23	3	44	47
FIVE WAYS	10½	36	25	2	15		40	17	33	60	61	53	22	30
	2½	36	21	2	10	3	45	46	6*	27	48	47	4L	18
	6	39	21	51	10	3	45	46	6s	27	48	47	4	18
NETHERTON	10½	39	57	42	4	60	38	21	56	4	59	28	41	44
	2½	2c	57	42	54	4	40	3	33	12*	26	46	41	3
	6	15c	11	18	54L	23	38	1	56	12	59	46s	34	44
GORNAL	10½	59	56	28	60	51	14	35	3	31	57	6	23	12
	2½	52	3c	48	34	2	14*	35	29	11	36	6L	32	12
	6	52	56c	48	34	51	19	21	29s	11	36	8	10	38
GORNAL WOOD	10½	6	10		61	26	22	27	40	30	24	60	31	58
	2½	29c	13	4	38	26	22	2	40c	8*	44	21	52	58
	6	29c	13L	1	38	50	16	27	3c	8s	44	21	52	56
WOODSIDE	10½	24	48	60	57	31	30	23	52	28	51	1	33	40
	2½	24	Rc	27	3	9	10*	18	47	4	8	3	13	2
	6	11L	46c	27	57	9	10	18s	52	53	8	1	13	16
PENSNETT	10½	8	R	14	53	52	1	11	2	21	15	26	2	2
	2½	8	46	14	18c	52	44*	11L	2	21	29	4	3	13
	6	47	12	10	3c	4s	44	2	47	4	29	39	18	13
ROWLEY-REGIS	2½	46c	14	40	50	28	17	15	45*	58	19	2	61	59
	6	25c	14L	40	50	28	53	31	45s	58	19	38	51	59
KATE'S HILL	11	58	61	8	12	14	19	42	50	10	4	15	11	60
	3	18c	4	8	39	14*	3	42	16	54	4	52	38	47
	6	18c	9	59L	39	21	13s	56	23	54	1	52	38	45
OLD HILL	11	17	35	51	55	48	28	16	49	61	26	24	36	36
	2½	17	35	45	4c	48	28	12*	49	52L	21	13	56	36
	6	22	40	45	55c	25	30	12	15	52	21	13s	58	29
TIVIDALE	2½	4c	49	21	46	57	43	26*	4L	56	2	50	9	10
	6	44c	49	21	17	56	43	26	48	56	22	61	9	10
LOWER GORNAL	10½	56	30	6	52	34	49	2	11	42	32	22	50	61
	2½	50	53	19*	44	36	49	41	3c	42	32	18	45	8
	6	58	53	19	44L	36	48	41	26c	34	25	18s	45	8
NEW WALL BROOK	11	61	34	41	32	33	50	57	22	48	31	40	6	34
	2½	61c	19	41	32	33	58	51	22*	43	31	16L	53	34
	6	10c	19	28	25	53	58	51	30	43	34	16	53	48
SEDGLEY	2½	57c	33	43	41	49	61	36	19	38	35	10	43	54
	6	57c	33	43	41	49	61	36	19L	38	35	10	43	54
WHITE HEATH GATE	2½	31	56c	11	30	24	2	34	14L	25	33	42	49	26
	6	31	56c	11s	30	24	59	34	14	25	33	42	49	26
WEDNESBURY	2½	48	17	7c	21	22	31L	24	9	36	47	27	14	57
	6	48	17	58c	21	22	31	24	9	36	47	27	14s	57
WESTBROMWICH	10½	34	18	31	43	27	7	34	57	51	41	17	42	35
	2½	31	2	31	43	30	56	60	38	51	41	44L	46c	4
	6	40	2	25	45s	30	56	60	38	47	14	44	46c	9
DARBY BANK	6	14	32	26	22	11	33	25	57	24	43	30	61	27

WEEK NIGHT SERVICES.

Day	Place	Hour	28	4	11	18	25	2	9	16	23	30	6	13	20
Monday.	Dudley	7	4	2	3	4	1	2	3	4	P	2	3	4	1
	Old Hill	7		1		3		4		2		1		3	
	Rowley Regis	7	3		2		3		4		P		1		4
	Tividale	7	44	4	1	2	40	3	2	3	25	4	46	2	14
	Westbromwich	7	2		4		2		1		P		4		3
Tuesday.	Oldbury	7	4	2	3	25	1	4	2	17	3	1	4	40	2
	Kate's Hill	7	3	4	29	1	2	3	12	4	1	2	10	1	4
	Dudley Port	7	1	16	4	2	47	2	3	48	4	3	1	18	3
	Woodside	7	P	1	2	26	3	P	4	1	16	4	3	2	60
	Lower Gornal	7	2	P	1	3	4	P	1	3	2	P	2	4	1
	New Wall Brook	7		3		4		1		2		57		3	
Wednesday.	Tipton	7	1	50	3	4	2	1	57	3	4	50	2	1	3
	Hill Top	7	3	2	4	41	1	2	3	42	2	4	3	49	2
	Pensnett	7	4	1	2		3	4	4		1	2		4	1
	Five Ways	7	2	P	1	3	4	P	1	4	3	39	P	2	4
	Sedgley	7		4					2				4		
	White Heath Gate	7	51	3	40	2	44	3	45	2	14	3	46	3	25
Thurs.	Darby Hand	7	2	3	4	39	1	3	2	15	4	3	1	24	3
	Netherton	7	15	4	3	1	19	2	4	3	13	2	3	1	53
	Gornal	7	1	P	2	3	4	P	1	2	39	P	4	3	4
	Gornal Wood	7	3	2	P	4	2	1	P	4	2	1	P	4	2
Fri.	New Mill-Street	8													

Preachers' Names & Residences.

1 S. Hulme, ..Dixon's Green, Dudley
2 A. Thompson, Watery Lane, Tipton
3 S. Jones, ..Church Square, Oldbury
4 B. Turnock, Queen's Cross, Dudley
R T. Robinson,........Stourbridge
5 A Gordon............Straits
6 W. Hardy............Gornal
7 S. Williams..........Hill Top
8 J. Adlington.........Brierly Hill
9 J. Griffiths..........Hill Top
10 W. Taylor...........Kates Hill
11 W. Starkey..........Dudley
12 P. Elwell............Kate's Hill
13 W. Male,............Dudley
14 S. Richards..........Oldbury
15 D. Ames..............Darby Hand
16 J. Round............Woodside
17 T. Warrs.............Oldbury
18 W. Finch............Dudley Port
19 J. Sheward..........Dudley
20 W. Hargrove.........Tipton
21 W. Harvey...........Dudley
22 J. Smith.............Dudley
23 T. H. Neracher....... do.
24 J. Walker...........Windmill End
25 R. Dutton...........Oldbury
26 J. Baker............Woodside
27 T. Smith............Spon Lane
28 N. Plant............Tipton
29 J. Forman...........Kate's Hill
30 T. Brown............Dudley
31 J. Rogers...........Dudley
32 J. Warley .... do.
33 J. Jones............Greet's Green
34 T. Williams.........Dudley
35 W. Payne............Westbromwich
36 Z. Barker ....Hill Top
38 J. Marsh............Dudley
39 T. Hipkins..........Darby Hand
40 T. Rollason.........Oldbury
41 J. Bradney..........Hill Top
42 J. Broom............ do.
43 R. [illegible]..........Wednesbury
44 J. Beck.............Oldbury
45 J. Beach............Oldbury
46 J. H. Crockett........ do
47 J. Williams..........Dudley Port
48 G. Deakin............ do
49 J. Howell............Hill Top
50 J. Roberts...........Tipton
51 J. Jeffries...........Oldbury
52 J. Green.............Brierly Hill
53 J. Hinton............Dudley
54 J. Keck..............Wolverhampton
55 W. Hewitt............Birmingham

ON TRIAL.

56 C. Jones............Tipton
57 T. Millard...........Tipton
58 T. Rudge............Wednesbury
59 W. [illegible]..........Westbromwich
60 D. Round............Woodside
61 T. Sheldon...........Dudley

REFERENCES.

S. Sacrament; L. Lovefeast; * Lecture to Sabbath Scholars; P. Prayer Meeting.

The Local Preachers' Meeting to be held at Tipton, Oct. 10th, at 2 o'clock in the Afternoon.

The Quarterly Meeting to be held at Dudley, New-Mill-street School, Oct. 24th, Dinner to be on the Table at One o'clock.

The Circuit Stewards will be in attendance, from Twelve to One o'clock, to receive the monies, and the Society Stewards are requested to make arrangements accordingly.

Any Preacher, when unable to attend his appointments, must, *himself*, provide duly authorised supplies.—*Gen. Rules*, page 20.

The Society Stewards must make arrangements for the giving of Tickets to the Classes as early after the 11th of Sept. as convenient. The Preacher will bring Tickets with him.

Open Air Services to commence at nine o'clock in the Morning, will be held at the following places: *Woodside*, Aug. 28, Nos. 11, 51, 53; *Gornal Wood*, Sept. 4, Nos. 13, 16, 60; *Rowley Regis*, Sept. 4, Nos. 59, 27, 58; *Kate's Hill*, Sept. 11 Nos. 8, 39, 29, 12; *Netherton*, Sept. 18, Nos. 16, 11, 18; *Lower Gornal*, Sept. 18, Nos. 50, 19, 31.

NOTICE. C. Collection for the "Distressed Chapel" and "Temporary Auxiliary" Funds. These funds have been instituted to relieve those Chapel Estates and Circuits, which have been injured by recent agitations and secessions. The Ministers have subscribed towards these funds £400. With this laudable example an appeal is made to our societies and congregations. "For I mean not that other men be eased, and ye burdened; but by an equality, that now at this time your abundance may be a supply for their want, that their abundance also may be a supply for your want: that there may be equality." 2 Cor. viii. 13, 14.

J. Goodwin, Printer, Dudley.

Figure 10: The 1842 Circuit Preaching Plan

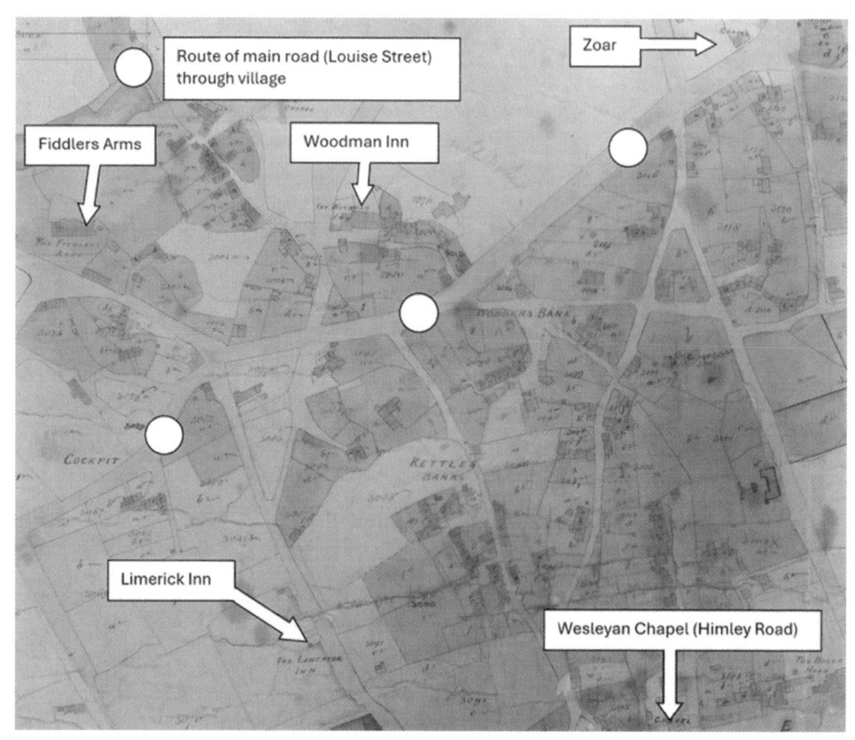

Figure 11: Location of the early meeting places

Figure 12: The Woodman Inn

The *'Club room'* of the Woodman Inn is believed to be the left-hand portion of the building.[96] The next two pictures show an old undated photograph of the Fiddler's Arms and then a modern view of its barn.

Figure 13: The Fiddler's Arms

Figure 14: The barn at the Fiddler's Arms

Figure 15: The Limerick Inn

The "Wooden Tabernacle" presents an interesting conundrum. No records or pictures of it are known to exist. The 1904 article talks of a temporary wooden structure being built. However, Barnett writes of, *'A small chapel erected in Summit Place near the site of the present Limerick Inn, and registered by William Horner on January 15th, 1805.'* [97] Given the location, this building could well have become the *Wooden Tabernacle* of the exiled Wesleyans, rather than their building a new structure and then immediately replacing it, as was to happen only a year or so later. Possibly the building had fallen into disuse, hence its availability, which would also help to explain both the claim that 'in the winter season preacher and hearers had to shelter under umbrellas during service' and also the fact that already by 1837 a new brick structure was being erected.[98]

Expenditure during 1836 included candles (13s-4d), ten candlesticks (9s-od), four collecting boxes (4s-od) and various payments relating to timber work (presumably to secure the inadequacies of the building, if this was not literally a new building). An account book entry for 25 December 1836 records a collection of £9/19/6d at the *"Opening of Tabernacle"*. Subsequent entries point to this being the formal opening of the Wooden Tabernacle.[99]

"The opening of a new building in Gornal Wood" was reported in the Minutes of the MNC Annual Conference for 1838:[100] the brick

Tabernacle. Mr Bate received £7/2/od for plans and specifications, the site was purchased for £54 and £35/6/od was expended on legal bills. Building work was undertaken by John and Joseph Addenbrook, masons who lived in the village, John Shenton of Upper Gornal was employed to complete the plaster work (expenditure totalling £31) and Preece and Millward were the carpenters. Palisades were erected on top of a wall and four trees planted in front of the building.

The inaugural service took place on 10 December 1837.[101] Notable expenditure on this special occasion included the preacher's travelling expenses, which were £4, and £2/7/6d spent on providing a *'Feast'* for the *'Singers'* who led the hymn singing. Collections on the day totalled £32/16/1d. The preacher was the Rev. Samuel Jones of London, who would have been known to the Tabernacle congregation, having been a minister in the Bilston MNC Circuit in 1835-36. He would return to serve in the Dudley MNC Circuit in 1842-43.[102]

A mortgage for £300 was taken out, along with a loan of £100 from a Mrs Hutchings, and members were invited to take out 'subscriptions' or shares, on which they received a small return by way of interest, to help defray the cost of the building. The mortgage was provided by Stephen Wilkes, who received interest of £15 p.a. Wilkes, a Sedgley Congregationalist, made his money as a local nail factor - someone who bought and sold nails.[103] The two loans were repaid in 1847 before the building of a successor to the Tabernacle and with the help of a £50 grant from MNC national funds (a grant conditional on the local Methodists raising £126 themselves).

The first trustees of *'the Methodist New Connexion Chapel'* between the Cock Pit and Himley Road, Gornal Wood' were recorded in 1837,

> *John Wasdell, Joseph Fellows, John Peyton, Titus Fellows, Samuel Whitehouse, John Waterfield, Francis Beddard , John Beddard, Michael Guest, John Hale, Alexander Turner, James Bradley, William Bradley, Reuben Jevon, Joseph Greenway, Endor (sic) Guest.*[104]

Who were these people? With the help of nineteenth century census records and newspaper articles it has been possible to piece together some information about them.

Titus Fellows was an example of those nineteenth century Methodists who advanced themselves in terms of employment, status and social class in ways rarely seen in previous generations, something acknowledged by historians, such as Asa Briggs, *'[As the] old forms of Nonconformity, like Quakerism, nurtured business virtues: [Methodism], too, by encouraging frugality and industry, helped to make [Methodists] 'successful'.*[105]

In 1841 Titus was a corn factor (someone who bought and sold corn on behalf of others). He progressed to become a *'coal miner and farmer employing some 180 men'* while still living in Pensnett in 1851. By 1861 he had moved to Great Wyrley where he was a mine owner and acquired Great Wyrley Hall. Following his death on Christmas Day 1890, an obituary published in the Walsall Observer newspaper said of him, *'... no one in the county probably stood higher in general estimation in the commercial world for probity, sound judgement, and kindly feeling.'* The same article explained that at some point in his life he had left Methodism and joined the Plymouth Brethren.[106]

Joseph Fellows may well have been a relative, possibly Titus's brother, given his occupation recorded in 1854 of *'corn dealer'*.

John Beddard There were two John Beddards living in Gornal at the time. It is not evident which one was a trustee,

• **John Beddard I** (1794-1858) was a farmer of some 65 acres and a copyholder of houses in Ruiton. In 1851 he was recorded as living at *Straits school house* where his wife, Elizabeth, ran a school with 8 pupils living there, along with the couples own 7 children and two *house servants.*

• **John Beddard II** (1806-1861) In 1851 he was working as a 'contractor' as were his two oldest sons, Joseph (17) and John (15). He was also married to Elizabeth, who did not have an occupation. They had eight children, four sons and four daughters.

The 1841 census listed **Eder Guest** as a miner. By 1859 he had become a coalmaster (i.e. a person in overall charge of a coalmine) *'of the coal and ironstone mining rights under land in Peacocks field, Dudley.'*[107] He was entitled to vote in elections as a copyholder of houses at Redhall (1838),[108] subsequently qualifying as a freeholder of property in Barrs Meadow (1861).[109] His wife, Ruth, was 8 years his senior, and they had four children, Ann Maria, who became a dressmaker, Murdy, who died young, Thomas and Esther. In old age Eder was cared for by his granddaughter, Esther Ann Bradley, who was executrix to his estate (total value £17) following his death in April 1889.

Michael Guest was the youngest trustee, age 21 in 1837. Two years later he married Druzilla Frost and they lived with her mother, Mary, a schoolmistress, in Musk Lane. They had 3 children, Mary Ann, Elizabeth and Esther. Michael worked as a banksman at a colliery in Kingswinford and died of suffocation in 1848 following a pit accident.[110] After his death, Druzilla married William Wakelam, a labourer, and continued to live in Musk Lane until her death in 1900.

Reuben Paul Jevon (1806-1880), a clerk, married Ruth in 1837 and in 1845 was listed as a copyholder and voter. By the time of the 1851 census, Ruth had died, possibly in childbirth as Reuben (*'widower'*), along with his 3-year-old daughter Elizabeth, was living with his brother Joseph in Coseley. The 1861 census noted him as a colliery clerk, now married to Sarah who was ten years his senior. Ten years later he had become an agent, living in Tipton Street, Sedgley and he and Sarah had a domestic servant living with them.

John Payton, born in 1791, was a tracemaker, someone who copied engineering diagrams for mining and manufacturing industries using tracing paper. He and his wife, Susannah, had three sons, Richard (b.1821) and twins John and Thomas (b.1826), and one daughter, Eliza (b. 1829). Thomas, an engineer, married Esther in his early twenties and joined the Tabernacle trustees when the trust was renewed in 1854.

John Wasdell (1804-1870) served on the 1837 and 1854 trust bodies. A colliery clerk, he was married to Ruth, with whom he had two children, Joseph (b. 1827) and Mary (b. 1838). Sometime after 1861 the family emigrated to Canada, where Joseph became a farmer.[111] When John died in 1870 he still had *'effects under £300'* in England.

Alexander Turner was a coal miner, living at Kettles Bank. Born in 1801, he was married to Mary (five years his junior) with whom he had six children.

Francis Beddard (1771-1846) was a bricklayer, who by 1841 was living with his daughter in Wordsley.

Of the other trustees, **William Bradley**,[112] **John Hale** and **Samuel Whitehouse** were employed as labourers, **James Bradley** as an agricultural labourer and **Joseph Greenway** as a clerk.

The annual Tabernacle income, using 1840 as a typical example, came primarily from the following sources,

Chapel Anniversary sermons	£9/9/4½d
Pew rents	£19/10/6d
Tea meeting profit	£3/17/2½d
Sabbath School rent	£6/19/6d

Evidently the trustees did not take up collections for heating and lighting, unlike their Wesleyan contemporaries. They did, however, introduce an annual tea meeting, an event which would become a fixture in the chapel calendar well on into the twentieth century. The *Sabbath School rent* indicates that from their earliest days, as was common among many nineteenth century churches and chapels, they were making possible a basic education for those who otherwise would have had no opportunity of schooling.

As to expenditure, the 1840s saw a communion table purchased at a cost of 5s-od, a stove installed for £3/10/od and an additional 19s-6d spent on a flue (this was in 1846, prior to which the building must have been unheated). In 1847 the interior of the chapel was repainted by Mr Shenton for £18/5/od, while the reopening service helped defray most of this, the collection raising £15/10/3d. Expenditure related to music in worship included a *'new double bass'* at a cost of £11/5/3d in 1849. Before this, there is evidence of the continued use of a bass viol, as a replacement string for the instrument was purchased in 1837, costing two shillings (10p), while a replacement bow in 1850 cost 5s-6d. Appreciation of the musical lead contributed by the *'singers'* continued to be recognised with an occasional *'feast'* paid for by the trustees. A *'book'* for the singers was purchased in 1850.

A C Pratt describes the way in which typically singing would be led in worship across the various strands of Methodism. The singers would sit apart from the main congregation either in a gallery or on special seats, often being trained by their leader whose standing would be 'of no small import' in the Society. What musical instruments were used in the Tabernacle apart from the bass viol is not known. In some chapels flutes, fiddles and even trombones were used.[113]

While most of the Trust accounts relate to the building and its internal activities, an entry for 1849 refers to a Camp Meeting taking place. The entry was for the hire of a waggon from a Mr Bradley for 2s-6d (12½p), which would have been used as a stage. Camp Meetings were open air outreach events with a waggon often used as a platform for the preacher, though sometimes they were held in large tents. These gatherings, while replicating a typical act of worship, were also intended to engage interest among non-churchgoers. Camp Meetings were a particular feature of Primitive Methodist activity,[114] however, the Wesleyan Methodists had some 30 caravans, known as Gospel Cars, built in the late nineteenth century and used to house evangelists who then were able to mission particularly in rural areas. The cars were also used for ministry in markets, fairgrounds, at overnight moorings for barge and boat people, and to visit traveller camps. The Wesleyan and Primitive Methodists and Church Army[115] all used 'Gospel cars' in the nineteenth and early twentieth century. They were most in demand during the period 1890 to 1907. Within Methodism, horse drawn wagons were partly replaced by hand-pushed 'trek carts' in the inter-war years, and finally by deaconess' caravans in the 1950s.[116]

Figure 16: A typical gospel car as the wagons were often known. This one is a reconstruction of the original gospel car "No. 11 Ebenezer", belonging to the Methodist Church and on loan to the Black Country Living Museum in Dudley.

When the descendants of those first Gornal MNC members looked back over the years of ministry based at the Tabernacle, *'the most memorable event'* was deemed to be, *'... a gracious revival under the ministry of the Rev. William Burrows, when the membership sprang up in a short time from about 40 to over 200.'*[117]

The period from the 1840s through to the late nineteenth century was one of widespread revivalism across England and clearly the local MNC congregation was part of that movement.[118] Mr Burrows was widely acknowledged for his contribution to the revival movement, as shown in a tribute paid to him in the centenary record of the MNC,

> *... He greatly enjoyed the atmosphere of revivals and was wont to exert himself amidst scenes of multiplied conversion, until he was ready to faint from exhaustion. His anxiety respecting the success of his ministry was extreme and led him to reproach himself with inefficiency while others were rejoicing in the large fruits of his labours.*[119]

He had spent two of his early years in ministry, 1826-27, in the Dudley MNC Circuit, prior to the 1836 Warrenite influx of chapels and members. He returned in 1848, immediately after having served the MNC Church nationally as its President of the Conference. [120] Possibly it was the Burrows-led revival which inspired the membership to make plans to build a Sunday School nearer the centre of the village - on a plot of land abutting what is now Abbey Road, known then as *Masons End* [121] - and for a new chapel shortly after at the same location. The account book for 1850 notes that on 6 May the Trustees *'lent £28-0-0 to school to buy land'* from Lord Dudley. A mere fifteen years after their exile from the Wesleyan Chapel in Gornal Wood, the MNC members had established a confident presence within the local community. It was about to become a visible presence at the very centre of the village.

PART TWO:
THE FIRST ZOAR

Chapter Three

The first Zoar, a significant presence

New buildings at the heart of the village

Mid-century witnessed a flurry of activity on the part of the Tabernacle trustees. It commenced with the building of the Sunday School at Mason's End. The builder was Mr William Millward, a prominent member of Wesley Chapel, Dudley and Mr James Bennett, aged 83, who laid the first brick, oversaw the contract.[122] Millward's employment was illustrative of the way in which, often, 'chapel' folk would be employed to undertake work on Methodist chapels and when the local parish church needed tradesmen then 'church' folk would often be employed.[123] The first appointed trustees,[124] who would also assume responsibility for the new chapel opened at the end of 1854, were:

	Occupation
Titus Fellows	Coal Miner and farmer employing 180 men
Joseph Fellows	Corn dealer
John Wasdell	Colliery bailiff
Eder Guest	Miner
John Hale	Labourer
James Bradley	Account clerk
William Bradley	Farmer and contractor
Benjamin Bradley	Account clerk
Richard Bradley	Farmer and contractor (brother to William)
Thomas Peyton	Engineer (son of John who was one of the 1837 trustees)
Henry Roberts	Butcher

The seven names ***in italics*** had also been trustees of the Tabernacle

The land at Mason's End had become available when Lord Dudley decided to sell several of his land holdings in the village in 1847. The tenant and sub-tenant chose not to take up the opportunity to buy it and so the Methodists stepped in. Figure 17 records the sub-tenant, John Cartwright, confirming this and pencilled at the foot of the page is the name Titus Fellows – evidently his interest had already been noted.

As a consequence of the hostility directed at Methodists by some landowners, magistrates and even Anglican clergy, who would go to great lengths to halt the progress of Methodism, it became common practice for Methodist Societies to nominate one person to make the initial land purchase to avoid attracting unwanted attention and opposition. It was Titus Fellows, the most socially prominent member

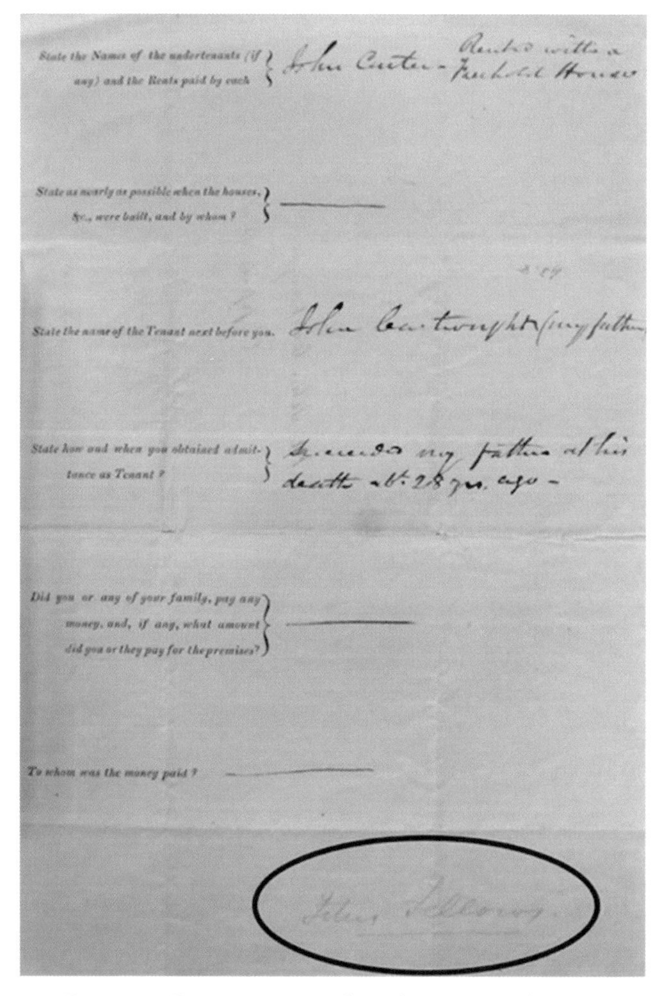

State the Names of the undertenants (if any) and the Rents paid by each } John Carter – Rented with a Freehold House

State as nearly as possible when the houses, &c., were built, and by whom? } ——

State the name of the Tenant next before you. John Cartwright (my father

State how and when you obtained admittance as Tenant? } Succeeded my father at his death ab.t 28 yrs. ago –

Did you or any of your family, pay any money, and, if any, what amount did you or they pay for the premises? } ——

To whom was the money paid? ——

Titus Fellows

Figure 17: Document recording the tenant's decision not to buy the land at Mason's End

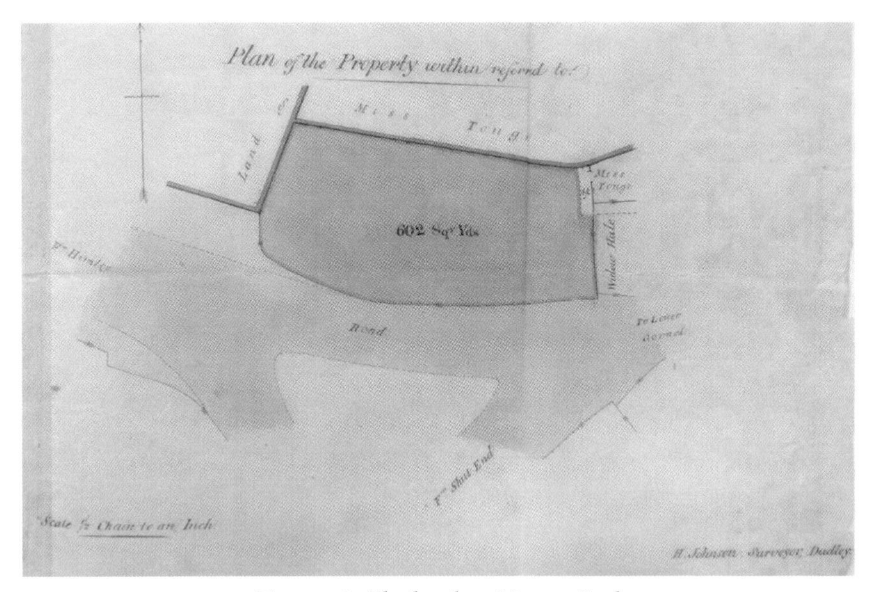

Figure 18: The land at Masons End

of the Tabernacle trustees, who was nominated to purchase the land at Mason's End. This was diplomatically reported in 1903. *One devoted brother, by almost sacrificial strategy, secured a piece of land to build "a house", but, to the surprise of the people, Zoar became the house that was built.*[125]

The original conveyance to Titus Fellows was dated 9 August 1850 and those named in the transfer began with the Revd T L Claughton, at that time vicar of Kidderminster, Worcestershire. A prominent Anglican clergyman in his day, Claughton was a fellow, lecturer and University preacher at Oxford prior to his incumbency at Kidderminster. He married the Hon. Susannah Julia Ward, daughter of Lord Ward and second cousin of a former Earl of Dudley. Later he became Bishop of Rochester and then the first Bishop of St Albans.[126] In December 1850 the property was conveyed by Titus to the chosen trustees.

Figure 19: the Revd T L Claughton

Figure 20: Zoar school and chapel

In a picture from around 1960, the front of the school building can be seen in Figure 20, facing onto the centre of the village, between the current chapel and the cottage to the right which housed the church caretaker. That part of the school visible in Figure 21 shows that the end wall was originally plain brick rather than rendered and there is a glimpse in that picture of the porch roof to the main door on the left-hand side of the school building.

When the caretaker's cottage was built or came into the ownership of the trustees is not known, though rental income for a *'Chapel house'* was first recorded in 1871. A Mrs Bennett may well have lived there as the accounts indicate regular sums paid to her, which may well be for caretaking duties, since she was reimbursed 2s-06d (7½p) for a broom in 1877.

With the completion of the school, a new chapel, *Zoar*, followed soon after. The builders were Messrs. Hinton and Meredith. William Hinton was a local preacher who lived in Pensnett and Sam Meredith was a well-known local builder.[127] The architect was a Mr. Wigginton who received a 4% fee of £32. A mortgage of £800 was secured from local businessman Mr Benjamin Gibbons (See Figure 22) and the foundation stone was laid on 24 April 1854. The mortgage was transferred in 1863 to Ralph Gough with half yearly interest payments of £20 (Figure 23).

Six months after building began opening services took place. The 'exiles' of 1835 now had a significant presence in the middle of Gornal

Figure 21: The first Zoar with the schoolroom alongside

Figure 22: Receipt relating to the £800 advanced by Mr Gibbons

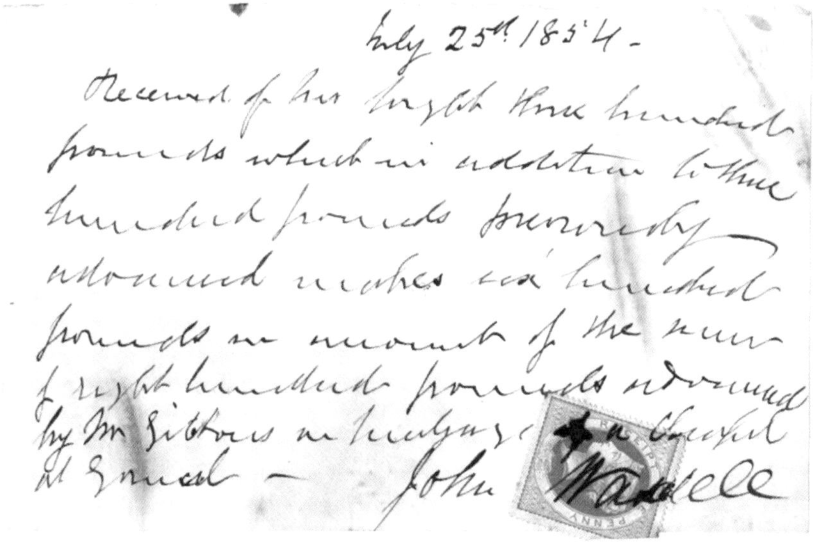

July 25th 1854 –

Received of Mr [illegible] three hundred pounds which in addition to three hundred pounds previously advanced makes six hundred pounds on account of the sum of eight hundred pounds advanced by Mr Gibbons on mortgage of the Chapel at [illegible] – John [illegible]

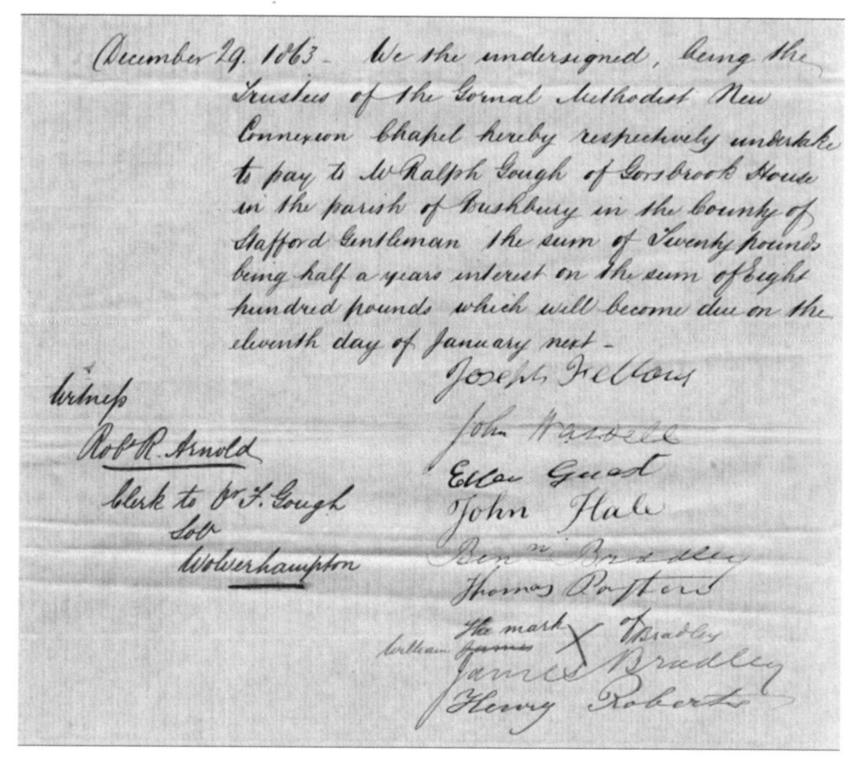
December 29. 1863 - We the undersigned, being the Trustees of the Gornal Methodist New Connexion Chapel hereby respectively undertake to pay to Mr Ralph Gough of Gorsbrook House in the parish of Bushbury in the County of Stafford Gentleman the sum of Seventy pounds being half a years interest on the sum of Eight hundred pounds which will become due on the eleventh day of January next -

Witness
Robt R. Arnold
Clerk to Mr F. Gough
Solr
Wolverhampton

Joseph Fellows
John Wassell
Ellas Guest
John Hale
Benn Bradley
Thomas Poffers
William ~~James~~ his mark X Bradley
James Bradley
Henry Roberts

Figure 23: Trustees acknowledgement of transfer of mortgage

Wood while the original Wesleyan congregation were still located on Himley Road, at the edge of the village. The trustees' achievement merited a detailed report in the national MNC Magazine for 1855:

DUDLEY WEST CIRCUIT

– THE OPENING OF A NEW CHAPEL AT GORNAL WOOD

The opening services of the above chapel were held on the 17th and 24th of December. On the first Sabbath the Rev. W. Cocker preached in the morning; and Dr. Melson, of Birmingham, in the afternoon and evening. On the second Sabbath the Rev. W. Mills preached in the morning and evening, and the Rev. S.M. Coombs (Independent) in the afternoon.

These two days were seasons of high and holy pleasure, and they were made the occasion of manifesting a spirit of Christian liberality which reflected great honour on our friends at this place.

The collections amounted to £110, and it is most gratifying to know that this truly handsome sum was not made up by the munificent donations of a few wealthy persons, but by the liberal gifts of working men, whose hearts God has touched, and who were disposed to render unto him according to the benefits they have received. And when we consider that divine declaration, "Them that honour me I will honour", we cannot but indulge the hope that God will bless a people thus inclined to honour him with their substance; and that in blessing them he will continue to make them a blessing. Our cause at this place has been marked by gradual progress amidst many difficulties and discouragements. The officers and members of the church have given themselves to earnest prayer and effort; and God has been graciously pleased to hear their prayers, and to crown their efforts with success. Some of the most profligate characters – men who were living regardless of all the duties and decencies of life, rushing headlong to the indulgence of every vicious inclination, and to the perpetration of the worst of crimes – have been converted from the error of their ways, and are now following after whatsoever is pure and lovely, and of good report.[128]

The Revd Dr William Cocker (1816-1902) was one of the ministers in the Dudley West Circuit[129] at the time. A prominent MNC minister with a distinguished ministry, including two terms as President of the national MNC Conference (1863 and 1880), he served in the MNC work in Canada for six years, including a year as its President in 1867. On his return to England, for ten years he was Principal of Ranmoor College, Sheffield, the MNC ministerial training college.[130]

Figure 24: William Cocker

Dr Melson was a well-respected physician and Wesleyan Local Preacher in Birmingham, whose father was a Wesleyan Methodist Minister.[131] The Rev. William Mills (1813-1864) had served in Dudley in 1837 and in 1854 was the President of the MNC Conference.[132] His expenses for the journey from Hanley, Stoke-on-Trent were 12 shillings (60p) and the Dudley West Circuit were required to send one of their own ministers, Joseph Milburn Chicken, to supply for Mr Mills in Hanley at a cost

Figure 25: William Mills

to Zoar of 10 shillings (50p). Such exchange arrangements were quite commonplace, even well into the twentieth century.

The MNC Magazine report went on to describe the building and comment on the name chosen for the chapel,

> *The chapel is 40 feet long, 36 feet wide, and 28 feet high from the floor to the ceiling: it has a gallery on three sides, is well furnished with pews in the bottom, and will contain about 450 persons. The architectural design is good; the work is creditable to the builders, and the structure is an honour to our people, and an ornament to the neighbourhood. About 6 yards from the chapel there is a substantial and spacious school room, capable of accommodating 400 children. The writer is not able to state with accuracy what will be the pecuniary position of the estate when all the expenses are paid; but it is confidently expected that there will be a yearly reduction of the debt. May the blessing of God continually attend the services of this sanctuary, that, in accordance with its name (Zoar), it may be a place of refuge to many a righteous Lot amidst the storms of life, and to many awakened souls fleeing from impending ruin; and may the same divine blessing rest upon the school, making it the means of augmenting, the church on earth and the church in heaven.*[133]

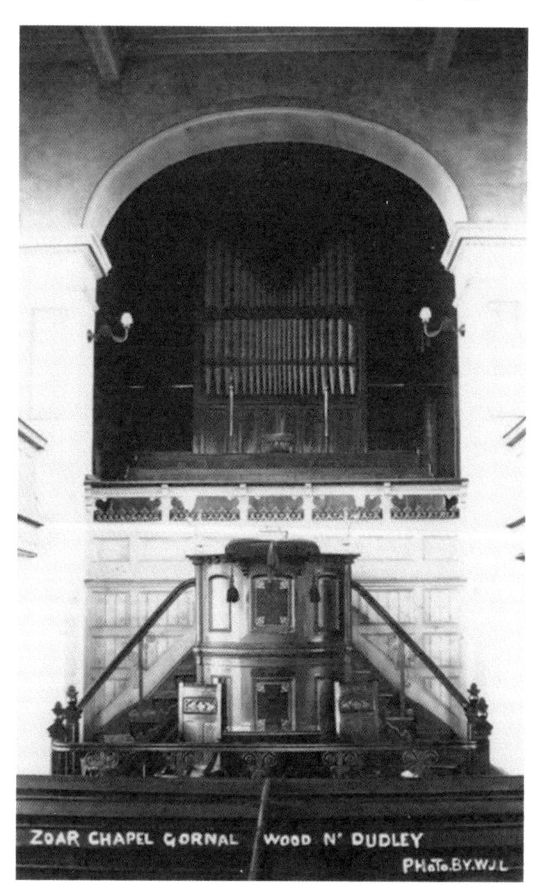

Figure 26: interior of 1854 Zoar

Considering how this MNC Society began with the expulsion of members from the Wesleyan congregation, the chosen name of '*Zoar*' for the building was particularly appropriate. In the Old Testament, Zoar, or Bela as it was also known, is mentioned in Genesis 14.8,

Then the king of Sodom, the king of Gomorrah, the king of Admah, the king of Zeboiim, and the king of Bela (that is, Zoar) went out, and they joined battle in the Valley of Siddim[134]

Zoar was to be the only one of the so-called "Cities of the Plain" to escape subsequent destruction. It became known as a place of refuge: Lot would hide near here (as noted in the MNC Magazine report);[135] and in Isaiah's oracle concerning Moab it is the place to which the refugees flee.[136] It is also mentioned at the end of the book of Deuteronomy as being at the furthest point of vision in the Promised Land as Moses looked out from mount Nebo.[137]

In 1855 the £300 loan debt for the Tabernacle was redeemed. What happened to the building is not known. However, there is an entry in the accounts, in December, detailing *'Rent for Jno. Tylers (sic) house Old Chapel Premises'* and *'Rent for Mr Bowles No 2 House.'* Either the building was converted into cottages or knocked down and replaced by two new buildings. Given the relative newness of the property, the former would probably be more likely. This was an action seen elsewhere in the locality: in Upper Gornal the Wesleyans converted a cottage into a chapel, restored it to a cottage when they acquired purpose-built premises, then, following an MNC breakaway from the Wesleyans, the new MNC congregation once more converted it to a chapel.

Zoar's cottages produced an initial annual rent of approximately £14. Letting was not always straightforward, for in 1858 there was a court case relating to non-payment of rent by a Mr. Hensey. The Hearing fee charge to the trustees was £2 and lawyer's advice cost 5s-0d (25p). In 1863 a Distraint Order was made against a Mr. Nicholds for rent arrears. Perhaps it was problems such as these which led the trustees to employ a rent collector, with Mr. Edward Wise receiving 1s-6d for every pound collected. An attempt was made to sell the cottages in 1857, when a notice board to advertise their sale was purchased for 1s-6d. Although the accounts for 1867 include a *'Deposit for two chapel houses'* of £7/0/0d, rent entries continued until 1873.The cottages may well have been sold in that year as there is a debit entry *'solicitor at Wolverhampton endorsing deeds 15/0d'*, however there is no evidence within the accounts of what sum was raised or what happened to it.

Trust renewal

The first trustees continued to fulfil their responsibilities until it became necessary in 1876 to renew membership.

The 1876 Trust

The trustees first met on 3 July 1876. There is no one complete listing of the trustees so the names below have been compiled from minutes of various trustees' meetings.

John Bate	Miner, died 1897
Edward Parkes	Engineer, d 1898
Thomas Hemmings	Labourer, d 1889
Isaac Greenway	Contractor, d 1897
Joseph Fellows	Farmer and Corn Dealer, d 1880. None of the minutes record him as actually attending a meeting. There is a note in the chapel accounts indicating a Joseph Fellows Senior, who served on the original and the 1854 trusts and a Joseph Fellows Junior.
Thomas Hale	Grocer, d 1899
John Tennant	Contractor, first Treasurer of the 1876 trustees, d 1896. Father of John Thomas (J T) Tennant.
Abraham Bradley	Miner, retired on formation of 1899 Trust.
John Thomas Tennant	Clerk, first Secretary of the 1876 Trust.
Adam Hale	Engineer
Richard Hemmings	Labourer
John Hyde	Grocer
David Hickman	Miner
Samuel Westwood	Stock Taker
Joseph Oakley	Engineer. Emigrated to America.
John Greenway Snr	Miner, retired on formation of 1899 Trust.
John Greenway the Younger	Miner
Henry Payton	Moulder, retired on formation of 1899 Trust.
William Sheen	Coke and Coal Merchant, first Chairman of the 1876 Trustees.

Income and Expenditure

Routine Trust income in the chapel's early years derived from four main sources. A typical example can be taken from 1857, when a total of £75 was raised from seat or pew rents (approximately £38), the annual Tea Meeting (£13), the Chapel Anniversary Sunday (£11) and house rents (£8). Expenditure included items such as mortgage interest (£40), fire Insurance (£3), colouring and whitewashing of 2 houses (£1), printing (£1), poor rate (16 shillings), a new bible for the chapel (£1) and general repairs (£3). This was one of the few years when no expenditure was incurred for window repairs, such frequent occurrences suggesting petty vandalism was the cause rather than occasional accidental damage. Typical entries included: *'two panes vestry window 6d [2½] and pane in chapel 6d'* for 1855 and *'repair to chapel windows £1/1/0d'* in 1892.

In 1870 the trustees spent some £125 on *'restoration'* work. The scale of this work can be appreciated when set alongside the total regular income for that year which was approximately £100. The cost was met from the following sources:

Collections	£29/01/01d
Ladies' Collection books	£89/10/08d
Collecting cards	£0/15/00d
First entertainment	£6/10/09d
Second entertainment	£2/11/00½d

The accounts published in 1896 and the activities related in them included three separate sets of figures. Firstly, the Trust Account ('Zoar Chapel and School Estate') already discussed (See Figure 27). Then there was the Society Account, administered not by the trustees, but by the Leaders' Meeting,[138] whose membership included class leaders, local preachers,[139] Sunday school teachers and stewards.[140] Its annual income was primarily derived from the ordinary weekly collections (approximately £90 in 1898). There were three main payments: a payment of £23 to *'Mr E P Hood, as Pastor'* [141]; the 'Quarterage', a three-monthly levy or Assessment due to the Circuit (£32) and a contribution for heating and lighting to the Trust account (£12). These two accounts and the activities related to them evidence a chapel which had changed dramatically from those days, mid-century, when the bold decision, as it then was, had been taken to build a schoolroom and then a chapel at the heart of Gornal Wood. The third account was the Improvement Fund, which stood at £279/5/6d, helped significantly by the money raised at the annual bazaar. It was this last account which

ZOAR CHAPEL AND SCHOOL ESTATE.

BALANCE SHEET from January 1st, to December 31st, 1897.

RICHARD HEMMINGS, Treasurer. GEORGE ROUND, Secretary.

RECEIPTS.

	£	s.	d.
Grant from Society towards Lighting and Cleaning (4 quarters)	12	0	0
Grant from Adult School	2	0	0
Grant for use of School and Vestries from various persons	5	4	6
Seat Rents (3 Quarters)	17	3	9
House Rent (2 Quarters)	2	18	6
Anniversary Collection	75	13	7¼
Harvest Festival	9	13	0
Trust Sermons	3	17	8
Grant from Jubilee Committee	9	16	0
	£138	7	0½

PAYMENTS.

	£	s.	d.	£	s.	d.
MUSIC, &c.						
Organist (3 quarters)	4	10	0			
Organ Blower (5 quarters)	1	3	0			
Music	2	4	2			
Grant to Choir	2	0	0			
Grant to Band	1	0	0			
Tuning Organ, &c.	1	11	3½			
GAS, &c.				12	8	5½
School and Chapel	8	6	1			
Coal and Coke	7	5	8½			
Gas Stove and Fitting	3	4	5			
Rates and Taxes	1	8	8½			
CHILDREN'S TREATS, &c.				20	4	11
Jubilee Treat	7	13	5½			
Jubilee Medals	1	11	0			
Grant to Jubilee Fund	0	10	6			
Annual School Treat	6	13	5			
Prizes for 1896	9	19	8			
INCIDENTALS.				26	8	1
Chapel Keeper, half year	5	3	0			
Commission to Seat Rent Collectors	1	0	6			
Fire Insurance	1	15	6			
Laying on Water	2	15	0			
Repairs	0	18	0			
Printing and Bill Posting (two years)	7	3	4			
Rev. M. Bartram, expenses	2	17	0			
Incidentals	1	0	8			
Interest on £200 at 4½ per cent. (1 year)	9	0	0			
Grant to Improvement Fund	40	0	0			
Balance in hand	4	11	5			
				76	4	5
				£138	7	0½

I have this day examined the Trustees' Accounts, &c., and found them correct.

(Signed) T. WILLETS ADSHEAD,
Circuit Auditor.

June 30th, 1898.

Figure 27: The Trust Account for 1897

would assume great significance at the start of the twentieth century, as will become clear as the story of Zoar continues.

Chapel Life

In the 1850s **SUNDAY WORSHIP** still involved a group of 'singers' leading the singing. They were allocated £2 yearly for their *'expenses'*. From 1869 they are recorded in the accounts as 'choir' rather than 'singers'. There is no indication as to why this change of designation occurred. What is evident is that by the 1880s their repertoire was broadening to include the singing of anthems and special music for Harvest Festivals, Christmas and even the Wake Tea entertainment (for all of which additional expenditure was recorded). The purchase of 20 chant books in 1886 suggests worship was developing a more formal pattern. Despite their increased contributions, even in 1896 the choir's annual allowance remained at £2.

Entries in the mid-1850s refer to *'books and strings etc.'* The mention of strings suggests the continuing use of a bass viol, supported by an 1864 entry referring to *'Repair dble. Bass, 12s-6d.'* Musical resources were expanded by the purchase of a harmonium for £37 in 1857 and a trumpet for £3/5/0d in 1861. The harmonium was sold in 1863 for £24/17/6d. The accounts do not detail a new one being purchased until 1872, costing £28/19/0d. A decision to purchase an organ was taken in 1880 when £50 was set aside in an organ fund, with annual sums of

£2/5/0d being added over the following two years. The new instrument was installed in 1883 and with it came the need for an organ blower and an organist, both of whom would be paid for their services. In 1894 the school organ was sold for £10, its replacement costing £13, plus another £7 to install it.

Through to the 1870s the **TRUST ANNIVERSARY SERMONS** [142] were the highlight in the Sunday calendar, delivered at morning, afternoon and evening services, sometime between September and December,[143] advertised by 250 or more *'circulars'* and 50 window *'bills'*. Typically, in 1861, Mr. Goodwin was paid 12s-6d for printing and A Turner 2s-6d for distributing them. The importance of the occasion is underlined by the amount of money realized by the collections taken at the services. Over the first 15 years of Zoar's existence, these amounted to between £7 and £11 at a time when the total annual trust income was between £60 and £80. Towards the end of the century two other special Sundays began to assume greater importance: the Harvest Festival[144] and the Sunday School Anniversary. The first recorded mention of the former at Zoar is July 1882 and for the latter April 1884. As the Trust accounts for 1897 indicate, both contributed significantly to the total income, while, compared to the 1850s, the main income sources had changed significantly.

SUNDAY SCHOOL ANNIVERSARIES became commonplace nationally during the nineteenth century,[145] with children singing hymns and reciting verse. These services were so popular that ***Repetition*** services were held, usually two to four weeks later. When they began at Zoar is difficult to establish. The 1884 entry states *'£20 received from the treasurer of the Sunday School committee'*, the amount suggesting a large-scale event such as an anniversary. Under expenditure, in 1886 is an entry, *'Provision of children's treat £7/19/5½d'*. Treat usually referred to the reward for participation in the anniversary. After 1892, when collections totalled £66/10/4d and £8/3/3d was spent on the treat, such entries regularly appeared in the Trust accounts, together with the cost of prizes for scholars three years later (cost £6/17/10d plus 3s-6d for presentation labels). Evidently the trustees realized the significant contribution that the anniversary collections could make to their regular income and decided to claim it for their funds as opposed to those of the Sunday School.

By the end of the nineteenth century there was a full weekly programme of **WORSHIP and CHRISTIAN FELLOWSHIP** advertised, which included,[146]

Sundays

Divine worship at 10.30 and 6.00 o'clock

School at 9.30 and 2.00 o'clock

Adult School (Male) at 7.30a.m.

Weekdays

Monday Public Prayer Meeting at 7.00p.m.

Wednesday Class Meetings at 7.00p.m.

Thursday Pleasant Evening at 7.00p.m.

CLASS MEETINGS were a significant feature of early Methodism, in which members met weekly in small groups to deepen their faith and commitment and offer mutual support. They are considered in detail in Chapter Six.[147] The **ADULT SCHOOL (MALE)** and **THURSDAY PLEASANT EVENING** will be considered in Chapter Four.

TEA MEETINGS provided the highlight of the year's social calendar. In the early Zoar years they helped to raise a significant portion of the Trust's income, but towards the end of the century the aim was simply to cover costs. Their popularity is evidenced in that 191 tickets were sold for the 1899 gathering.

In the later years of the nineteenth century the **CHAPEL BAZAAR** became another important fund raiser and social occasion for the Zoar Society, as it did across Methodism nationally. Arnold Bennett offers a literary account of what was involved and the interaction of different stall holders in his novel *'Anna of the Five Towns'*.[148] Figure 28 shows the detail of the stalls and the income produced for Zoar in 1896. While Bazaars were held annually in some places, the Zoar trustees only used them occasionally and mainly to stimulate interest and income for major projects.

PROPERTY MATTERS demanded a significant amount of trustees' attention towards the end of the century. In 1883 there were new negotiations about land purchase. The growth of the Sunday School necessitated more space and Thomas Griffin, owner of the neighbouring Abbey Farm estate, was approached. A modest scheme was proposed, requiring a two-yard strip of land along the rear of the chapel grounds in order to build onto the back of the school. Agreement was reached, but not before Mr Griffin had pushed the price up to 5s-6d (27½p) per square yard, significantly in excess of the 4s (20p) maximum that the trustees had hoped to pay.

In 1898 the trustees took the decision to apply to register the building for marriages. Earlier that year Parliament had passed a Marriage Act which provided for the appointment, by the governing body of

.. GENERAL STATEMENT OF BAZAAR. ..

RECEIPTS.

	£	s.	d.
Congregational Stall	34	17	4
do.	21	16	5
Sunday School Stall	25	5	0½
Confectionery Stall	13	6	4
Refreshment Stall	1	11	0
do.	1	11	0
Entertainments	2	13	5
do.	0	16	11
Ironworks	0	6	5
Money at Door	1	3	[illegible]
do.	1	1	[illegible]
Sale of Tickets	10	3	0
Proceeds of Tea given by Mrs. Smith	0	16	0
Balance of Donations from Congregational Stall	0	5	0
do. do. Sunday School „	0	3	6¼
Grant by Mrs. Smith to Congregational Stall	10	0	0
do. do. Sunday School „	5	0	0
do. do. Confectionery „	2	10	0
Total ...	133	5	5¾

EXPENDITURE.

	£	s.	d.
36 yards Art Muslins at 5½d. per yard	0	16	6
366 do. do. 1½d. „	1	14	3½
30 yards W. Calico at 3d. per yard ...	0	7	6
Bill Posting	0	3	0
do.	0	3	0
Police Officer	0	5	0
Grant to Band	0	2	6
do.	0	5	0
Higgins' Printing Account	2	3	6
Joshua Jones, Timber	1	0	1
Paper	0	2	0
String	0	0	6
Advertisement in "Dudley Herald"	0	4	6
Stamps for Circulars	0	4	6
	7	11	10½
Balance in Treasurer's hands ...	125	13	7¼
Total ...	133	5	5¾

Examined and found correct, JNO. SHEEN, GEORGE ROUND, } Auditors.

Figure 28: 1896 Bazaar Account

a building already registered for public worship, of an authorised person in whose presence a marriage could legally be solemnized and registered. It was the usual practice to register buildings for public worship when they opened, but the original Zoar trustees had evidently failed to do so, as the local registrar sent the necessary forms in July 1898,[149] with the registration obtained on 22 November, 44 years after the opening.

217

Certificate of Place of Meeting for Religious Worship having been certified to the Registrar General.

No. of Registry	Name of Building	Where situated: Parish or Place	Where situated: County	Superintendent Registrar's District	Religious Denomination	Date of Registry
[illegible].888	Zoar Chapel	Abbey-road, Gornal Wood, Sedgley	Stafford	Dudley	Methodist New Connexion	22nd November 1898.

IT IS HEREBY CERTIFIED that the Place of Meeting for Religious Worship above described was, on the Nineteenth day of November 1898, duly certified to the Registrar General of Births, Deaths, and Marriages in England, and was on the Twenty-second day of November 1898, duly recorded as required by the Act of 18 & 19 Victoria, Chapter 81; and also that the Record of such certification remains uncancelled at the date hereof.

GIVEN under the Seal of the GENERAL REGISTER OFFICE this Twenty-third day of November 19[illegible].

(SEE BACK.)

Figure 29: the 1898 registration document

Chapter Four

The first Zoar, establishing itself at the heart of the village

With the building in the 1850s of a substantial suite of premises in the middle of the village, how did the trustees and members of Zoar engage with villagers and what can we learn from that engagement about village life? [150]

Attendance at worship

The main services, open to all, were held on Sundays at 10.30 am and 6.00 pm. While hymns were sung and prayers said, the main focus was on the bible and the sermon, with its detailed reflection on the chosen readings. However, when Holy Communion was being celebrated, only those who were members were admitted. Even as late as the 1960s it was the usual practice at Zoar for a shortened service of Holy

ARRANGEMENT OF SUBJECTS.

PART I.

SECTION I.—The Existence, Attributes, and Works of God, 1—37.
II.—The Incarnation, &c., Offices, and Characters of Christ, 38—109.
III.—The Characters and Influences of the Holy Spirit, 110—121. [See also Section iv. Part iii.—Praise to the Holy Spirit.]
IV.—The Apostacy of Man, 122—124.

PART II.

SECTION I.—Death, 125—144.
II.—Resurrection, 145—146.
III.—Judgment, 147—159.
IV.—Heaven, 160—179.
V.—Hell, 180—181.

PART III.

SECTION I.—Praise, 182—189.
II.—To the Father, 190—191.
III.—To the Son, 192—203.
IV.—To the Holy Spirit, 204.
V.—To the Trinity, 205—208. (See also Doxologies at the end of the Book.)
VI.—For Temporal Benefits, 209—211.
VII.—For Spiritual Mercies, 212—219.

PART IV.

SECTION I.—Petition.—General, 220—224.
II.—For Divine Guidance, 225—227.
III.—For Holiness, 228—274.

xii ARRANGEMENT OF SUBJECTS.

SECTION IV.—For the King. The Nation. Universal Peace. The Jews, 275—280.
V.—For Christ's Universal Reign, 281—291.

PART V.

RELIGIOUS ORDINANCES.

SECTION I.—The Scriptures, 292—296.
II.—The Sabbath, 297—305.
III.—Public Worship, 306—350.
IV.—Domestic Worship, 351—353.
V.—Private Devotion, 354—357.
VI.—Baptism. The Lord's Supper, 358—372.
VII.—Love Feasts, 373—379.
VIII.—Society Meetings, 380—411.

PART VI.

PARTICULAR CLASSES OF PERSONS.

SECTION I.—Sinners, 412—423.
II.—Penitents, 424—462.
III.—Backsliders, 463—479.
IV.—The Lukewarm, 480—484.
V.—Christian Believers: their Privileges, &c., 485—620.
VI.—Mariners, 621—623.
VII.—The Young, 624—626.

PART VII.

PARTICULAR OCCASIONS.

SECTION I.—Revival of Religion, 627—633.
II.—Morning and Evening, 634—640.
III.—Birth-Day and New-Year, 641—645.
IV.—National Calamities. Fasts. Friendly Society Anniversary, 646—656.
V.—Doxologies, 657—660.

Figure 30: the contents of the MNC hymn book published in 1859

Communion to follow immediately after the main service. Although membership was no longer required, there was still a handful of people who would leave before this second service began.[151]

Membership

Membership was conferred on those who had made a public profession of faith and had been received formally as members of the Methodist Church, following a course of instruction and reaffirmed in the annual or quarterly distribution of membership or class tickets.[152] In the earliest days of the Church, ministers and class leaders would review the membership lists, considering the standing of each member in turn, before tickets were issued. In 1855 the Zoar Society recorded a membership of 77, a figure which varied little for the rest of the century and stood at 78 in 1901. These figures imply that the Society's influence within the village was not particularly significant. However, average congregations at the time were recorded as some 300. This was equivalent to 5% of the population of the local parish, or at least 10% of Gornal Wood itself.[153]

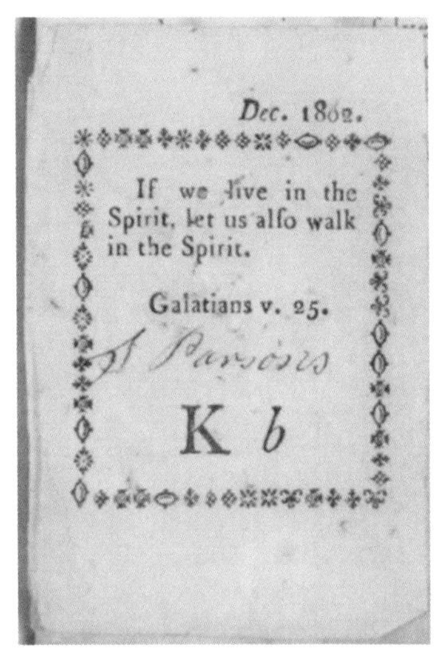

Figure 31 - an example of an early class ticket

A further indication of the chapel's strength was the 211 pew lettings which were in place in 1855. The prestige of having one's 'own' pew clearly persisted. For Zoar in 1858 the four Quarterly pew rental income totals were: £6/9/0d, £6/17/0d, £8/5/0d and £5/2/0d. The relative importance of this particular income stream can be appreciated in that the total trust income for that year was approximately £60. Not that all pew or seat holders were good at settling their accounts. In June 1877 the trustees noted some seat holders were *'considerably behind'* with their payments, a minute book entry repeated on several occasions in future years.

Evangelical outreach

Evangelical outreach activity took place on an occasional basis, with the camp meetings mentioned earlier repeated in 1857 and 1858. Their timing reflects a period of nationwide evangelistic activity, referred to by some commentators as the 'Second Evangelical Awakening' which reached its peak in 1859-60.[154] At Zoar in 1857, 4s-6d was spent on hand bills to advertise the meetings and the following year 14 shillings. While co-operation or shared activities between the different denominations was rare at the time, the 1858 event was sponsored jointly by Zoar along with the local Wesleyans and Primitive Methodists, who shared the cost of the publicity, the Wesleyans contributing 4s-8d and the Primitive Methodists 2s-4d.

In 1864 special events known as Revival Meetings[155] were held, their aim being *'a revival of godliness and Christian grace'*. Meetings would take place each evening for a week or a fortnight, with a specially invited preacher. Everyone would be encouraged to invite non-church attenders and Sunday School teachers would be expected to ensure their scholars knew of the special gatherings for young people. The meetings involved hymn singing and prayer, building up to the preacher's address. Then, typically, as illustrated by Arnold Bennett,

> *The voice of the revivalist ceased, but he kept the attitude of supplication. Sobs were heard in various quarters, and here and there the elders of the chapel could be seen talking to some convicted sinner. The revivalist began softly to sing 'Jesu lover of my soul' and most of the congregation, standing up, joined him; but the sinners, stricken of the Spirit remained abjectly bent, tortured by conscience, pulled this way by Christ and that by Satan. A few rose and went to the Communion rails, there to kneel in sight of all. [the minister] descended from the pulpit and opening the wicket which led to the Communion table spoke to these over the rails, reassuringly, as a nurse to a child. Other sinners, desirous of fuller and more intimate guidance, passed down the aisles and so into the preacher's vestry ... and were followed thither by class leaders and other proved servants of God.* [156]

The intensity and high-profile impact of such occasions is well described by Bennett.[157] His account underlines the novelty and powerful impact of the meetings, which usually enjoyed a significant profile within the local community, not least, perhaps, because there was little else to invite people's attention.

Thursday Pleasant Evening

By the end of the century, a regular mid-week meeting with this name was taking place on Thursdays at 7.00 pm. This was probably a spin-off from the Pleasant Sunday Afternoon movement. The PSA was the idea of John Blackham, a Congregational Church deacon in nearby West Bromwich, who recognised that many non-churchgoers, especially among the working classes of the 1870s, were at a loose end on Sunday afternoons. He introduced meetings which included a variety of activities offering fellowship, social contact, entertainment and worship. The symbol used by the organisation was that of two hands, one giving and one receiving a friendly welcome.

Evidently those who attended Zoar's meetings were rewarded with book prizes, as the label below indicates. The book awarded in 1895 to Elizabeth Stoddart was entitled *Friendly Visitor*.

Figure 32: The PSA Logo on a Victorian watch chain fob

Figure 33: PTE prize label

Use of the chapel premises

Over time lettings were made to a large cross-section of local organisations and events. These lettings give some insight into community life in Gornal Wood. They included,

- a ***Women's Club***, so called, but about which nothing else is known.
- ***Miners' Union***
- the ***Lower Gornal Protestant Churchmen's Mission*** was presumably

a group representing the different non-Anglican and non-Catholic denominations active in the locality.

• the ***Liberal Association***.

• a ***Death Club***, which was most probably a Friendly Society, one of many such societies in Victorian times. Epidemics and high mortality rates among children meant death was very much a part of everyday community life for the Black Country working classes. There was no National Insurance or National Health Service and the only way of planning for unexpected expenditure on health care, times when workers were laid off during periods of Depression or for funerals was to join a Friendly Society, with members typically paying a penny or more per week into its funds. Without such provision death might mean a pauper's burial in an unmarked grave. In the 1860s the average cost of a working man's funeral was £5, with a handcart, or bier cart, carried by 2-4 men being the most common form of transport for the coffin. By way of comparison, a black lacquered carriage pulled by horses could be hired for £100 in 1887.[158]

• ***the Rechabites*** was another Friendly Society, committed to the Temperance Movement,[159] flourishing from the second quarter of the nineteenth century. The name was taken from the Old Testament Rechabites who were a nomadic people known for their strict rules to abstain from wine, from building houses, from sowing seed, and from planting vineyards (Jeremiah 35:6–7).

• ***the Free Gardeners Friendly Society*** The Ancient Order of Free Gardeners originated in Scotland in the seventeenth century as an organisation to regulate the gardening profession. Whilst its history reflects elements of freemasonry, by the mid-nineteenth century most lodges were, primarily, mutual benefit societies, open to non-gardeners.[160] Zoar records show that there was an active lodge in Dudley and, evidently, meetings took place in Gornal Wood.[161] One time trustee, John Greenway was a member.

• ***Local doctors*** Beginning with Dr Walker in 1872, the premises were used as a vaccination clinic. This particular letting probably came about as a consequence of the Government's 1867 and 1871 Vaccination Acts requiring parents to have their children vaccinated against smallpox. The 1867 Act required local poor-law guardians to manage vaccination districts, which were formed out of the parishes, and pay vaccinators from 1s to 3s per child vaccinated in the district, the amount paid being determined by how far they had to travel. The 1871 Act required the appointment of Vaccination Officers.

• ***Public meetings*** Typical, and intriguing, was the holding of a meeting in 1877 *'to protest against the action taken by the Returning Officer in the recent Local Board Election and to consider what steps shall be taken to obtain a proper scrutiny of the voting papers.'* [162]

The Zoar trustees were not always in agreement as to whom the premises should or should not be let. So, for example, in September 1877 there was a debate concerning letting to non-chapel organisations (or *'for public purposes'* as the Minutes have it). The outcome was the appointment of a sub-committee to supervise such lettings and a decision to charge 1/- (5p) per hour for gas.

Education

The erecting of a Sunday School at the heart of the village was presumably inspired by a wish to provide better facilities in order to engage more effectively with young people. No early records exist chronicling its activities. Most probably it would have followed the pattern made popular by the pioneering work of Robert Raikes in Gloucester in the last quarter of the eighteenth century, providing basic lessons in literacy alongside religious instruction. By 1831 Sunday Schools in Great Britain were being attended weekly by some 1.25 million children, or about 25 per cent of the eligible population.[163]

The internal layout of the Zoar Sunday School was to be little changed over more than a century with rows of benches, with moveable backs, laid out in one large hall.[164] Everyone could face forward when the Sunday School Superintendent or anyone else was speaking from the desk at the front and then, when individual classes were taking place, along each alternate row the backs could be tilted the other way to make small individual classes.

By the end of the nineteenth century, in addition to the work of

Figure 34: a typical Victorian Sunday School bench

the Sunday School, there also existed what was known as an Adult School (Male) which met at 7.30 am on Sundays. Such meetings were not uncommon at the time but have not achieved a significant profile in the recording of the history of the Sunday School movement. Adult schools began to develop from the end of the eighteenth century, but their most successful years were from around 1850, with a peak in the years prior to the First World War. Their original aim was to teach reading using the Bible and writing by copying out passages or from dictation. Over time the range of activities expanded to include lectures, discussions and study circles. They took place at one of the few times when young working men were free and able to attend and provided an environment in which they could develop their self-confidence, debating ability and an awareness of the world beyond their own limited working environment. Arnold Bennett's novel Clayhanger offers an illustration of these gatherings. He devotes several pages recording the experience of the young Edwin Clayhanger in preparing for and contributing to such a meeting.[165] These schools were found across a number of denominations and at their peak some 1900 schools were active, involving over 114,000 adults.[166]

Nationally, churches and chapels became increasingly involved in the general field of education during the nineteenth century, as a complex and often haphazard pattern of education provision emerged. iii In the early years of the century, provision in Gornal Wood was minimal. Charles Girdlestone, vicar of Sedgley Parish Church (1826-37), writing in 1832 offered an explanation,

> *... whilst the population ... has increased ... scarce any persons of property reside, except such as are actively engaged in business. Thus the poor are deprived of that instruction and help, which it should be the chief occupation of the rich to impart. And with the exception of the ministers of religion, scarce anyone of education and leisure can be found, to devote himself to the work of doing good.* [167]

Not that everyone considered it a good thing to educate the children of working-class families. When the Parochial Schools Bill of 1807 was debated in the Commons, Tory MP Davies Giddy said,

> *[to educate the poor] would be prejudicial to their morals and happiness: it would teach them to despise their lot in life, instead of making them good servants in agriculture and other laborious employments. Instead of teaching them subordination it would render them fractious and refractory... it would enable them to read seditious pamphlets, vicious books and publications against Christianity and render them insolent to their superiors.*[169]

In the village, St. James' parish church sponsored a National School, following the establishment by the Church of England of the National Society for Promoting the Education of the Poor in the Principles of the Established Church in England and Wales. The society's aim was,

[that] the National Religion should be made the foundation of National Education, and should be the first and chief thing taught to the poor, according to the excellent Liturgy and Catechism provided by our Church.

An 1847 Inspection report on the St James's school described it as '*... by no means in a fitting condition, but the salary [of the teachers] is so low it is hardly more than can be expected.*' In that year there were only 138 children (57 boys and 81 infants and girls) in school, along with a male and female teacher who together received an annual wage of £30. Among the miners and nailers there was little appreciation of the value of education, summed up in two comments recorded in an 1861 report, prepared by George Coode,[170] on education in the locality, '*It is a common thing to say "The father went to the pit and he made a fortune, his son went to school and he lost it."*'

Coode commented further on what he encountered in Gornal,

Education has made but little progress, indeed in the district of lower Gornall (sic), where the men are all pitmen or quarries, and the women, boys and girls all nailers or small chain makers ... in three days spent among them I found no adult in this class who could write; and although some confessed to be able to read a little, in each case when I examined the parties the pretention proved false.

Mid-century, Zoar housed a small day school. Following the chapel opening, in 1855-56 the vestry was rented for use as a school by a Miss Wasdell, at one shilling (5p).[171] This letting disappeared until 1863 when a Miss Bradley was recorded as pursuing the same activity at the same rental. As with many other schools of the day, it is probably true to say that the standard of education offered was minimal.[172] Estimated calculations suggest local working-class children received an average two years of education which ended before the age of 10.[173]

As early as 1851 the Methodist New Connexion Annual Conference had encouraged chapels to look at their accommodation, insisting that Sunday Schools should not remain '*wholly unoccupied between Sabbath and Sabbath*' when they could be '*fitted up for day schools at very little expense.*'[174] Following Gladstone's Liberal Government's Education Act of 1870, intended to establish a national scheme of education,[175] the Zoar trustees decided that their school,

.. be offered to the [local Sedgley] school board for the sum of £20 per Annum,

free of all tax, for educational purposes provided that they elect Managers from our Society to carry out the arrangements of the said school board.

The Board asked for an additional building to be provided for an Infants school along with extra classrooms and space for a playground. Despite the evident wish of both Board and trustees to make it happen, the scheme failed to materialise due to the refusal, on this occasion, of Zoar's immediate neighbour, Mr Griffin, to sell or lease part of his land to make possible the additional requirements. In 1880 the Board opened Red Hall school on Zoar Street in Gornal Wood adding a new set of buildings on the other side of the road in 1890.[176] It would appear that additional accommodation was still required, as, despite the failure of previous plans, the Zoar Trust accounts indicate that their premises were being rented on a regular basis by the Sedgley Urban District Council for schooling purposes through much of the 1890s.

Paying taxes

Property ownership required the trustees to pay a number of taxes, all of which highlight the changing face of English society in the second half of the nineteenth century. Poor Rate varying from 10 to 18 shillings (50-90p) was levied on the trust property through the second half of the nineteenth century, used to provide poor relief.[177]

In 1867 the trustees were required to pay a special tax, levied on top of the Poor Rate, *'for cattle plague'*, after England had been hit by a particularly extensive and virulent outbreak of rinderpest or cattle plague in 1865-67.[178] The tax was intended to provide funds in order to mitigate the consequences, which were so devastating nationally that churches were asked to make use of a specially circulated prayer.[179]

A Highway Rate, charged to help maintain and improve local roads, varied between four and eight shillings (20 - 40p) and was last listed in the Zoar Trust accounts in 1873. Local parishes had been made responsible for roads other than turnpikes following the General Highways Act of 1835. After the Local Government Act of 1888, the responsibility was handed over to newly constituted County Councils.

Following a series of Acts of Parliament passed in the 1860s and 1870s, culminating in the 1875 Public Health Act, the trustees also became liable to pay a General District Rate to the local authority. The 1875 Act sought to coordinate various previously approved pieces of legislation to do with matters such as sewerage and drains, water supply, housing and disease. For example, local authorities were ordered to cover sewers, keep them in good condition, supply fresh water to their citizens, collect rubbish and provide street lighting.

Utilities

By the end of the century the trustees had begun paying a Water Rate. Initially water for the chapel cottages was supplied from a pump. The account books indicate that it regularly required attention. Typical examples were 6s-od paid to Thomas Payton in 1859 for repair work and 2s-od and 1s-6d in 1867 to John Payton. However, the pump also helped produce a regular annual income of around 30 shillings (£1-50p) from *'supply of water to Mrs. Bennett,'* an arrangement which continued through into the 1880s. In 1859 a 'soft water pump' was installed at the chapel. Its use was superseded in 1897 when a mains water supply was laid on by the South Staffordshire Water Works Company[180] and the opportunity taken to connect the supply to the chapel house, as £2/15/od was paid for *'putting in water to house.'* From this time a Water Rate, initially 1s-8d, was paid each Quarter.

When the chapel opened, the interior was lit by Camphine lamps, four of which were purchased from Messrs. Salt and Lloyd of Birmingham for 24 shillings each, along with a gallon of Camphine at 5 shillings and two bottles at 1 shilling each (5p). Camphine was the trade name of a purified spirit of turpentine prepared by distilling turpentine with quicklime.

Figure 35: a typical Camphine lamp

In 1865 gas lighting was installed by James Fuller of Wolverhampton at a cost of £34, met by special collections on 15 October which raised £13/14/07d, entertainment by the 'Pensnett Lifeboat Crew' raised £1/14/06d and £21/16/01d came from collecting cards, which had been issued to individuals who then had to seek subscriptions. The use of collecting cards or books was a common and effective way of widening the number of people contributing to a project. Money also came from the sale of three of the old lamps at 4 shillings each.

Chapel heating was provided by coke and coal. In 1876 it was decided to pay the chapel keeper extra for lighting the fire on a Saturday evening, when required. By 1878, the *heating apparatus* was deemed to be in *a very unsatisfactory and even a very dangerous condition* and so plans were agreed to upgrade it.

What has been written up to this point reveals why, as one century ended and another commenced, the trustees could look back over 65 years of significant growth and development. The little band who had met in the open air on the first Sunday after their expulsion from the Wesleyan congregation on Himley Road could not have imagined that their successors would be part of a lively vibrant congregation, based in substantial premises, at the centre of the village and intimately involved in the life of the local community.

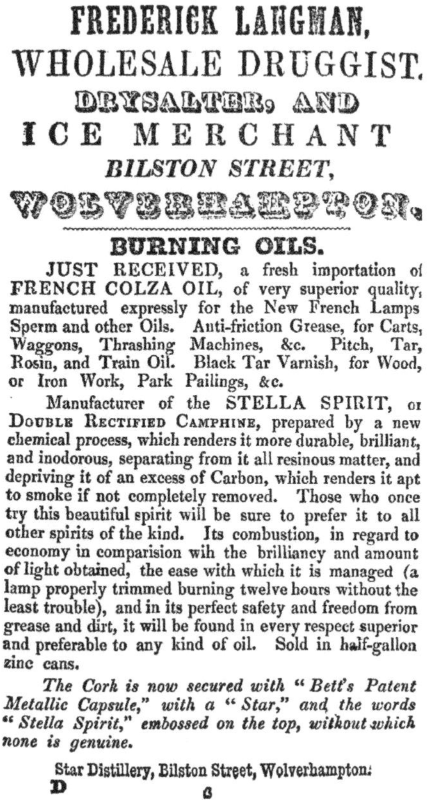

FREDERICK LANGMAN,
WHOLESALE DRUGGIST,
DRYSALTER, AND
ICE MERCHANT
BILSTON STREET,
WOLVERHAMPTON.

BURNING OILS.

JUST RECEIVED, a fresh importation of FRENCH COLZA OIL, of very superior quality, manufactured expressly for the New French Lamps Sperm and other Oils. Anti-friction Grease, for Carts, Waggons, Thrashing Machines, &c. Pitch, Tar, Rosin, and Train Oil. Black Tar Varnish, for Wood, or Iron Work, Park Pailings, &c.

Manufacturer of the STELLA SPIRIT, or DOUBLE RECTIFIED CAMPHINE, prepared by a new chemical process, which renders it more durable, brilliant, and inodorous, separating from it all resinous matter, and depriving it of an excess of Carbon, which renders it apt to smoke if not completely removed. Those who once try this beautiful spirit will be sure to prefer it to all other spirits of the kind. Its combustion, in regard to economy in comparision wih the brilliancy and amount of light obtained, the ease with which it is managed (a lamp properly trimmed burning twelve hours without the least trouble), and in its perfect safety and freedom from grease and dirt, it will be found in every respect superior and preferable to any kind of oil. Sold in half-gallon zinc cans.

The Cork is now secured with "Bett's Patent Metallic Capsule," with a "Star," and the words "Stella Spirit," embossed on the top, without which none is genuine.

Star Distillery, Bilston Street, Wolverhampton.

Figure 36: Promoting Camphine Oil

PART THREE:
THE SECOND ZOAR

CHAPTER FIVE

Managing the Zoar Trust Estate in the twentieth and twenty-first centuries

The *'Zoar Trust Estate'* was the title in use at the turn of the century to describe all the property owned by the church, principally the church and Sunday School buildings and the caretaker's house. Successive

[This Document when signed should be carefully preserved with Memorandum of Appointment of New Trustees.]

Form "B."—Consent to Act as Trustees.

(1) Insert Full Name of Property, Street or Road, Parish, Town, and County, where situate.

We, the undersigned, are willing to be appointed and to act as Trustees of the Methodist New Connexion (1) Zoar Chapel and School, situate in Abbey Road Gornal Wood, parish of Sedgeley, County of Stafford.

As Witness our hands the First day of November 1899.

NAME (IN FULL).	RESIDENCE (IN FULL).	OCCUPATION.
William Smith	Fair View Lower Gornal	Contractor
George Round	107 Ruiton Street	Grocer &c
Joseph Brettle	The Gas works	Retort Setter.
John Bowyer	5 Straits Road Gornal Wood	Store keeper
Henry Dayton	38 Himley Road Gornal Wood.	Grocer
Benjamin Parkes	3. Bull St Gornal Wood	Engineer
Joseph Gilbert	5 Bull St Gornal Wood	Miner
John Hemmings	19 Zoar Street Lower Gornal.	Clerk.
Charles Henry Smith	7 Prices Road	Engineer
Herbert Hickman	Temple Street Lower Gornal	Draper.
Job Hale	2 Burr Street Gornal Wood	Retort Worker

Figure 37 - The Memorandum recording new trustees in 1899

Trust bodies owned and managed the Estate through to 1974 when the *Methodist Church Act* was approved by Parliament, abolishing local Trusts.

At the start of the twentieth century a renewed Trust was in place. In 1898 a decision had been taken to review Trust membership as several trustees had either died, moved away from the locality, including Joseph Oakley who emigrated to the USA, or asked to be discharged from their responsibilities. Ten trustees were prepared to continue:

Benjamin Bradley	Wrens Nest, Woodsetton	Accountant clerk
John Thomas Tennant	39 Himley Road	Draper
John Hyde	51 New Street	Agent
Samuel Westwood	51 & 52 Graveyard Road	Stocktaker
David Hickman	6 Water Road	Miner
William Sheen	Cape Hill, Smethwick	Traveller
Richard Hemmings	12 & 13 Church Street	Grocer's manager
Adam Hale	4 Hopyard Lane	Engineer
John Greenway	10 Barrs Street	Retort Worker[181]

New trustees were appointed as recorded on the necessary consent form.

Renovating the Sunday School Building

During the early years of the twentieth century the trustees considered various plans to renovate the premises. Their thinking as to what was achievable changed over time. Initially, an architect was asked to submit *'plans and specifications for improvements, alterations and additions ... at the Chapel and premises.'*[182] The renovation of the Sunday School was soon agreed, to include *'ventilation, sanitation, reseating, stripping walls of plaster, roof, putting of windows in end of school in Abbey Road, glazing windows.'* At the same time, repairs were put in hand to the roof and boiler.

A tender was accepted from Joshua Jones, who had been approached about joining the recently reformed trust, but, for whatever reason, did not become a trustee. Sedgley Urban District Council was to be responsible for the gas fittings and Fisher, Son and Weaver for the seating - plans to use fixed seating were changed as the project unfolded. As part of the renovation, it was decided to replace the organ, which was advertised for sale *'in the Dudley Herald twice and in the Express and Star for one week'* and sold to a Mr. Holden for £1. The choice of a replacement rumbled on in meetings for some time, with a substitute hired on a temporary basis and a permanent replacement finally purchased from Messrs. Nicholson and Lord of Walsall in 1902 at a cost of £50. The cost-conscious trustees asked the company to include an organ stool as part of the deal.

Various events were arranged to raise money for the renovations, beginning with a special appeal at the Sunday School Anniversary of 1901 and including a series of Sunday afternoon musical concerts, a sale of work and a special effort in connection with the annual Tea Meeting. As the work moved forward, it was decided that costs needed to be cut. For example, the number of lamps to be installed was reduced and the trustees also undertook a review of regular expenditure to see where other savings could be made. The premises were re-opened by Mrs. William Smith, wife of the newly appointed Trust Chairman. The trustees initially talked of inviting the Revd. Joseph Odell as guest preacher, a notable Primitive Methodist minister, who at the time was in charge of the 'Evangelists' Home' in Birmingham,[183] but the final choice was the President of the MNC Conference, with Circuit ministers and officials *'and the leading ladies and gentlemen' invited ... by special circular ...'.*

The chapel: renovate or replace?

With the Sunday School renovated, the trustees turned their attention to the chapel itself. 1903 saw the calling of a meeting of Leaders, Trustees and Teachers to discuss the question of improvement or replacement. On 22 April this *'representative assembly ...,' so the subsequent*

Figure 38: The Jubilee Celebration Preachers

Trust minutes record, '... after considerable discussion ...' agreed to the suggestion of '... a new Chapel with end gallery only', but further reflection and discussion led the trustees to conclude that replacement would be too costly and so improvement or 'reconstruction' became the focus of everyone's attention. The following year would be the chapel's Jubilee and it was decided that the celebrations would be used to promote the reconstruction scheme. Special services were planned for December 1904, with specially invited preachers, Revd. Thomas Rider from Southport, who had been in the circuit in 1863-65 and served as MNC President in 1883, Revd. Michael Bartram from Darlington, who had been in the circuit as a probationary minister in 1886-87 and served as MNC President in 1894 and the Revd. Francis Jewell of Prestatyn.

Publicity for these celebrations included an appeal from the trustees,

> *After the lapse of "Fifty Years" it is almost needless to say that the Chapel has become very inadequate, inconvenient, and entirely out of date. The trustees have before them a plan of Reconstruction, and specially appeal to all old scholars and friends for their presence at one or all of these services and for their very generous help to carry out these alterations.*

As well as special Sunday services, a *'Great United Tea Meeting'* was planned for the Monday following the first anniversary service, *'Under the distinguished patronage of Alderman J Hughes, JP'*. Hughes was the son of the innkeepers of the Woodman Inn who in 1835 had invited the Wesleyan exiles to meet for worship at their premises.[184]

The trustees' meetings of March and May 1905 revisited the question of a new church building. They were advised that the cost was estimated at

Figure 39: the Jubilee Tea Meeting of 1904

£3,000. Given that the *'Improvement Fund'* contained £600 at that time, they held to reconstruction at £1,800.

For a Society whose membership stood at just over 80, fund raising now became a challenging priority. A "Grand Bazaar" was arranged for the Monday and Tuesday of Easter Week in 1905, with all proceeds intended for the reconstruction scheme. Along with the Circuit ministers, a galaxy of important local people was associated with the event, including two local Members of Parliament, William George Webb, a Conservative who represented the neighbouring Kingswinford constituency, and the local Wolverhampton South MP, Henry Norman,[185] plus prominent local politician Alderman J T Homer.[186] Also present was Mr. J W Sankey of Sankey's Iron Works in Bilston and W P Gibbons of the local Gibbons Brothers' Manufacturing Works.

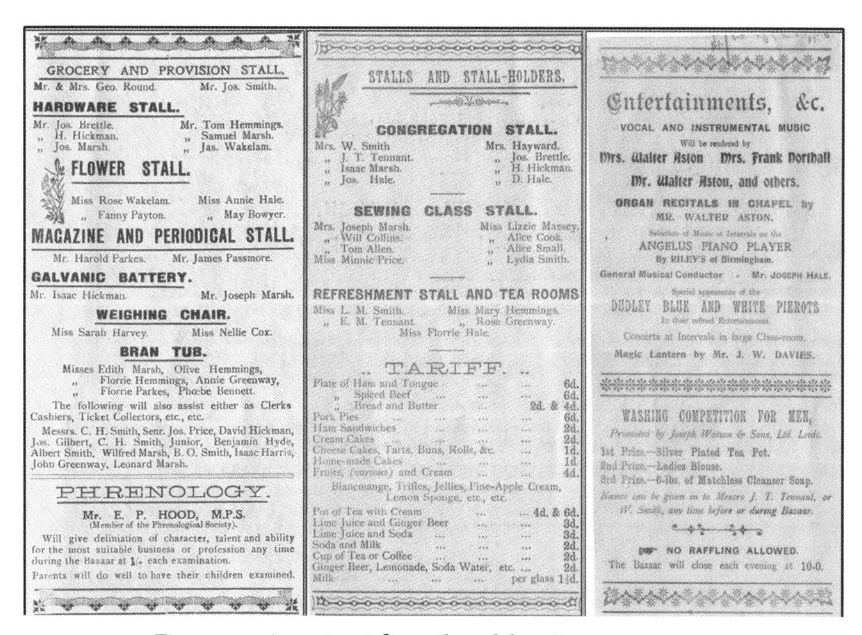

GROCERY AND PROVISION STALL.

Mr. & Mrs. Geo. Round. Mr. Jos. Smith.

HARDWARE STALL.

Mr. Jos. Brettle. Mr. Tom Hemmings.
„ H. Hickman. „ Samuel Marsh.
„ Jos. Marsh. „ Jas. Wakelam.

FLOWER STALL.

Miss Rose Wakelam. Miss Annie Hale.
„ Fanny Payton. „ May Bowyer.

MAGAZINE AND PERIODICAL STALL.

Mr. Harold Parkes. Mr. James Passmore.

GALVANIC BATTERY.

Mr. Isaac Hickman. Mr. Joseph Marsh.

WEIGHING CHAIR.

Miss Sarah Harvey. Miss Nellie Cox.

BRAN TUB.

Misses Edith Marsh, Olive Hemmings,
„ Florrie Hemmings, Annie Greenway,
„ Florrie Parkes, Phœbe Bennett.

The following will also assist either as Clerks Cashiers, Ticket Collectors, etc., etc.

Messrs. C. H. Smith, Senr. Jos. Price, David Hickman, Jos. Gilbert, C. H. Smith, Junior, Benjamin Hyde, Albert Smith, Wilfred Marsh, B. O. Smith, Isaac Harris, John Greenway, Leonard Marsh.

PHRENOLOGY.

Mr. E. P. HOOD, M.P.S.
(Member of the Phrenological Society).

Will give deliniation of character, talent and ability for the most suitable business or profession any time during the Bazaar at 1/- each examination.

Parents will do well to have their children examined.

STALLS AND STALL-HOLDERS.

CONGREGATION STALL.

Mrs. W. Smith Mrs. Hayward.
„ J. T. Tennant. „ Jos. Brettle.
„ Isaac Marsh. „ H. Hickman.
„ Jos. Hale. „ D. Hale.

SEWING CLASS STALL.

Mrs. Joseph Marsh. Miss Lizzie Massey.
„ Will Collins. „ Alice Cook.
„ Tom Allen. „ Alice Small.
Miss Minnie Price. „ Lydia Smith.

REFRESHMENT STALL AND TEA ROOMS

Miss L. M. Smith. Miss Mary Hemmings.
„ E. M. Tennant. „ Rose Greenway.
Miss Florrie Hale.

.. TARIFF. ..

Plate of Ham and Tongue	6d.
„ Spiced Beef	6d.
„ Bread and Butter ...	2d. & 4d.
Pork Pies	6d.
Ham Sandwiches	2d.
Cream Cakes	2d.
Cheese Cakes, Tarts, Buns, Rolls, &c. ...	1d.
Home-made Cakes	1d.
Fruits, *(various)* and Cream	4d.
Blancmange, Trifles, Jellies, Pine-Apple Cream, Lemon Sponge, etc., etc.	
Pot of Tea with Cream	4d. & 6d.
Lime Juice and Ginger Beer	3d.
Lime Juice and Soda	3d.
Soda and Milk	2d.
Cup of Tea or Coffee	2d.
Ginger Beer, Lemonade, Soda Water, etc. ...	2d.
Milk	per glass 1½d.

Entertainments, &c.

VOCAL AND INSTRUMENTAL MUSIC
Will be rendered by
Mrs. Walter Aston Mrs. Frank Northall
Mr. Walter Aston, and others.

ORGAN RECITALS IN CHAPEL by
MR. WALTER ASTON.

Selection of Music at Intervals on the
ANGELUS PIANO PLAYER
By RILEY'S of Birmingham.

General Musical Conductor - Mr. JOSEPH HALE.

Special appearance of the
DUDLEY BLUE AND WHITE PIEROTS
In their refined Entertainments.

Concerts at Intervals in large Class-room.

Magic Lantern by Mr. J. W. DAVIES.

WASHING COMPETITION FOR MEN,
Promoted by Joseph Watson & Sons, Ltd. Leeds.

1st Prize.—Silver Plated Tea Pot.
2nd Prize.—Ladies Blouse.
3rd Prize.—6-lbs. of Matchless Cleanser Soap.

Names can be given in to Messrs J. T. Tennant, or W. Smith, any time before or during Bazaar.

NO RAFFLING ALLOWED.

The Bazaar will close each evening at 10-0.

Figure 40: An extract from the celebration programme

The two days followed the same pattern, beginning in the early afternoon with an opening ceremony which included a hymn, prayers, introductory remarks by the chairman for the day, a speech by the opener, who was then presented with a bouquet, a vote of thanks to the opener, with a proposer, seconder and the chairman and concluding with the singing of the National Anthem.

The bazaar raised £212/2/1d (equivalent to nearly £25,000 in 2024). The trustees were able to add £51/1/8d from funds already held, £50 from the Anniversaries of 1903 and 1904, and £150 from the Jubilee celebrations. By the June trust meeting in 1905 £1,100 was available for reconstruction. However, when plans were submitted to the MNC's Connexional Chapel Committee, the trustees were encouraged to pursue *'a larger and more satisfactory scheme'*. A £250 grant was

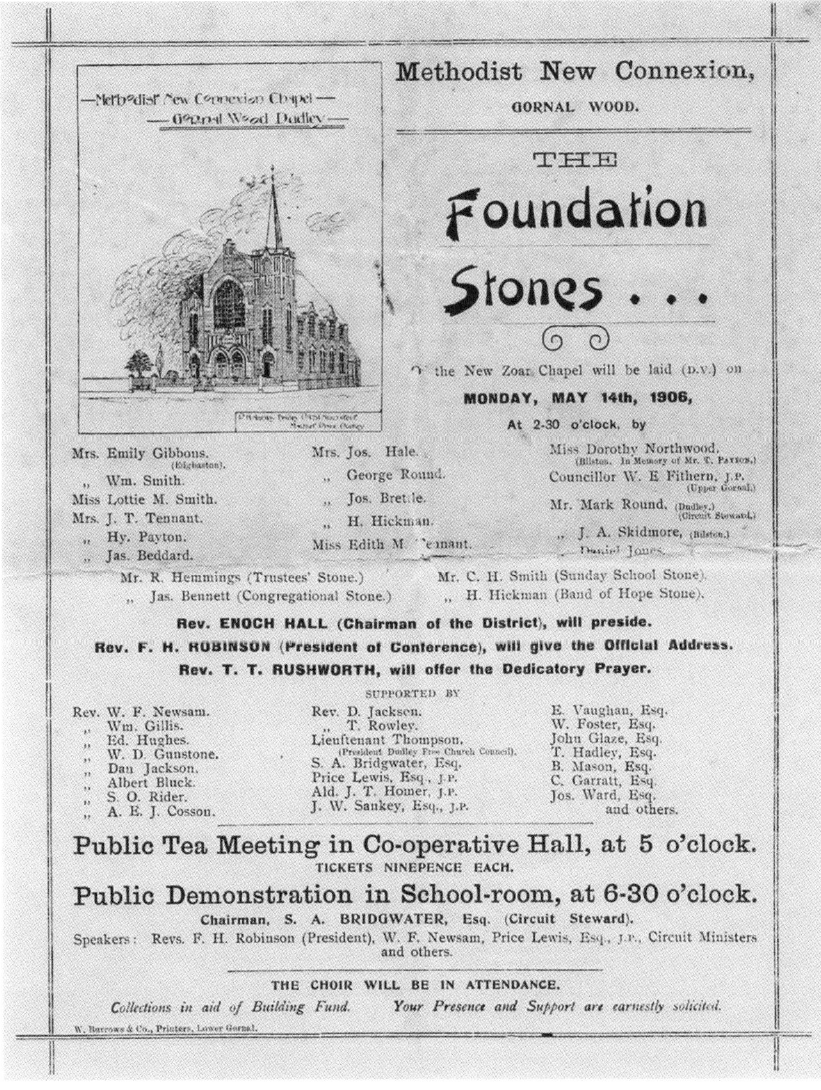

Figure 41: Celebrations to mark the Laying the Foundation Stones

promised from the MNC Extension Fund, as this was deemed to be a qualifying scheme for what was known as a *'secondary extension'*: a project qualifying because of the growth and expansion of an already established Society.[187] The trustees responded positively and swiftly to this challenge. At a meeting held on 28 February 1906 they agreed to rescind the previous decision to renovate and instead to opt for replacement. By July church members had given another £200 and promised a further £700. A loan of £300 was secured from the MNC Chapel Loan Fund. At the end of that year, to help meet the total cost, a mortgage of £500 would be taken out, provided by local Mine Agent, John Hughes.

On Monday 14 May 1906 the foundation stones for the new church were laid during an afternoon service involving the President of the Methodist New Connexion, Revd F H Robinson, and the Chairman of the District, the Revd Enoch Hall, along with many other Church and community representatives. The service took place at 2.30 pm and was followed by a *'Public Tea Meeting'* in the nearby Co-operative Hall, with tickets at 9d. each, and then a *'Public Demonstration'* at 6.30 pm. The evening gathering was essentially another service, with timings against each item. There were five hymns, a 15-minute report by the trust secretary, George Round, and three addresses, by the President (30 minutes), the Chairman (25 minutes) and the Revd W F Newsam, a former minister, (25 minutes), ending a day of great hope and expectation.

The opening of the new chapel

Contractor for the new building was Mark Round of New Street, Dudley, a leading member of the Dudley MNC Circuit. 12,000 *Ketleys Best Red bricks*[188] were used, a late decision by the trustees to use a better-quality brick than was first planned. The building was different from that of today in one important respect, which is evident from Figure 44: there was no clock in the tower when the building was erected. Evidently the intention was to have one, as the matter was discussed, but a decision deferred.

Figure 42: Mark Round

Figure 43: Revd Luke Wiseman

The *'New Zoar Chapel'*[189] was opened on Wednesday 28 November 1906, by Mrs. William Smith, who had previously opened the refurbished Sunday School. The service took place, perhaps surprisingly, not only in mid-week, but at 3.30pm. The dedication sermon was preached by Revd. Luke Wiseman, at that time the minister of the new Wesleyan Central Hall in Birmingham and future President of both the Wesleyan Conference (1912) and the Methodist Conference (of which he was the second President) established after the coming together of the Wesleyan, Primitive and United Methodist Churches in 1932.

Many of the leading local figures who had offered their support at the Grand Bazaar and the stone laying were in attendance and following the service there was a tea at 5.30pm (cost 9d) and then a *'Public Meeting'* in the chapel at 6.30pm. As on the occasion of the stone laying, the order of service for the evening listed the time at which every item was due to be delivered. There were four main speakers, Revd F H Robinson (Ex-President of the Conference), Revd W D Gunstone of Birmingham, along with Sir Henry Norman MP and Alderman Price Lewis of Wolverhampton. The first three were allotted 25 minutes each, with Alderman Lewis given 20 minutes. The choir sang the anthem *'I have surely built thee an house'*. Councillor W E Fithern JP[190] chaired the evening, being given 10 minutes for his remarks and the doxology was timed to be sung at 9.00pm! In order to reduce the debt on the building, the publicity for the opening set a target of £300 to be raised on the day. On the three following Sundays, the Revds Rider, Bartram and Jewell returned to lead special services.

This time the trustees ensured that the chapel was properly registered, both for public worship and for the conduct of weddings.[191]

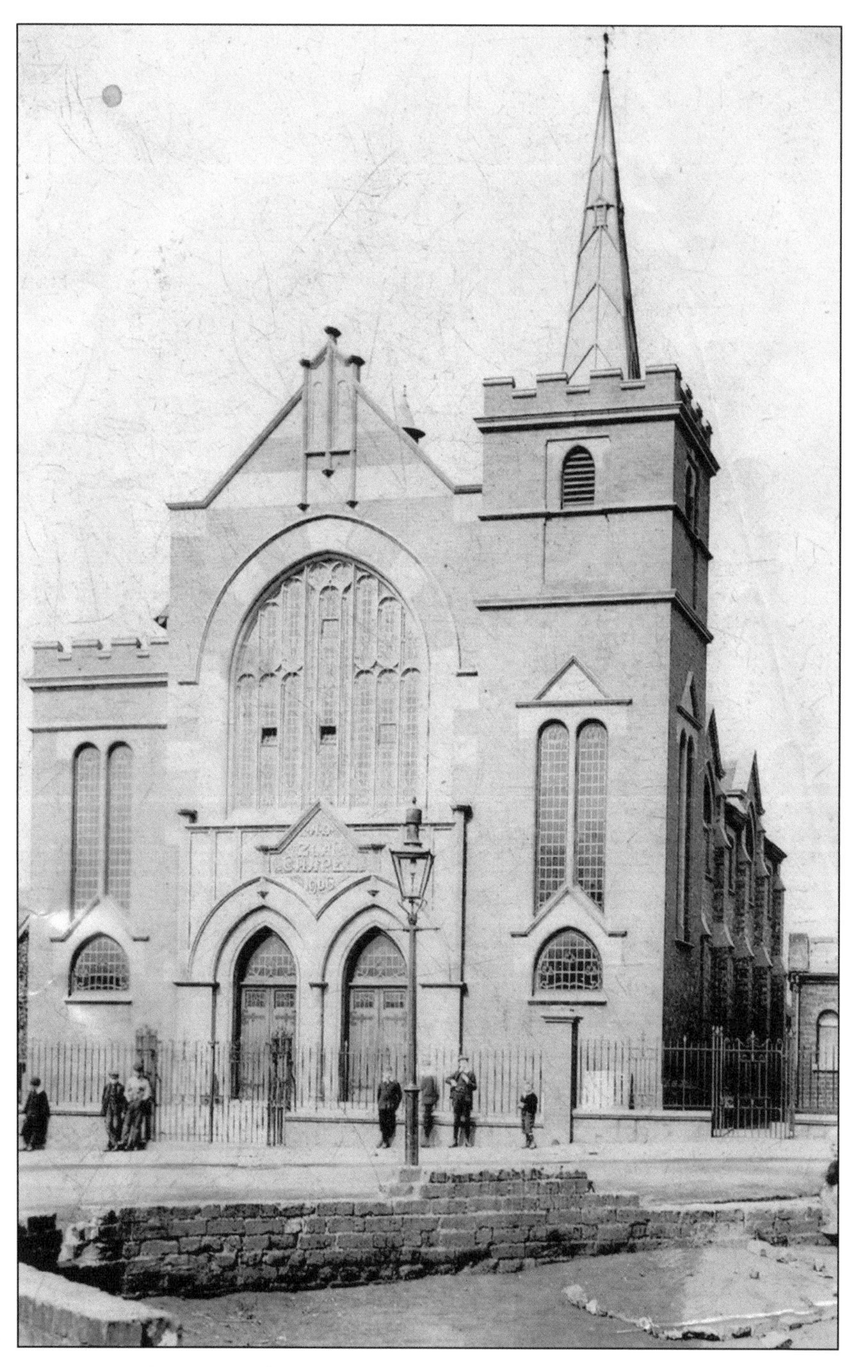

Figure 44: The 1906 Zoar before the addition of the clock

[Form for Certifying a Place of Meeting for Religious Worship under the Act 18 & 19 Vict., c. 81, to be signed *in Duplicate* by the person certifying.]

TO THE REGISTRAR GENERAL OF BIRTHS, DEATHS, AND MARRIAGES IN ENGLAND.

DIRECTIONS for filling up this Form.

(a) Insert in the blank spaces the Name, Residence, and County or County Borough, and the Rank or Profession of the Person certifying.

I, the undersigned, (a) John Lyddon Hookins of Fernleigh, Russell Street, Dudley in the County Borough of Dudley

Do HEREBY, under and by virtue of an Act passed in the Nineteenth year of Her late Majesty Queen Victoria, intituled "An Act to amend the law concerning "the certifying and registering of Places of Religious Worship in England," CERTIFY that a certain Building known by the name of (b) Zoar Chapel

(b) Here insert "Congregational Church," "Baptist Chapel," or whatever name the building may be called or known by.

(c) Describe the locality of the Building so as clearly to identify it.

situated at (c) Abbey Road, Gornal Wood

in the Civil Parish of Sedgley

(d) If in a County Borough insert "Borough."

in the County (d) of Stafford

in the Sub-district of Sedgley

in the Registration District of Dudley

is intended to be used (e) and will accordingly be forthwith used as a Place of Meeting for Religious Worship by a Congregation or Assembly of persons calling themselves Methodist New Connexion

(e) If the Building has been previously used as a Place of Worship, add the words, "as heretofore."

And I request that this Certificate may be recorded in the General Register Office pursuant to the said Act. Dated this 24th day of November 1906

(*Signature of the Person Certifying*) J. L. Hookins

(f) Insert on the line immediately under the signature, the word "Minister," "Proprietor," "A Trustee," "Occupier," "An Attendant," or such other words as will clearly show the connection subsisting between the Person certifying and the Place of Meeting.

(f) Chairman of Trustees of the Place of Meeting above described.

N.B.—When the Building to be Certified as a place of meeting for Religious Worship is intended to be used in lieu of a building previously Certified to, and recorded by the Registrar General, a form of "Notice of disuse" of the latter building should also be filled up and forwarded to the General Register Office, to ensure cancellation of the original certificate and Record. (Act 18 & 19 Vict., c. 81, s. 6.)

33.

Figure 45: Registration for Public Worship

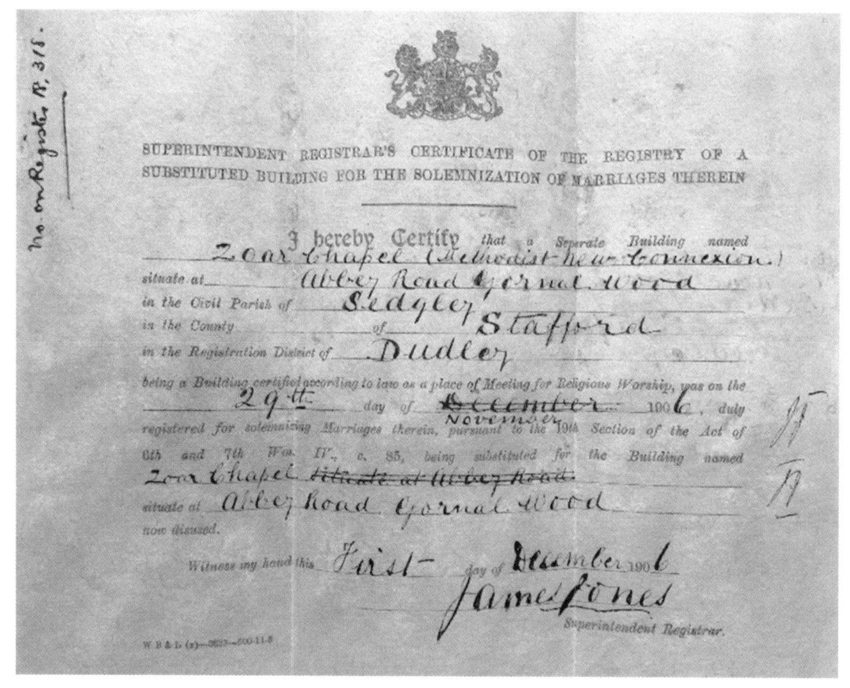
no. on Register R, 318.

SUPERINTENDENT REGISTRAR'S CERTIFICATE OF THE REGISTRY OF A SUBSTITUTED BUILDING FOR THE SOLEMNIZATION OF MARRIAGES THEREIN

I hereby Certify that a Separate Building named Zoar Chapel (Methodist New Connexion) situate at Abbey Road Gornal Wood in the Civil Parish of Sedgley in the County of Stafford in the Registration District of Dudley being a Building certified according to law as a place of Meeting for Religious Worship, was on the 29th day of ~~December~~ November 1906, duly registered for solemnizing Marriages therein, pursuant to the 10th Section of the Act of 6th and 7th Wm. IV., c. 85, being substituted for the Building named Zoar Chapel ~~situate at Abbey Road~~ situate at Abbey Road Gornal Wood now disused.

Witness my hand this First day of December 1906

James Jones

Superintendent Registrar.

Figure 46: Marriage Registration Certificate

Pew or Seat Rents

At the chapel's opening, the service booklet included a note that *'Applications for sittings are invited and every effort will be made to accommodate.'* The caretaker held a list of previous seat-holders, and it was decided to check his records to establish who had been paying their pew rents and then open a new list. Initial applications were taken up for 203 'sittings'. Rates varied between four (20p) and six shillings (30p) per Quarter for a whole pew, with the best seats deemed to be the back side pews. Individual 'sittings' could be had for 1/- (5p) per Quarter or 1/3d for sittings in the rear five centre rows. As many pew holders were in the habit of putting their own cushions on the seats, the trustees decided to pass a resolution requiring that *'all cushions put into new church be as near as possible the colour of the cushion around the communion rail'.*

Pew holders would again be issued with cards recording their payments and a seat rent ledger was to be purchased. It was also decided that the caretaker's salary would be increased to £9 per annum from January 1907 and for this he would be expected to collect the pew rents, 'without commission'. Despite this arrangement, as early as 1910 circular letters had to be sent out to defaulters and in 1914 the trustees agreed *'the caretaker be asked to become seat rent collector' at 5% commission on the amount collected'*. Presumably they felt that the commission would prove an incentive to help reduce the number of defaulters.

The popularity of 'your own seat' was still evident in 1931, when Mr. B Hyde wanted to give up his seat. The Pew Stewards were unwilling to arbitrate as to who should take it over and referred the matter to the trustees. In March 1936 a discussion took place on the abolition of pew rents, when *'It was suggested that if this was brought about an appreciable increase in the congregations would result.'* However, following a seat holders' meeting, pew rents were retained. Conservatism had won the day.

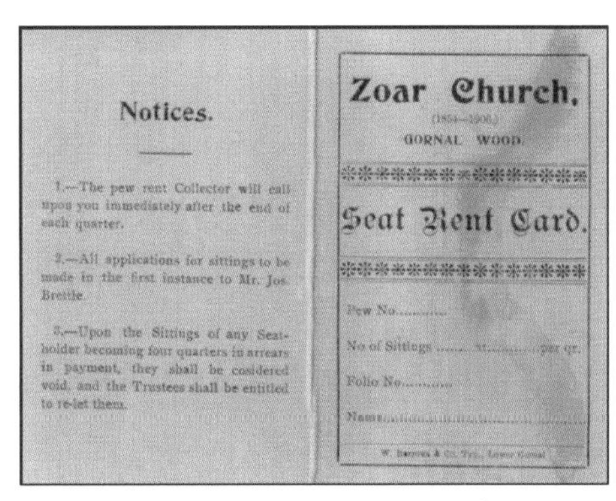
Notices.

1.—The pew rent Collector will call upon you immediately after the end of each quarter.

2.—All applications for sittings to be made in the first instance to Mr. Jos. Brettle.

3.—Upon the Sittings of any Seat-holder becoming four quarters in arrears in payment, they shall be considered void, and the Trustees shall be entitled to re-let them.

Zoar Church,

GORNAL WOOD.

Seat Rent Card.

Pew No............

No of Sittings .... at............ per qr.

Folio No............

Name............

Figure 47: Seat Rent Card

ZOAR CHURCH, GORNAL WOOD.

Seat Rent Card.

RENT DUE.							CASH PAID.				SIGNATURE.
Date	*Arrears*		*Rent due*		*Total.*		*Date.*	*Amount.*			
	s.	d.	s.	d.	s.	d.		£	s.	d.	
19 Lady-Day											
Midsummer											
Michaelmas											
Christmas											
19 Lady-Day											
Midsummer											
Michaelmas											
Christmas											
19 Lady-Day											
Midsummer											
Michaelmas											
Christmas											
19 Lady-Day											
Midsummer											
Michaelmas											
Christmas											

Figure 48: Seat Rent Record

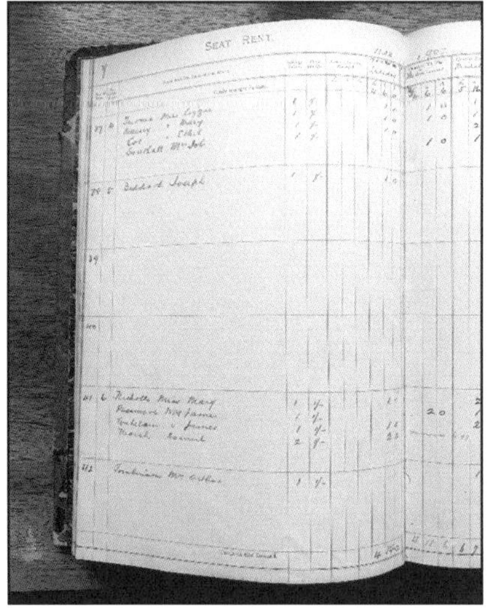

Figure 49: page from the Seat Rent Book

Caretaking the buildings

The appointment of caretakers was one of the many responsibilities which fell to the trustees. A new caretaker had to be appointed in 1912, following the resignation of the long serving Mr. and Mrs. Joseph Scranage. From five applications, Mr. and Mrs. William Flavell were appointed *'at the present salary'* (£9), although this was increased by £2/10/0d in 1914 for as long as a weekly letting on Thursday afternoons to the 'Compensation Authority' [192] continued. The Flavells resigned in 1915 and it was decided that any replacement should be *'under 50 years and with no more than two children'*. Mr. John Jones was the successful applicant. Granted a *'war bonus'* of £2 in 1918, the following year he resigned, despite being offered a £2 salary increase. The agreed intention was to make a new appointment at £12 plus the house, but the May 1919 Minutes record the re-appointment of Joseph Scranage at £16 p.a. with the house rent free. In 1921 the salary was increased to £20 plus 10% commission on the collected seat rent payments. The Scranages served as caretakers until Mrs. Scranage died in 1934. A joint committee of trustees and leaders reviewed the duties to be undertaken before making a new appointment, with Mr. and Mrs. J Marsh taking over. They were followed by Mr and Mrs Hunt, the first caretakers to be given a legal contract of employment. Successive caretakers included Mr and Mrs Ken Powell, Mr and Mrs L. Priest, Mr and Mrs Houghton, Mrs Williams, Mr and Mrs Alan Morgan and Mr and Mrs Jackson.

Figure 50: Joan and Ken Powell

In 1938 the trustees authorised a significant internal renovation of the caretakers' cottage, which included taking up the quarry floor in the sitting room, replastering various rooms and replacing the grate with a boiler to provide hot water to the kitchen sink. Privacy for any of the caretakers was not easy as, for many years, they had to share their kitchen facilities with the church. In 1946 the Women's Owni asked the trustees to replace the wash boiler in the caretaker's house with a gas boiler, 'enumerating the several advantages such action would effect.' An expert on kitchen planning was to be consulted and a committee of eight (four trustees and four members of the Women's Own) was appointed to take the project forward. In 1952 it was agreed to put an electricity supply into the house.

The Clock

After the First World War individual trustees, church members and senior classes of the Sunday School undertook to raise money for a church clock. Built and installed by W F Evans and Sons in 1919 at a

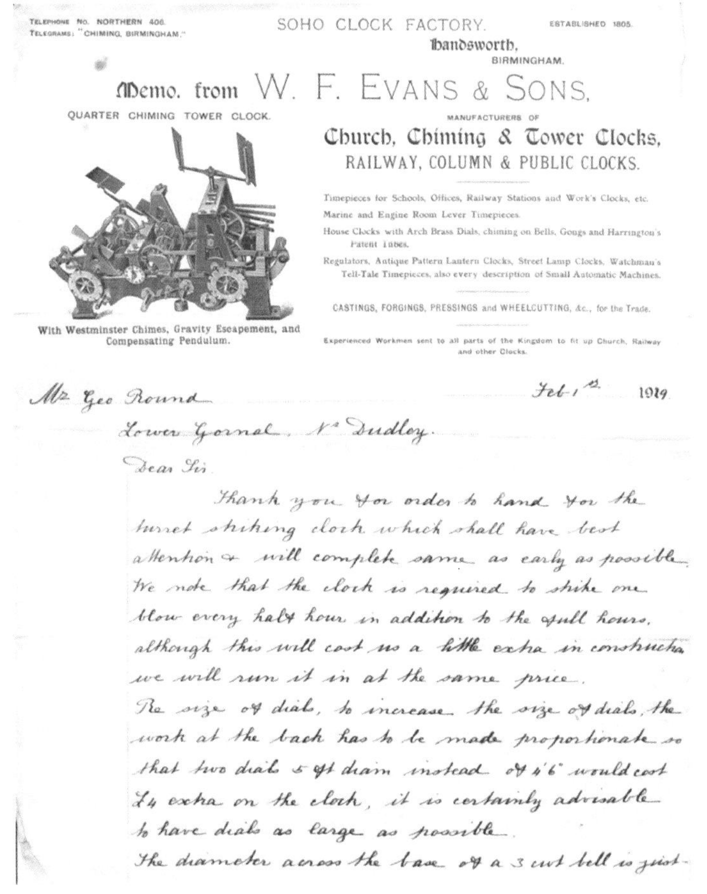

TELEPHONE No. NORTHERN 406.
TELEGRAMS: "CHIMING, BIRMINGHAM."

SOHO CLOCK FACTORY. ESTABLISHED 1805.

Handsworth,
BIRMINGHAM.

Memo. from W. F. EVANS & SONS,

QUARTER CHIMING TOWER CLOCK.

With Westminster Chimes, Gravity Escapement, and Compensating Pendulum.

MANUFACTURERS OF

Church, Chiming & Tower Clocks,
RAILWAY, COLUMN & PUBLIC CLOCKS.

Timepieces for Schools, Offices, Railway Stations and Work's Clocks, etc.
Marine and Engine Room Lever Timepieces.
House Clocks with Arch Brass Dials, chiming on Bells, Gongs and Harrington's Patent Tubes.
Regulators, Antique Pattern Lantern Clocks, Street Lamp Clocks, Watchman's Tell-Tale Timepieces, also every description of Small Automatic Machines.

CASTINGS, FORGINGS, PRESSINGS and WHEELCUTTING, &c., for the Trade.

Experienced Workmen sent to all parts of the Kingdom to fit up Church, Railway and other Clocks.

Mr Geo Round Feb 1st 1919
Lower Gornal, Nr Dudley.

Dear Sir

Thank you for order to hand for the turret striking clock which shall have best attention & will complete same as early as possible.
We note that the clock is required to strike one blow every half hour in addition to the full hours, although this will cost us a little extra in construction we will run it in at the same price.
Re size of dials, to increase the size of dials, the work at the back has to be made proportionate so that two dials 5 ft diam instead of 4'6" would cost £4 extra on the clock, it is certainly advisable to have dials as large as possible.
The diameter across the base of a 3 cwt bell is just-

Figure 51: Clock order

cost of £158, the clock was dedicated to those who had fallen in the Great War. Sedgley Gas Works laid on a gas supply to light the clock for £4/12/4d and a commemorative tablet, made by Mark Round and Sons who had built the church, was placed on the wall at the foot of the tower. It was unveiled on 21 July 1919 and followed by a special service chaired by William Lees followed, with addresses given by Mr Lees, the two Circuit ministers, R H Little and Kaye Garthwaite, along with Mr J T Tennant, JP (Chair of the Trustees). Miss Florrie Hale sang two solos and the choir rendered the Hallelujah Chorus.

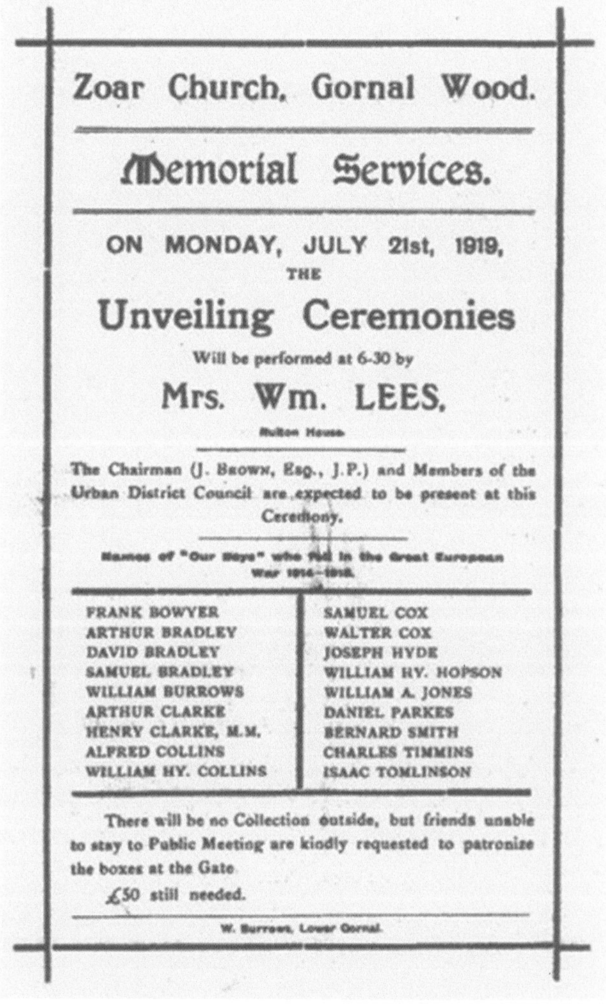

Zoar Church, Gornal Wood.

Memorial Services.

ON MONDAY, JULY 21st, 1919,

THE

Unveiling Ceremonies

Will be performed at 6-30 by

Mrs. Wm. LEES,

Ruiton House

The Chairman (J. Brown, Esq., J.P.) and Members of the Urban District Council are expected to be present at this Ceremony.

Names of "Our Boys" who fell in the Great European War 1914–1918.

FRANK BOWYER	SAMUEL COX
ARTHUR BRADLEY	WALTER COX
DAVID BRADLEY	JOSEPH HYDE
SAMUEL BRADLEY	WILLIAM HY. HOPSON
WILLIAM BURROWS	WILLIAM A. JONES
ARTHUR CLARKE	DANIEL PARKES
HENRY CLARKE, M.M.	BERNARD SMITH
ALFRED COLLINS	CHARLES TIMMINS
WILLIAM HY. COLLINS	ISAAC TOMLINSON

There will be no Collection outside, but friends unable to stay to Public Meeting are kindly requested to patronize the boxes at the Gate

£50 still needed.

W. Burrows, Lower Gornal.

Figure 52: War Memorial Dedication

Trust Renewal

1920 was marked by the death of four long-standing trustees, Adam Hale, David Hickman, William Sheen and William Smith, JP. This led the remaining trustees to consider the matter of renewing the Trust, as Benjamin Bradley, John Hyde, Samuel Westwood, Richard Hemmings, John Bowyer and Henry Payton had all died prior to this. A continuation Trust was agreed and when renewal was undertaken in 1923 John Greenway, John Hemmings and Job Hale asked to be discharged from their responsibilities.

1923 TRUST

Name	Occupation	Address
John Thomas Tennant **		The Limes, Lower Gornal
Charles Henry Smith **		7 Prices Road, Lower Gornal
Benjamin Parkes **		9 Bull Street
George Round **		Five Ways
Joseph Gilbert **		15a Brook Street
Joseph Brettle **		8b Red Hall Road
[***continuing trustees***]		
Albert Arthur Smith	Clerk	19 Zoar Street
Benjamin Hyde	Clerk	Red Hall Road
Isaac Harris	Clerk	11 Tipton St Sedgley
Isaac Hickman	Fitter	13B Humphrey St.
Thomas Davies	School Teacher	18 Zoar Street
William Collins	Shop Assistant	13 Zoar Street
Joseph Bate	Chartermaster	47 Zoar Street
Simeon Hemmings	Grocer	New Street
James Henry Wakelam	Miner	4 Bird Street
Herbert Bate	Miner	31 Summit Place
John Howard Hemmings	Draughtsman	53 Red Hall Road
Thomas Marsh	Draughtsman	2 Graveyard Road
John Henry Payton	School Teacher	38 Himley Road
John Granville Tennant	Tailor & Draper	39 Himley Road

William Lees	Solicitor	Ruiton House, Dudley
Joseph John Marsh	Company Director	Woodthorne
Noah Westwood	Gas Retort Builder	34 Graveyard Road
Joseph Walsh	Meter Inspector	41 Summit Place
William Bradley	Gas Retort Builder	3 Musk Lane
James Passmore	Bricklayer	Bull Street
Howard Smith	Gas Retort Builder	23 Prospect Road
William Howard Flavell	Assistant Superintendent Insurance Co.	32 Himley Road
John Thomas Greenway	Insurance Agent	24 Smithy Lane, Pensnett
Sidney Marsh Hale	Clerk	44 Zoar Street
Joseph John Baker	Miner	5 Bird Street

This body was renewed again in 1949, the last renewal of the trust prior to the major changes in the governance and oversight of local churches which were introduced nationally by the 1974 Methodist Church Act.

1949 TRUST

Name	**Occupation**	**Address**
Benjamin Charles Smith		75 Summer Lane
Harold Fletcher	Manager	71 St James Road, Dudley
William Henry Fletcher	Cycle Dealer	33 Red Hall Road, Lower Gornal
Ernest Cox	Colliery Deputy	66 Red Hall Road, Lower Gornal
John Eric Davies	Assurance Agent	50 Highland Road, Dudley
Eric Vincent Harris	Engineering Draughtsman	The 'Bungalow', Long Common, Claverley
William Harold Jones	Colliery Clerk	1 Bird Street, Gornal Wood

Joseph Bate	Butcher	5A Louise St, Gornal Wood
William Clifford Collins	Accounts Clerk	8 Ashford Drive, Dudley Rd, Sedgley
Geoffrey Thomas Marsh	Engineering Draughtsman	46 Brookdale, Lower Gornal, Nr. Dudley
John Geoffrey Tennant	Time Clerk	39 Himley Rd, Gornal Wood, Dudley
Arthur Norman Round	Colliery Deputy	93 The Broadway, Dudley
Harold Desmond Bate	Electrician	5A Louise St. Gornal Wood
Norman Marsh	Engineer	12 Cinder Road
William Arthur Nock	Draughtsman	12 Bank Road, Lower Gornal
Albert Norman Round	Clerk	65 Barker Street, Lozells, Birmingham
Percy Russell	Blacksmith	72 Robert Street, Lower Gornal
Alfred Pounder	Workhouse Manager	?? Vale Street, Upper Gornal
William Jones	Colliery Weighman	48 New Street, Lower Gornal
Joseph John Jones	Water Gas Operator	1 Bird St. Gornal Wood
Reginald Arthur Marsh	Plater	12 Cinder Road
Frank Fletcher	Clerk	37 Brookdale, Gornal Wood
John Alfred Jones	Engineering Draughtsman	14 Louise St. Gornal Wood
William Timmins	Tailors Cutter	Hill Dene, Summer Lane, Lower Gornal
***Joseph Gilbert* ***	Retired	31 Red Hall Road, Lower Gornal

Joseph Brettle*	Retired	13 Red Hall Road, Lower Gornal
Albert Arthur Smith*	Cashier	21 Patrecia Avenue, Goldthorne Park, Wolverhampton
Benjamin Hyde*	Clerk	101 Tipton Road, Sedgley
Isaac Harris*	Clerk	The Bungalow, Long Common, Claverley
Isaac Hickman*	Retired	95 Lake Street, Lower Gornal
Thomas Davies*	Retired	50 Highland Road, Dudley
William Collins*	Retired	24 Zoar Street, Lower Gornal
James Henry Wakelam*	Miner	23 Bull Street, Gornal Wood
Herbert Bate*	Miner	5A Louise Street, Gornal Wood
John Howard Hemmings*	Manager	The Limes, Lower Gornal
Thomas Marsh*	Contract Manager	“Imbant” Whitehall Road, Stourbridge
John Granville Tennant*	Taylor & Draper	39 Himley Road, Gornal Wood
Joseph John Marsh*	Director	“Woodthorne” Grosvenor Road, Lower Gornal
Noah Westwood*	Clerk	34 Grosvenor Road, Lower Gornal
Joseph Marsh*	Retired	17 Abbey Road, Gornal Wood
William Bradley*	Gas Retort Builder	3 Musk Lane, Gornal Wood

Howard Smith**	Gas Retort Builder	21 Robert Street, Lower Gornal
William Howard Flavell**	Retired	"Halcyon" Oakham Road, Dudley
John Thomas Greenway**	Insurance Agent	"Sandon" Cinder Road, Gornal Wood
Sidney Marsh Hale**	Clerk	50 Robert Street, Lower Gornal

[***continuing trustees**]

Building Renovations

Less than ten years after the Sunday School had been renovated at the turn of the century there was concern about lack of space. In 1912 the Leaders' Meeting learned of a corrugated chapel building that was being sold in Wolverhampton. They asked the trustees to make an offer, suggesting £25 as a possible bid. The trustees did put in a successful offer - of £21. The building was erected to the rear of the Sunday School and became the room used by the youngest members.

Zoar Church, Gornal Wood.

COST OF ADDITIONAL CLASSROOMS.

To Purchase of All Souls' School		£21 0 0
Messrs. M. Round & Sons:—		
To taking down School, removing here, putting in new foundations, erecting classrooms, making good faulty work, putting in two moveable partitions, general repairs, painting inside and all woodwork outside (three coats), erecting store room and other work		112 12 0
To Paint for Corrugated Work	£2 13 6	
Labour for same	2 15 0	
		5 8 6
To 111 New Chairs at 2/6 each		13 17 6
To Gas Fittings		8 10 11
To New Radiators and fixing same ...		16 0 0
		£177 8 11

Figure 53: The cost of the additional classroom

In 1920 the trustees appointed a sub-committee to plan for the renovation of the Sunday School *'as early as possible.'* The following year the caretaker's house was added to the renovation agenda. At the same time discussions followed on the state of the finances and, once again, cost cutting measures were sought from regular expenditure, including cutting the annual remuneration of the organist and choirmaster by £4. Mr. Aston agreed and Mr. Hale offered to serve without remuneration.

The financial belt tightening must have been effective because in 1922 the Trust decided to *'convene a special meeting with a view to co-opting 14 members of the church and congregation'* whose shared remit was to prepare renovation plans and put them into action. Alterations and repairs were made to the caretaker's house, which was also repainted and decorated and a boiler installed to replace the fire-grate for hot water supply to the kitchen. The school building was repaired and repainted, the front gable end was cemented over (having previously been a brick finish, see Figures 20 and 21) and two new windows were installed, work undertaken by two Dudley firms, chapel builders Messrs. Mark Round and Sons and H. Wythes and Sons. The gas lighting was remodelled by workers from the Sedgley Urban District Council and the organ taken down, repaired and rebuilt by Nicholson and Lord of Walsall. The total cost was £511/7/1d, a bill met by the trustees with £396/5/7d from their deposit account, £73/0/6d raised at the re-opening services held in October of 1922 and for the rest they had to arrange an increase in their bank overdraft.

In October 1923 the new trust body discussed the renovation of the church, but it was not until 1926 that a sub-committee of trustees was appointed with a brief to consider,

> *Alterations to minister's vestry and infants (sic) room. Lighting. Cleaning and decorating of church generally. Font cleaning and renovating and adding new stop to organ.*

Proposals were presented and accepted later in the year which included building work by Messrs. Mark Round and Sons (£160); painting and decorating by H. Wythes and Sons (£232); organ renovation by Nicholson and Lord (£66); a new font (£25/15/0d); a new safe (£19/8/0d); the provision of umbrella holders and pans, to be fixed on the ends of the pews (£7/2/6d) and carpeting, presumably of the area at the front of the church around the communion table.[194] The trustees agreed that the carpets being replaced should be fitted in the caretaker's house! There was debate as to whether gas or electricity should be used to light the church and it was decided to go with the latter. The electricity supply was connected by the Midland Electric Corporation for Power Distribution, whose HQ was in Birmingham, while the wiring work was undertaken by Joseph Smith (£117/11/0d). With other smaller items, the total bill amounted to £831/11/2d). Mrs J T Tennant kindly offered to meet the cost of the font.

Acceptance of Application for Supply of Electricity.

From

Midland Electric Corporation for Power Distribution, Limited,

27, TEMPLE STREET,
BIRMINGHAM.

Reference
Job No. 100

4 NOV 1926 192

To Mr J Brettle,
Red Hall Road,
Lower Gornal,
Near Dudley

Sir,

We beg to acknowledge receipt of your application dated 10 Oct 1926 for a supply of Electrical energy, at Zoar Church, Lower Gornal and hereby accept same, subject to the terms and conditions as set out therein.

The rate to be charged will be :—

For Power No.

For Light No. 1

This rate to be subject to any further increase or decrease which may be made by the Company to consumers generally from time to time.

The minimum amount to be paid for energy supplied shall be not less than £1 per annum.

All Service Cable on private property will be charged at 10/- per yard run.

Notice in writing should be given when the wiring is completed.

For MIDLAND ELECTRIC CORPORATION
FOR POWER DISTRIBUTION, LIMITED.

Figure 54: Electricity Arrangements

Arrangements were made for the church to be closed for nine weeks while the work was carried out, with a hoped-for reopening service in January 1927, the President of Conference as preacher. The first modest fund raiser involved a series of organ recitals. A grand bazaar was planned for 1926 as the major effort, enjoying the patronage of various local politicians, including the local sitting Member of Parliament, John Baker.[195] '*The Objects of the Bazaar*' were set out in the official programme,

> *For some time past the necessity for cleaning and renovating the Church, and making a few necessary alterations and improvements has been felt by the Trustees and all interested in its welfare.*
>
> *The present Church was built and opened nearly 20 years ago, since which nothing has been done to it in the manner suggested. To meet this desire the ladies of the congregation have been working for well over 12 months, and this Bazaar is the result.*

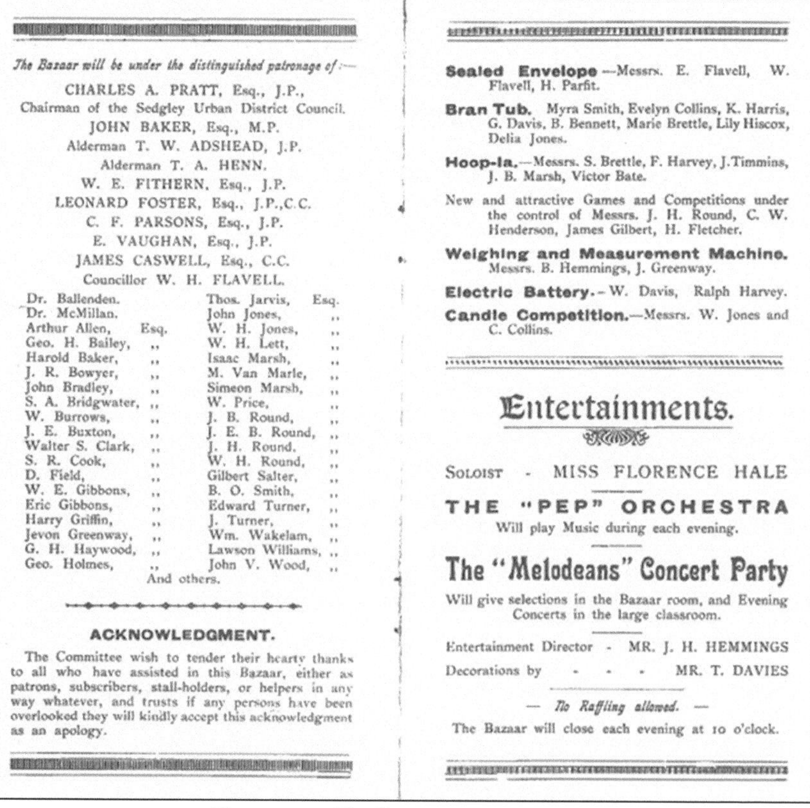

The Bazaar will be under the distinguished patronage of:—

CHARLES A. PRATT, Esq., J.P.,
Chairman of the Sedgley Urban District Council.
JOHN BAKER, Esq., M.P.
Alderman T. W. ADSHEAD, J.P.
Alderman T. A. HENN.
W. E. FITHERN, Esq., J.P.
LEONARD FOSTER, Esq., J.P., C.C.
C. F. PARSONS, Esq., J.P.
E. VAUGHAN, Esq., J.P.
JAMES CASWELL, Esq., C.C.
Councillor W. H. FLAVELL.

Dr. Ballenden.	Thos. Jarvis, Esq.
Dr. McMillan.	John Jones, ,,
Arthur Allen, Esq.	W. H. Jones, ,,
Geo. H. Bailey, ,,	W. H. Lett, ,,
Harold Baker, ,,	Isaac Marsh, ,,
J. R. Bowyer, ,,	M. Van Marle, ,,
John Bradley, ,,	Simeon Marsh, ,,
S. A. Bridgwater, ,,	W. Price, ,,
W. Burrows, ,,	J. B. Round, ,,
J. E. Buxton, ,,	J. E. B. Round, ,,
Walter S. Clark, ,,	J. H. Round, ,,
S. R. Cook, ,,	W. H. Round, ,,
D. Field, ,,	Gilbert Salter, ,,
W. E. Gibbons, ,,	B. O. Smith, ,,
Eric Gibbons, ,,	Edward Turner, ,,
Harry Griffin, ,,	J. Turner, ,,
Jevon Greenway, ,,	Wm. Wakelam, ,,
G. H. Haywood, ,,	Lawson Williams, ,,
Geo. Holmes, ,,	John V. Wood, ,,

And others.

ACKNOWLEDGMENT.

The Committee wish to tender their hearty thanks to all who have assisted in this Bazaar, either as patrons, subscribers, stall-holders, or helpers in any way whatever, and trusts if any persons have been overlooked they will kindly accept this acknowledgment as an apology.

Sealed Envelope—Messrs. E. Flavell, W. Flavell, H. Parfit.

Bran Tub. Myra Smith, Evelyn Collins, K. Harris, G. Davis, B. Bennett, Marie Brettle, Lily Hiscox, Delia Jones.

Hoop-la.—Messrs. S. Brettle, F. Harvey, J. Timmins, J. B. Marsh, Victor Bate.

New and attractive Games and Competitions under the control of Messrs. J. H. Round, C. W. Henderson, James Gilbert, H. Fletcher.

Weighing and Measurement Machine. Messrs. B. Hemmings, J. Greenway.

Electric Battery.—W. Davis, Ralph Harvey.

Candle Competition.—Messrs. W. Jones and C. Collins.

Entertainments.

SOLOIST - MISS FLORENCE HALE

THE "PEP" ORCHESTRA
Will play Music during each evening.

The "Melodeans" Concert Party
Will give selections in the Bazaar room, and Evening Concerts in the large classroom.

Entertainment Director - MR. J. H. HEMMINGS
Decorations by - - - MR. T. DAVIES

— *No Raffling allowed.* —

The Bazaar will close each evening at 10 o'clock.

Figure 55 – The Bazaar programme I

To do what is needed some six hundred pounds will be required, and it is hoped to raise a goodly sum by this effort.

The event itself was planned along the same lines as the last major bazaar, that of 1905. The format of the day was virtually identical although the make-up of the stalls, entertainment and refreshments offer interesting comparisons. The bazaar realized £518/0/3d.

The one other major property project in the 1920s was the introduction of mains drainage to the premises. In 1928 deep drainage was installed in the centre of the village and it was decided to connect the Sunday School and the caretaker's house to the mains sewer. However, the renovation sub-committee reported,

As to the church lavatories, these were considered to be satisfactory and the committee recommend that they remain as present pending a requisition from the Local Sanitary Authority for their alteration.

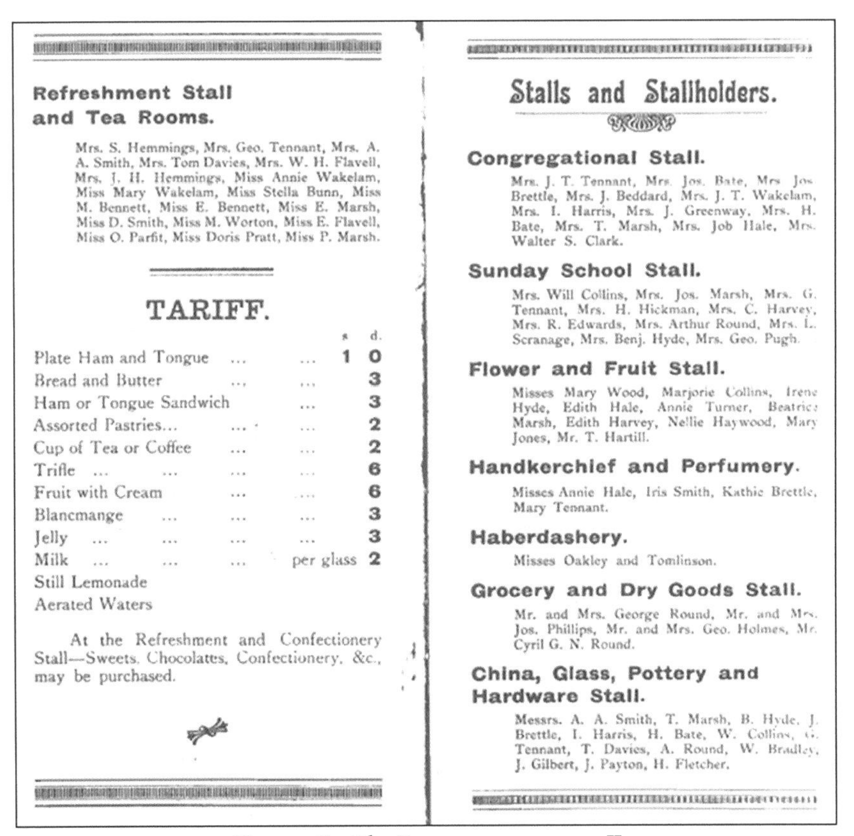

Refreshment Stall and Tea Rooms.

Mrs. S. Hemmings, Mrs. Geo. Tennant, Mrs. A. A. Smith, Mrs. Tom Davies, Mrs. W. H. Flavell, Mrs. J. H. Hemmings, Miss Annie Wakelam, Miss Mary Wakelam, Miss Stella Bunn, Miss M. Bennett, Miss E. Bennett, Miss E. Marsh, Miss D. Smith, Miss M. Worton, Miss E. Flavell, Miss O. Parfit, Miss Doris Pratt, Miss P. Marsh.

TARIFF.

	s.	d.
Plate Ham and Tongue	1	0
Bread and Butter		3
Ham or Tongue Sandwich ...		3
Assorted Pastries...		2
Cup of Tea or Coffee		2
Trifle		6
Fruit with Cream		6
Blancmange		3
Jelly		3
Milk ... ... per glass		2
Still Lemonade		
Aerated Waters		

At the Refreshment and Confectionery Stall—Sweets, Chocolates, Confectionery, &c., may be purchased.

Stalls and Stallholders.

Congregational Stall.

Mrs. J. T. Tennant, Mrs. Jos. Bate, Mrs Jos. Brettle, Mrs. J. Beddard, Mrs. J. T. Wakelam, Mrs. I. Harris, Mrs. J. Greenway, Mrs. H. Bate, Mrs. T. Marsh, Mrs. Job Hale, Mrs. Walter S. Clark.

Sunday School Stall.

Mrs. Will Collins, Mrs. Jos. Marsh, Mrs. G. Tennant, Mrs. H. Hickman, Mrs. C. Harvey, Mrs. R. Edwards, Mrs. Arthur Round, Mrs. L. Scranage, Mrs. Benj. Hyde, Mrs. Geo. Pugh.

Flower and Fruit Stall.

Misses Mary Wood, Marjorie Collins, Irene Hyde, Edith Hale, Annie Turner, Beatrice Marsh, Edith Harvey, Nellie Haywood, Mary Jones, Mr. T. Hartill.

Handkerchief and Perfumery.

Misses Annie Hale, Iris Smith, Kathie Brettle, Mary Tennant.

Haberdashery.

Misses Oakley and Tomlinson.

Grocery and Dry Goods Stall.

Mr. and Mrs. George Round, Mr. and Mrs. Jos. Phillips, Mr. and Mrs. Geo. Holmes, Mr. Cyril G. N. Round.

China, Glass, Pottery and Hardware Stall.

Messrs. A. A. Smith, T. Marsh, B. Hyde, J. Brettle, I. Harris, H. Bate, W. Collins, G. Tennant, T. Davies, A. Round, W. Bradley, J. Gilbert, J. Payton, H. Fletcher.

Figure 56 – The Bazaar programme II

Opening Ceremony

FIRST DAY,
TUESDAY, MARCH 9th.
The Bazaar will be opened at 3 o'clock by:

MISS MARY LEES,
NEWBRIDGE.

CHAIRMAN: J. J. MARSH, ESQ.
Woodthorne.

Supported by the Circuit Ministers and others.

HYMN No. 2. — REV. A. F. VINEY

All people that on earth do dwell,
Sing to the Lord with cheerful voice:
Him serve with fear, His praise forth tell;
Come ye before Him and rejoice.

The Lord, ye know, is God indeed;
Without our aid He did us make;
We are His flock, He doth us feed;
And for His sheep He doth us take.

O enter then His gates with praise;
Approach with joy His courts unto:
Praise, laud, and bless His name always,
For it is seemly so to do.

For Why? The Lord our God is good,
His mercy is for ever sure;
His truth at all times firmly stood,
And shall from age to age endure.

PRAYER. — REV. W. H. MAY

Secretary's Statement
Introductory Remarks ... ... THE CHAIRMAN
Bazaar Opening ... ... MISS MARY LEES
Presentation of Bouquet ... SHEILA TENNANT
Song ... .. MISS FLORENCE HALE
Resolution of thanks to Lady Opener and Chairman
Proposed by ... ... J. T. TENNANT, ESQ., J.P.
Seconded by ... ... REV. W. H. MAY

Opening Ceremony

SECOND DAY,
WEDNESDAY, MARCH 10th.
The Bazaar will be opened at 3 o'clock by:

MISS LOTTIE M. MARSH,
WOODTHORNE.

CHAIRMAN: T. ALLEN, ESQ., *Dudley.*

Supported by the Circuit Ministers and others.

HYMN No. 299. — REV. W. H. MAY

We love Thy kingdom, Lord,
The house of Thine abode,
The Church our blest Redeemer saved
With His own precious blood.

We love Thy Church, O God;
Her saints before Thee stand,
Dear as the apple of Thine eye,
And graven on Thy hand.

For her our tears shall fall,
For her our prayers ascend,
To her our cares and toils be given,
Till toils and cares shall end.

Beyond our highest joy
We prize her heavenly ways,
Her sweet communion, solemn vows,
Her hymns of love and praise.

Sure as Thy truth shall last,
To Zion shall be given
The brightest glories earth can yield
And brighter bliss of heaven.

PRAYER. — REV. A F. VINEY

Secretary's Statement
Introductory Remarks .. ... THE CHAIRMAN
Bazaar Opening ... MISS LOTTIE M. MARSH
Presentation of Bouquet .. MARGARET MARSH
Song .. .. MISS F. HALE
Resolution of thanks to Lady Opener and Chairman
Proposed by ... ... REV. A. F. VINEY
Seconded by ... . MR. JOS. BRETTLE

At 5-30 the Children will present Purses of Money to Miss Lottie M. Marsh.

Hymn: "What are your hands for—little hands?" THE CHILDREN.

PRESENTATION OF PURSES.

Hymn: "Though to-day we are but children weak and small." THE CHILDREN.

Figure 57 – The Bazaar programme III

The 1935 Centenary Celebrations make possible renovation and improvements to the estate's buildings

In 1923, J T Tennant, referring to the *Chapel Account Book for 1827-1869*, had claimed that the foundation of the Zoar cause had taken place in 1826 and so the centenary should be marked on the occasion of the 1926 Church Anniversary. Discussions continued at subsequent meetings when it was agreed that the centenary be celebrated in November 1926 and *'that the Ladies of the congregation be called together to consider the centenary celebrations.'* However, the matter was dropped in April 1926 when it was decided *'that no real trace of our establishment in 1827 (sic.) was available.'* The misunderstanding had come about because the account book referred to had been begun in 1827, the foundation year of the Himley Road cause.[196] The establishment of the Society which was to become Zoar was not formed until 1835 by those expelled from Himley

Road. So, in March 1934 and evidently with greater confidence this time, the trustees agreed,

'In the year 1935 it will be 100 years since the society from which we have developed was started.'

A special committee was set up to make plans for celebrating this anniversary. It was made up of five choir members, nineteen trustees and twenty-six members of the Women's Own. Various ideas emerged, including the floodlighting of the church, although this was not implemented because it was deemed too costly. A souvenir booklet was published and sold for 6d (2½p). Some of the early recorded detail is open to question, as dates and details in the original account book suggest the writers of the booklet confused the date of the opening of the wooden Tabernacle with that of its replacement brick structure.

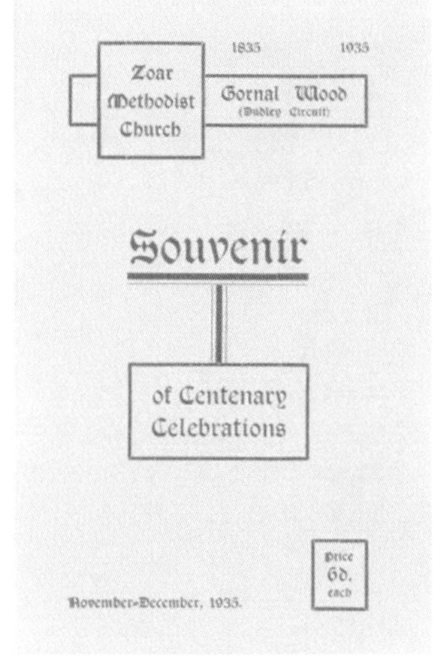

Figure 58: Centenary Celebration booklet

Anniversary publicity included 1000 circulars, 100 window bills[197] and 50 posters, plus a large streamer for the front of the building, along with adverts in the local Dudley Herald and Express and Star newspapers. Celebrations were planned around three special Sundays at the end of November and early December, with 700 hymn sheets ordered from the Methodist Book Room in London. A full account of the special services was reported in the local Free Church Council Messenger of January 1936,

Our Centenary Celebrations will ever be remembered as an outstanding event in the history of our Church. Some of Methodism's greatest preachers have visited us, with golden words of heavenly wisdom and truth, and we trust the inspiration of these services will long remain.

The Celebrations commenced on Nov 17th with the visit of the Rev. Wm. Younger. In the morning he spoke on the futility of being anxious about the future, for which we should trust the Holy Spirit, and consult Him about all our projects. In the evening, speaking on the text "Rise", in connection with the healing of the paralysed man, he said we were living in a world of culpable contentment with moderate attainments, and only the shadows of what God intended us to be. He urged us to "Rise" and strive to attain the full standards of life that are possible only through the presence of Christ in us. After the evening Service Mr. Younger administered the Sacrament to a large number of worshippers. On Nov. 18th, at 5.30pm, a Tea was held followed at 7pm by a Public Meeting, Mr J.H. Round was the chairman. He made a strong appeal to the younger members to carry on the work of the Church, so well upheld by noble men and women in the past. The Rev. T.J. Morgan proffered greetings and best wishes on behalf of the local Free Churches. The principal speaker, the Rev. W. Younger, gave an address on the various aspects of Biblical revelation of human personality. It was a great privilege to hear Mr Younger's masterly exposition of this subject. The chairman of the District, the Rev. W.J. Ward, also made a brief address.

Figure 59: Rev William Younger

On Nov 20th, the Rev Luke Wiseman visited us. At 4pm he preached on the value of the Old Testament, and brought us face to face with Christ as the fulfilment of the Scriptures. The presence of Jesus, he said, is the only infallible fact of the Church. Even if the Bible were destroyed Jesus would for ever remain the same. At 7pm at a Meeting presided over by Mr. P.L. Crook, the Rev. Wiseman gave his popular Lecture "The Christian Pilgrimage by the Daylight Route", basing his remarks on the second part of Bunyan's Pilgrim's Progress. The Lecture, which was interspersed with hymns by Mr. Wiseman and the audience, was exceptionally enjoyable and uplifting.

On Nov 24th, the preacher was Mr. J. Rounsfell, of Weston. He brought us vital messages on "Faith" and the vision of the New Jerusalem. On Nov 27th, an augmented choir rendered, with great success, Haydn's "Creation", the soloists being Dorothy Merrick, Alfred Dickin and Samuel Saul, with Winifrid Aston at the Organ and Florence Hale conducting. The performance was well attended, and was further graced by the presence of Mr. T. Allen as chairman.

On Dec 1st , the preacher was the Rev. W. Madgen, who spoke in the morning about the things the Church stands for, and in the evening contrasted the religious and general outlook of our forefathers one hundred years ago with that of the present day.

The concluding Services were held on Dec 8th. In the morning the Rev.T. H.

Johnston interpreted to us various ways in which the reappearance of Christ is manifested. At the evening Service the Rev. W.E. Walker spoke on peace, and the means of its practical realisation in the present unsettled state of the world. Throughout the Celebrations the Services were very well attended. We pray that, inspired and blessed by these Centenary experiences, we may, with God's help, press forward in His Service, ever eager to do all we can towards the extension of His Kingdom.

Financially the Centenary activities were a success. A 'Silver Tree' organized by the ladies raised £54, the Sunday School Anniversary produced £176/10/0d and the net proceeds of the celebrations amounted to £122/13/3d. Estimates were sought for repairs to the

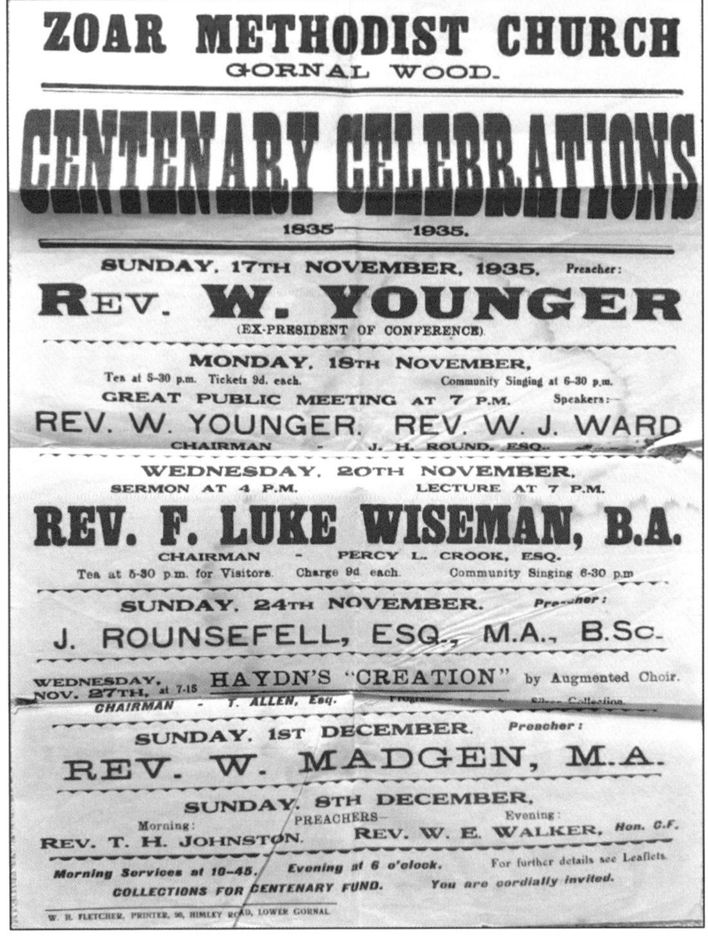

Figure 60: Window Poster for the celebrations

church and school, repairs and redecoration for the caretaker's house, tarmacking of the land in front and to the side of the church, installation of an electric blower for the church organ, a set of small chairs for the infants' room and improvements to the heating system. It took until 1938 for all of this to be implemented, thanks to much debate regarding estimates and, later, disputing the bills submitted for payment. The account for the heating system work was only accepted *'after some severe criticism of the account and of the secretary for having given instructions for the work to be done at the high prices charged.'*

Messrs. Arthur Nelson & Co of Durham were appointed to install the organ blower at a cost of £45, a *British Silent Electric Blowing Unit* which the trustees insisted was being purchased on the understanding that if it was deemed too noisy, it would be removed at Nelson's expense. It did not need removing. Just over ten years later an organ fund was set up to make possible a major overhaul and upgrading of the organ at the substantial cost of £860. The work was undertaken by Messrs Walter James Bird and Son.

At the suggestion of the Women's Own meeting *'the possibility of installing amplifiers in the church for the convenience of members of the congregation whose hearing is not good'* was taken up. However, when the report came back it was decided not to proceed, as, *'this would be too expensive a matter to undertake at present'*.

Abbey Farm estate

The Abbey Farm estate consisted of a substantial plot of agricultural land, a set of farm buildings and a farmhouse[198] to the left and rear of the church. It was in the early twentieth century that the trustees first

Figure 61: the Abbey Farmhouse mid-twentieth century

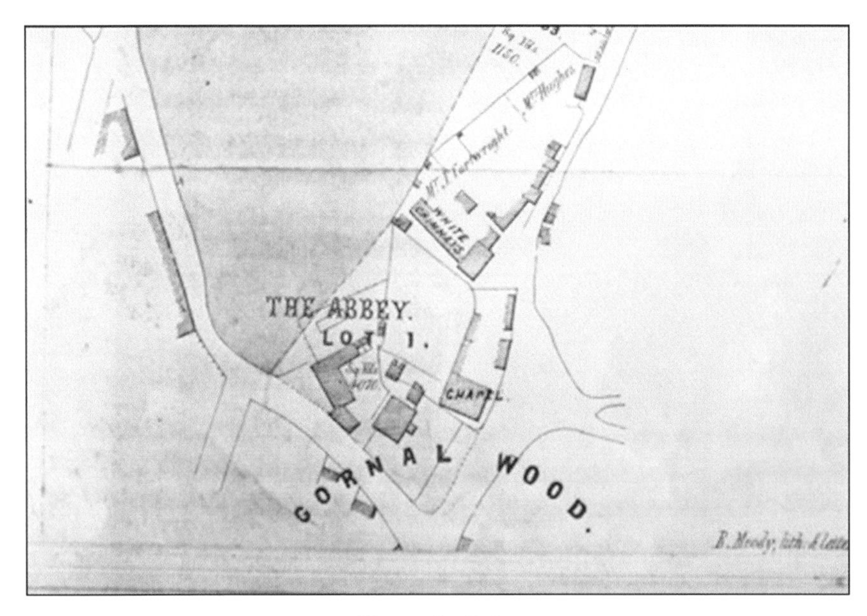

Figure 62: Lot 1

took an interest in the property, as over several years the question of buying the farmhouse regularly reappeared on the Trust's agendas.

In the early years of the twentieth century, the Abbey Farm's owner was William Lees, solicitor, Zoar member and trustee, who died in 1925. Conversations took place with his widow, Charlotte Marion, as to the future possible sale of the farmhouse. She gave an undertaking that the trustees would be given first refusal, at a figure of £600, should she decide to sell. Nothing definite followed until there was evidence of some renovation work on the building. The trustees were reassured that their interest was not forgotten. When in 1931 the property was put up for sale, they made tentative enquiries but did not proceed to purchase the building and again were reassured by the solicitors involved that certain restrictions protecting their interest had been put into the legal sale documents.

Joseph John Baker,[199] member and trustee and employer in the coal mining industry, eventually purchased Abbey Farmhouse. In April 1937 the trustees were offered the property for £775 by Mr. Baker. When the matter came to the meeting he was asked to retire, but to *'keep within hail'* should they wish him to *'clear up any points that may arise'*. A lengthy discussion followed which revealed a *'diversity of opinion'*, but no decision. Before the trustees had come to a mind, in June they were asked to meet a deputation from the local Miners' Welfare, accompanied by a representative from their London HQ, to hear about a proposed scheme to buy and *'reconstruct the whole of the Abbey Estate to include many social amenities'*. The outcome was agreement in principle to accept this idea, subject to the buyers agreeing to certain conditions covering matters such as protecting rights of light and access, *'no singing, dancing or music of any kind during any service, Sundays or otherwise'*, and the guarantee of a contribution to the development of the planned children's playground, which bordered the Abbey farmhouse. Nothing came of this scheme.

After J J Baker died in 1948, his sons William and Benjamin and daughters Lydia (Hartill) and Mary (Hayward), who were his executors, offered the Abbey farmhouse to the newly formed trust for £1,000. As their first major decision, they agreed to purchase the property at £950, having obtained a loan of £600 from the Connexional Chapel Committee in Manchester (which they found a challenge to pay back on time). The first tenants were Harold Jones, a trustee, and his new wife Joan, who were joined in 1950 by a new-born son, Anthony Ward Jones. They stayed for a further two years.

The trustees were approached in 1959 with an offer to buy the farmhouse in order to build a garage and petrol station on the site, while, in 1963, a property developer offered £15,000 for the property. Both offers were declined. In 1964 the farmhouse was condemned as unfit for human habitation and the following year a demolition order was issued. The land was then used as a carpark. Aware of the poor condition of the Sunday School building and pressed by the teachers, in 1970, to do something about it, the trustees agreed in 1972 to sell the land and put the money raised towards providing a replacement. Conversations began with a supermarket chain. Two sets of plans were prepared, one showed the supermarket along with several small shop units on the old Sunday School site and a new Sunday School on the farmhouse site, the other reversed the locations, but the Sedgley Urban District Council rejected both options. When the council came back to the trustees and announced they planned to place a compulsory purchase order on the property, involving a compensation payment of £15,000, the decision was challenged. What could have become an interesting legal dispute over council rights was averted when an increased offer of £22,000 was made and accepted. The council erected a library on the farmhouse site and a new Sunday School building was located where the old building, the caretakers' cottage and neighbouring cottages had stood.[200] Built by S. Capewell and Sons of Netherton, the new building cost £29,800. Original plans for the new premises included a caretakers' flat over the top of the public spaces, however, the proposal was abandoned because of the additional cost.

Financial Matters

The routine income and expenditure of the Trust through the first half of the century is illustrated in Figures 63-65. While annual accounts were usually printed for distribution, the 1945 statement, like all those issued during the Second World War, is handwritten and duplicated on cheap paper, illustrating the way in which the war affected even routine and inconsequential activities in daily life.

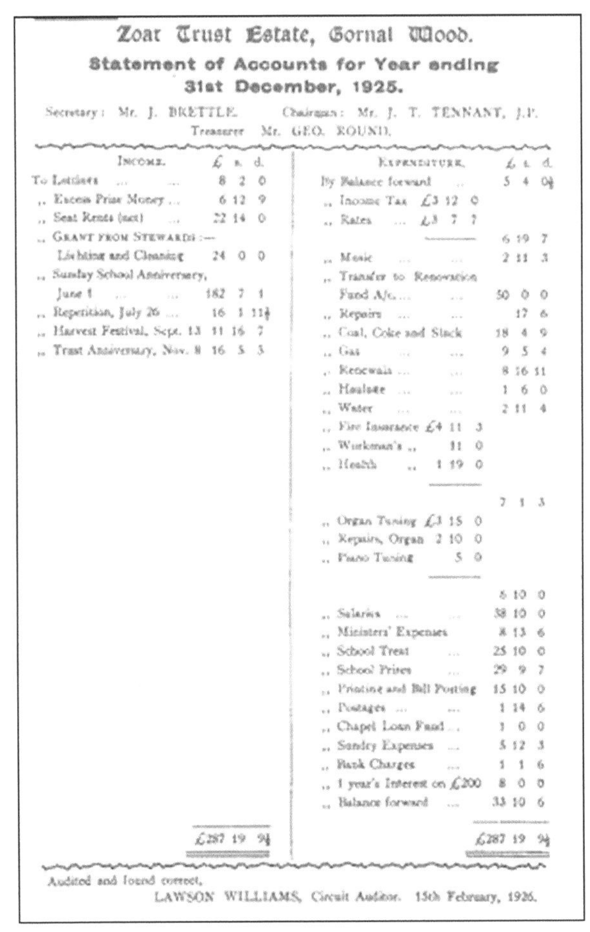

Zoar Trust Estate, Gornal Wood.

Statement of Accounts for Year ending 31st December, 1925.

Secretary: Mr. J. BRETTLE. Chairman: Mr. J. T. TENNANT, J.P.
Treasurer Mr. GEO. ROUND.

INCOME.	£	s.	d.
To Lettings	8	2	0
,, Excess Prize Money ...	6	12	9
,, Seat Rents (net) ...	22	14	0
,, GRANT FROM STEWARDS :— Lighting and Cleaning	24	0	0
,, Sunday School Anniversary, June 1	182	7	1
,, Repetition, July 26 ...	16	1	11¾
,, Harvest Festival, Sept. 13	11	16	7
,, Trust Anniversary, Nov. 8	16	5	3
	£287	19	9¾

EXPENDITURE.		£	s.	d.
By Balance forward ...		5	4	0¾
,, Income Tax	£3 12 0			
,, Rates ...	£3 7 7			
		6	19	7
,, Music		2	11	3
,, Transfer to Renovation Fund A/c... ...		50	0	0
,, Repairs			17	6
,, Coal, Coke and Slack		18	4	9
,, Gas		9	5	4
,, Renewals		8	16	11
,, Haulage		1	6	0
,, Water		2	11	4
,, Fire Insurance	£4 11 3			
,, Workman's ,,	11 0			
,, Health ,,	1 19 0			
		7	1	3
,, Organ Tuning	£3 15 0			
,, Repairs, Organ	2 10 0			
,, Piano Tuning	5 0			
		6	10	0
,, Salaries		38	10	0
,, Ministers' Expenses		8	13	6
,, School Treat ...		25	10	0
,, School Prizes ...		29	9	7
,, Printing and Bill Posting		15	10	0
,, Postages		1	14	6
,, Chapel Loan Fund ...		1	0	0
,, Sundry Expenses ...		5	12	3
,, Bank Charges ...		1	1	6
,, 1 year's Interest on £200		8	0	0
,, Balance forward ...		33	10	6
		£287	19	9¾

Audited and found correct,
LAWSON WILLIAMS, Circuit Auditor. 15th February, 1926.

Figure 63: The 1925 Account

ZOAR TRUST ESTATE, GORNAL WOOD.

STATEMENT OF ACCOUNTS

For the year ending December 31st, 1936.

Hon. Treasurer - Mr. ALBERT A. SMITH. Hon. Secretary - Mr. JOSEPH BRETTLE.

1936 EXPENDITURE	£ s. d.	£ s. d.	£ s. d.
District Rate ...			4 6 9
Income Tax ...			1 9 3
Music ...			12 10
Hymn Books (Choir) ...			1 16 0
Printing ...			9 15 1
Repairs and Renewals ...			6 9 9
Gas and Coke ...		37 8 7	
Coal ...		1 0 0	
Haulage ...		2 5 0	
Electric Supply ...		6 17 6	
			47 11 7
Water Rate ...			4 2 8
Insurances ...			7 14 10
Organ and Piano Tuning			8 10 0
Salaries ...			46 10 0
Preachers' Expenses ...			4 4 0
Sunday School Prizes ...	24 17 11		
Less Excess Prize Money	4 4 6		
		20 13 5	
Sunday School Treats ...		17 6 9	
Chars-a-banc for Singers		3 4 0	
Sunday School (New Bibles)		4 3 4	
			45 7 6
Temporary Loan to Circuit			9 0 0
Hospital Sunday ...			2 9 4
Stamps ...			10 9
Sundry Expenses ...			5 14 2
Cash in Hand and at Bank			269 10 5
			£470 15 0

1936 INCOME.	£ s. d.	£ s. d.
Balance brought forward ...		74 19 6
Lettings ...		15 10 0
Seat Rents ...		18 14 0
Sunday School Anniversary ...		171 3 10
Special Donation ...		10 0 0
Repetition Services ...		14 1 6
Harvest Festival Services ...		11 19 6
Trust Anniversary ...		7 18 5
From Stewards ...		24 0 0
Centenary Fund ...		122 18 3
		£470 15 0

Audited and found correct, LAWSON WILLIAMS, Circuit Auditor. February 15th, 1937.

Figure 64: The 1936 Account

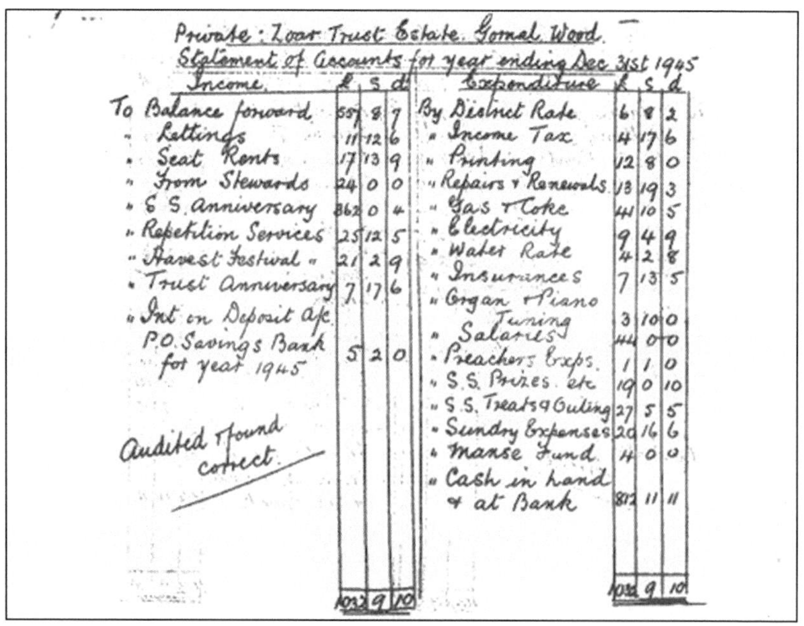

Private: Zoar Trust Estate. Gornal Wood.

Statement of Accounts for year ending Dec 31st 1945

Income.	£	s	d
To Balance forward	557	8	7
" Lettings	11	12	6
" Seat Rents	17	13	9
" From Stewards	24	0	0
" S S. anniversary	362	0	4
" Repetition Services	25	12	5
" Harvest Festival "	21	2	9
" Trust anniversary	7	17	6
" Int on Deposit a/c P.O. Savings Bank for year 1945	5	2	0
	1032	9	10

Expenditure	£	s	d
By District Rate	6	8	2
" Income Tax	4	17	6
" Printing	12	8	0
" Repairs + Renewals	13	19	3
" Gas + Coke	41	10	5
" Electricity	9	4	9
" Water Rate	4	2	8
" Insurances	7	13	5
" Organ + Piano Tuning	3	10	0
" Salaries	44	0	0
" Preachers Exps.	1	1	0
" S.S. Prizes etc	19	0	10
" S.S. Treats + Outing	27	5	5
" Sundry Expenses	20	16	6
" Manse Fund	4	0	0
" Cash in hand + at Bank	812	11	11
	1032	9	10

Audited + found correct

Figure 65: The 1945 Account

After the First World War, the trustees become very insurance conscious, regularly reviewing and increasing the Estate policies, from £5,000 in 1931 to £10,000 in 1946 and £25,000 in 1950. In the 1930s, possibly for the first time, it was decided to insure the caretakers, both Mr. and Mrs. Marsh against accident and Mrs. Marsh against sickness. Next came accident insurance for teachers and scholars of the Sunday School and in the 1950s comprehensive policies for the church boiler and heating system and to cover theft of church monies up to £1,500.

In 1954 the Zoar Estate was added to when Leonard Evans, a former Zoar Sunday School scholar who had moved to the USA and whose grandfather was James Bennett who had laid the first foundation

ZOAR METHODIST CHURCH

ACCOUNTS FOR YEAR ENDING 31st August 2000

INCOME

1998/9		1999/2000
£14,317.47	Offerings	£13,842.12
£1,557.10	Anniversary	£1,608.24
£609.02	Income Bond Dividend	£539.67
£187.30	Bank Interest	£61.06
£2,642.68	Donations	£1,950.00
£300.00	Play Group	£300.00
£40.00	Hire of Hall	£70.00
	Covenants / Tax Credits	£1,572.58
	Quarterage Refund	£3,192.00
	Mothers & Toddlers Group	£45.00
£50.00	Harvest Supper	
£169.90	Coffee Morning	
£122.89	Luncheon Club	
£549.20	Collection - Rev. H. Le Ruez	
£2,533.00	Special Gift Day	
£23,078.56	Total Income	£23,180.67
£12,333.54	Cash at Bank 1/9/99	£8,128.28
£35,412.10		£31,308.95

EXPENDITURE

1998/9		1999/2000
£12,536.00	Quarterage / Plans	£11,736.50
£202.00	Methodist Property Fund	£196.00
£49.95	Printing / Photocopying	£399.74
£54.32	Envelope Scheme	£55.68
£10.00	Women's Work	£10.00
£10.00	Ladies Class	£10.00
£50.00	Alpha Course Expenses	£50.00
£213.00	Speakers' Expenses	£485.00
£18.66	Communion Wine	£10.40
£54.92	Water Rates	£18.57
£304.61	Electricity (Church)	£270.03
£197.52	Telephone	£202.90
£976.33	Insurance	£1,006.23
£1,083.39	Gas	£499.55
	Sunday School	
£105.99	Prizes	£60.04
£298.30	Electricity	£453.05
£367.91	Teaching Materials	£344.04
£330.00	Youth Work	£256.75
£67.46	Party	£57.50
£118.50	Anniversary	£74.94
£356.48	Trip	£259.65
£247.63	Organ Maintenance	£165.10
£12.75	Remembrance Sunday Wreath	£13.00
£228.00	Donations	£1,156.00
£5,749.19	Property Repairs	£5,722.35
£120.00	Copyright Fee	£196.00
£66.00	Piano Tuning	£72.00
£365.60	Cleaning & Materials	£657.21
	Vacuum Cleaner	£327.67
	Millenium Sign	£73.25
	Bibles for Church	£235.68
	Bibles for New Members	£34.98
£628.00	Gift - Rev. H. Le Ruez	
£113.76	Brownie Flag	
£14.00	Baptismal Gift	
£2,333.55	Organ Repairs	
£27,283.82	Total Expenditure	£25,109.81
£8,128.28	Cash at Bank 31/8/2000	£6,199.14
£35,412.10		£31,308.95

Figure 66: Accounts for 2000

stone of the Sunday School, gave his late grandfather's house at 22 The Alley, along with an additional property at 34 Musk Lane, to the trustees. Mr Evans paid a visit to England in the course of which he personally handed over the deeds to these properties at a trustees' meeting and expressed his appreciation of all that Zoar had meant to him in his early years. The trustees rented out the properties until 1969 when they were sold for £2,725, the money being ring-fenced for redevelopment or renovation work and used in 1975 to help fund the new Sunday School building.

By 2000 a much more complex set of income and expenditure figures required the attention of the Church Council, which, after the changes to local church governance in 1975, had become responsible for all financial and property matters. The contribution of the Sunday School Anniversary collections to income was still significant, underlining the way in which it continued to attract large congregations. The annual financial returns show that anniversary collections peaked in 1994 when £2,618.03 was raised.

Maintaining the Property

Perhaps inspired by a post-war spirit of optimism, in 1952 the trustees decided to redecorate the church and began fundraising with a bazaar. The only evidence of this event is contained in a programme marking the occasion which was evidently a scaled down version of previous bazaars. *'The Grand Bazaar and Sale of Work'* took place mid-week on Wednesday 19 November, opened at 3.00pm by Mrs Tom Marsh, wife of the long-serving former Sunday School Secretary. Stalls offered drapery, fancy goods, groceries, china, glass, pottery, hardware, fruit, vegetables, bulbs, plants, fancy goods and bran tub, along with a refreshment stall and tea rooms. While the purpose of the bazaar was described in the 6d. programme, no further mention is made in any of the church records.

The Objects of the Bazaar

The decoration of our Church has been the subject of considerable discussion for some time past, and it is generally agreed that the time has come for us to carry out our decisions.

The Church was last decorated 26 years ago, so that the work is long overdue.

To do what is needed, some four hundred Pounds will be required, and it is hoped to raise a substantial sum by this effort.

We thank all our friends for their kindly assistance, and in launching this Bazaar, and stating our objects, we appeal for your patronage and support.

Rev. G. F. Hunt, Minister.
J. Brettle, Sec.
W. H. Fletcher, Treas.
I. Harris, S. M. Hale, G. Marsh — Stewards.
H. Fletcher, S.S. Superintendent.
B. C. Smith, " "
H. Jones, S.S. Sec.

Figure 67: The 1952 Bazaar

The extent of this redecoration must have been minimal, because, anticipating the 60th Anniversary of the church in 1966, the trustees decided to make plans for an extensive interior redecoration. The church was closed for several weeks in 1967 while the work took place and, on completion, a special service was planned for the first Saturday in September. Invitation leaflets encouraged thanksgiving gifts of money towards the redecoration. The Superintendent Minister, the Revd Alan Fisher, conducted the service and four young people, Margaret Bate, Janett Malpass, the author and John Powell led the procession which entered the church prior to the opening hymn. They were mentioned in the order of service as representing *'The future Church'*.

Figure 68: 'The Future Church' [201]

CHAPTER SIX

The internal life of the church: Governance, Worship and Fellowship

Governance: the Leaders' Meeting [202]

Following the Methodist Union Scheme of 1907 the churches of the Methodist New Connexion, including Zoar, became part of the United Methodist Church. The Leaders' Meeting, which dealt with all non-property matters, was required to reconstitute itself according to a new and detailed constitution,

> *The powers and duties of the meeting were – to determine the order of service; to fix the hours of worship; to arrange the various week night meetings; to appoint the times for public collections; to receive persons into and to suspend or exclude persons from membership; to record in a book or roll the names of the members of the local church and to examine that roll, name by name, not less than twice a year and to exercise general supervision of the membership of the church; to recommend persons as candidates for the ministry; to nominate persons to the Church Meeting for appointment by that meeting as representatives to the Circuit Quarterly Meeting; to recommend to the Church Meeting persons as local preachers, to administer the fund for the poor; to receive reports from the various societies connected with the church and generally to consider and devise plans for promoting the prosperity of the church; to appoint such committees as it might deem necessary for the dispatch of its business and to delegate to them such of its powers or duties as it deemed fit.*[203]

For Zoar membership consisted of seven Class Leaders, two Society Stewards, one Poor Steward, a representative from the Trustees, Sunday School, Christian Endeavour and Band of Hope, plus twelve representatives elected by the congregation. The Leaders met frequently with more than 20 meetings a year being the norm for a long time and usually taking place after Sunday worship, until, in 1911, it was proposed and agreed that in future meetings be held mid-week.

Their decisions established the way in which the church was to and would function, until a new Methodist Union scheme was formulated in the 1930s.

Sunday Worship

The Leaders Meeting minutes indicate a considerable amount of time was devoted to matters relating to Sunday services, from hymn book requirements to the format and content of the services themselves.

• To begin with, the Sacrament of the Lord's Supper was held as and when the Leaders requested it, then, in 1910, they agreed to plan for a celebration every time a minister was appointed to lead worship.

• In 1911 the choir were asked to sing an anthem at least every fortnight and to teach new hymn tunes to the congregation when the offertory was being collected.

• A new pulpit hymn book was purchased in 1913 and it was decided to seek someone to provide it. Evidently well used, in 1916 it required rebinding.

• Also in 1913, a pulpit fall was made after it was agreed *'... that drapery be purchased for the pulpit for use on the death of any member, teacher or trustee and that same remain on pulpit for one month.'*

• In January 1915, Leaders decided to place the collection boxes on the communion table after the offering had been taken up, then three years later the decision was reversed and they chose to revert to the previous practice of counting the collection immediately it was taken up.

• Also in 1915, it was agreed *'that the Lord's Supper be observed on the first Sunday of every month.'*

• In August 1916 two dozen hymn books *'for the use of visitors'* were purchased. The stated expectation was that seat holders would supply their own.

• In 1917 the Leaders decided that an Amen should be sung at the end of each hymn and 'instructed' the choir *'to carry this into effect forthwith'*.

• In the early years of the twentieth century, it was quite common for children to attend evening worship and evidently this created challenges for the stewards as in November 1918 it was resolved that the children should leave during the singing of the hymn before the sermon, while shortly afterwards the Leaders appointed a rota of *'Officers of Order'* to supervise them. This wasn't as effective as they had hoped, because in 1922 it was agreed that *'small children be debarred from attending evening worship unless accompanied by someone to look after them.'* Additionally on Sunday mornings an experiment was introduced by which the boys and girls were kept on the side seats downstairs. Two years on and it was minuted *'that as a consequence of the bad behaviour in the gallery that portion leading to big windows be closed for general use.'*

ZOAR CHURCH, GORNAL WOOD.

OFFICERS OF ORDER

For Evening Services during 1924.

GROUP 1.	GROUP 2.	GROUP 3.	GROUP 4.	GROUP 5.	GROUP 6.
Mr. J. Brettle	Mr W. H. Fletcher	Mr. T. Davies	Mr. J. Jones	Mr. H. Bate	Mr. J. Wakelam
Mr L. Scranage	Mr J. Payton	Mr. W. Price	Mr W. Jones	Mr. A. Round	Mr. J. H. Hemmings
Mrs. W. Collins	Mrs. G. Tennant	Mrs. J. Massey	Miss E. Bennett	Mr. S. Brettle	Mr. S. M. Hale
Miss L. Cox	Miss D. Smith	Miss M. A. Hale	Miss E. Marsh	Mr. F. Harvey	Mr. J. Scranage

Date	Group No.	Date	Group No.	Date	Group No.	Date	Group No.
January 6	1	April 6	2	July 6	3	October 5	4
13	2	13	3	13	4	12	5
20	3	20	4	20	5	19	6
27	4	27	5	27	6	26	1
February 3	5	May 4	6	August 3	1	N'vember 2	2
10	6	11	1	10	2	9	3
17	1	18	2	17	3	16	4
24	2	25	3	24	4	23	5
March 2	3	June 1	4	31	5	30	6
9	4	8	5	Sept'mb'r 7	6	D'cember 7	1
16	5	15	6	14	1	14	2
23	6	22	1	21	2	21	3
30	1	29	2	28	3	28	4

Officers should be present 10 minutes before Services commence, and also see to the children leaving as quietly as possible. It is requested that Officers unable to be on duty provide substitutes.

The Leaders depend upon the co-operation and assistance of Officers in maintaining order during Divine Service.

Figure 69: Officers of Order

- Plans to buy a further 50 hymn books in 1919 were scaled back to 36 once the cost was known.
- An Offering was evidently not taken up at morning services prior to 1919 as in that year it was proposed and agreed by the Church Meeting[204] to begin doing so in view of the church's financial situation at the time.
- In 1919 the choir asked permission *'to chant the Lord's Prayer and sing the Psalms'*. The implementation of this request is shown in the blank orders of service provided for preachers by the Leaders.[205] Additionally, the congregation were to be asked to stand for the Benediction and then sit for the Vesper.

Zoar Church, Gornal Wood.

Order of Evening Service.

	No.	Tune.
HYMN		
SHORT PRAYER AND LORD'S PRAYER (Chanted)		
HYMN		
FIRST LESSON		
HYMN		
SECOND LESSON		
ANTHEM		
PRAYER		
NOTICES AND OFFERTORY		
HYMN		
SERMON		
HYMN		
BENEDICTION AND VESPER		

Figure 70: Order of Service

• In 1920 the Leaders decided to have flowers on the communion table and a rota was prepared of people willing to provide them.
• In 1922 the choir were asked to consider the musical portion of the service with the young people in mind.[206]
• 1924 brought a decision *'that a look out committee be formed to secure a better attendance of the young people at the evening services.'*
• The choir, in 1926, requested the trustees to supply them with 24 new tune books plus a large music book for the organ.
• The two senior women's classes were asked *'to seek to secure a larger attendance at evening services'* in 1927. No guidance was offered as to how they might go about this task.
• Following the Methodist Union of 1932 (the final union scheme which involved bringing together the three main strands of Methodism: Wesleyan, Primitive and United Methodists), a new hymn book was published and in 1934 Zoar decided to acquire copies. First used in February 1935, there was a debate in the Leaders' Meeting about their use, with a decision taken, *'that under supervision the children be allowed to use the visitors' hymn books on Sunday mornings'*.
• In 1935 *'it was resolved that the children be encouraged to attend divine service on Sunday mornings and that a prize be awarded to each one making 60% attendances.'* Three registrars were appointed to keep the records.
• 1935 witnessed a change to the Vesper. It was decided to use 688 (*'O God our Father who doest make us one'*) from the new hymn book.
• Beginning with the 1935 Centenary celebrations, the Leaders decided to change the start time for worship from 10.30am to 10.45am.
• In 1938 more of the new hymn books were purchased, a further 12 choir editions and 36 additional books *'for the use of visitors'*. Shortly afterwards the caretaker reported that they had started disappearing. The explanation given was that they had not been stamped with the name of the church, so it was decided to purchase a new handstamp. This created an indented impression of the words on the front cover. A pulpit hymn book was provided in memory of the late Thomas Hemmings.
• A seven-fold *'Amen'* was practiced by the choir with a view to it replacing the Vesper in 1938, the year in which they were also asked to try out intoning the Lord's Prayer.
• During 1941 a Vesper considered appropriate for the difficult war years was introduced, *'Lord keep us safe this night'* and approval given for the seven-fold *'Amen'* to be sung after the prayers at both morning and evening worship.

• 1944 witnessed yet more change, when it was agreed to say the Lord's Prayer and move the singing of the seven-fold Amen to the end of the service, with this latter practice surviving through into the 1960s.
• Another 50 hymn books *'for visitors'* were purchased in 1945 and the old ones assessed for wear and tear and missing pages.
• Zoar Leaders agreed the church should host a United Youth Service in November 1945. It took place at 8.00pm on a Sunday evening.
• The idea was floated in 1945, by the minister, Revd. J W Webb, that Welcome Stewards be appointed to greet people on arrival. Mr Webb also suggested it would be a good idea to use more young people when seeking to fill offices in the church.
• In 1947 two verses of MHB 684, *'Jesus stand among us, in this hallowed hour'* were introduced as an introit to the evening service. Also, the congregation were asked to stand when the minister entered the pulpit at the commencement of the service and it was agreed to continue saying the Lord's Prayer.
• In the 1950s as children left the morning service, following the notices and offering and before the sermon, they were given a stamp as evidence of their attendance. The stamps had a bible scene on them and had to be stuck into an album, which was then handed in at the end of the year and, as with Sunday School attendance, book prizes were then awarded.

Figure 71: Four examples of the weekly 'stamps'

• Chanting the Lord's Prayer was back in 1955.
• In 1969 concern was expressed that *'our church was growing old and that our young people tended to go round the churches and not always attend their own church as much as they might.'*
• In the 1970s the need for those leading the Sunday morning services to consider the presence of children became a regular agenda item

at teachers' meetings. One idea proposed was to gather together a collection of hymns which, it was believed, would appeal more to them. The increasing use across Methodism of 'Family Services'[207] was first discussed in 1970. It wasn't until 1984, when the then minister, the Revd Keith Rowbottom, announced he intended to begin holding such services monthly, that the practice became a regular occurrence.

The Choir, Choirmaster and Organist

The choir played an important role in worship and, at times, it sought to make clear what it considered its role to be in determining the content of the Sunday services. For example, in 1912 the Leaders received and agreed a resolution from the choir, *'that ministers be requested not to interfere with the musical part of the service and that no hymns be curtailed'* and then *'that after the hymn has been announced the tune be played through and the first verse read.'*

Highly significant in shaping and leading the choir were the choirmaster and organist. Both appointments were the responsibility of the Trustees, appearing more often than might have been expected on their agendas. For some thirty years in the second half of the nineteenth century, the role of choirmaster had been held by trustee John Tennant. He was followed by Joseph Hale, who also took on the role of organist, resigning in 1911. The roles were separated again at this point, with Arthur Tomlinson appointed choirmaster. In 1919 he also resigned. Tom Hemmings took over temporarily as organist until Mr. S Millington was appointed at an annual salary of £6 (increased to £8 in 1912). He resigned in 1917 and was replaced by Wilfred Aston, who was to be paid £10p.a. (raised to £15 in 1918). He resigned after two years, the post being advertised in the local press,[208] and attracting seven applicants from Upper and Lower Gornal, Sedgley, Coseley, Tipton and Pensnett. The trustees decided that applicants would be required to play the organ on one Sunday and *'submit to a test under a judge to be appointed by the trustees'*. Evidently none of the applicants was deemed suitable as Wilfred Aston was asked and agreed to withdraw his resignation *'for three months'*.

Figure 72: Joseph Hale

In October 1919 John Hemmings[209] was offered the post at a reduced salary of £8 p.a. with the proviso that *'he take at least two years training under a competent organist* [and that] *at the expiration of that period the matter come up for confirmation.'* The same meeting also made a recommendation for a replacement choirmaster,[210] reappointing Joseph Hale, with a salary of £8, and agreed that *'he be given plenary powers to make such arrangements as shall lead to greater efficiency in the musical portions of the services.'* In 1921 Wilfred Aston was reappointed organist at a salary of £16 p.a. with a rise to £20 after 12 months in post. John Hemmings had agreed to stand down and was appointed *honorary* deputy organist. A problem arose concerning Mr. Aston's absences from the organ which led to a decision that, *'a letter be sent to the organist (Mr. W Aston) pointing out the desirability of his making definite arrangements for his place to be filled at the organ in case he is unable to be present.'* This evidently proved to be an ongoing problem which would lead to more heated correspondence a few years later, including a complaint in 1924 that he was leaving the church before the end of the service. Resignations were offered but eventually withdrawn.

The trustees conceded that there was a lack of certainty as to what was actually expected of the organist, so they decided to compile a list of duties: attendance at all Sunday Services, the weekday evening practice and the necessary practices for the preparation of any special events including the Sunday School Anniversary.

In 1930 'an assistant choirmaster [sic.]' was appointed, Miss Florence Hale, Joseph's daughter. Shortly after this move the trustees agreed to pay her an honorarium of £8 p.a., which was subsequently reduced to £4.

Figure 73: Florence Hale

Later in the 1930s and through until 1954 Miss Hale took on the leadership of the choir, which, alongside its weekly duties, performed major works such as Mendelssohn's Elijah and Hymn of Praise, and Handel's Messiah, augmented and supported by invited soloists. In 1948, at the invitation of the choir committee, the world-renowned soloist Isabel Baillie paid what was a second visit to Zoar. Such events underlined the way in which

Zoar became well-known for its musical contribution to life in the village and beyond.

Use of the organ was tightly controlled by the trustees. Sidney Hale asked permission to practice on it but was not allowed to do so until his appointment as deputy organist in 1936.

ZOAR METHODIST CHURCH
Isobel
Baillie
SECOND VISIT OF WORLD RENOWNED SOPRANO
On Friday, 24th September, 1948, at 7-30 p.m.
Organist: Wm. TIMMINS
AUGMENTED CHOIR CONDUCTED BY
FLORENCE HALE
Chairman (to be announced in Press).
PROGRAMME: TWO SHILLINGS AND SIX PENCE.
PROCEEDS FOR ORGAN AND CHOIR FUNDS

Figure 74: Isobel Baillie's visit

Subsequent organists included William Timmins, who took over from Wilfred Aston in 1946, with Ernest Cox as his deputy, Mrs Kirkland, appointed at a salary of £20 per annum but who resigned after one year and Geoff Marsh who served as a temporary stand-in on more than one occasion. William Timmins returned in 1954, when he was appointed organist, choirmaster and director of music. In 1968 he resigned in order to take over musical leadership at the prestigious Carr's Lane church in Birmingham. The final regular organist, serving for a number of years, was Brian Jones.

In 1957 William Timmins proposed that Gwen Browne, a gifted

Figure 75: Gwen Marsh (nee Browne)

Figure 76: Long serving Choir Member Vi Millward

soloist, who would serve the church in a variety of capacities into the twenty-first century, should take over the musical directorship. The choir continued to make significant contributions to worship over many years, benefiting from individual choristers who gave long years of service. A newspaper article in 1978 highlighted the particular contribution of May York, a chorister for 46 years, and Vi Millward who had chalked up 48 years.[211]

By 2000 a music group was regularly leading the singing in worship.

The Organ blowers

For many years, vital to the performance of the organists was the appointment of the organ blowers. Typical were Benjamin Greenway for the chapel at £1/5/0d per annum and Ernest Cox for the Sunday School at 15 shillings, appointed by the trustees, who also decided, that *'an insurance policy be taken out on the Trustees' servants to include the caretaker, organist and organ blower.'* [212] The last post-holder was Mr. Lees who was granted two quarters extra pay as an expression of thanks for his services, as in 1938 an electric organ blower was installed in the church. In 1949 the church organ underwent a major overhaul along with the fitting of a new and more powerful electric blower. The Sunday School organ was still being manually pumped in the 1950s when the author undertook the task as his first job in the life of the church. Alas, there was no longer an honorarium. An electric blower was fitted to this organ in 1968.

The organ in the Sunday School had an interesting history. It was originally donated to the trustees by the Earl of Dudley, having previously been housed in the Dudley family's residence at Himley Hall. When the Sunday School was demolished in 1975 it was cleaned and renovated, then returned and reassembled in its original setting.[213]

The Spiritual Life of the Church

Historically within Methodism it was the weekly Class Meeting which was seen as the key to sustaining the spiritual life of its members. There is no record of the vitality or otherwise of Class Meetings at Zoar in the nineteenth century. When the United Methodist Church was established in 1906, its Foundation Deed Poll document included the following paragraph,

> *EVERY church forming part of the United Methodist Church ... shall be divided into classes to meet for Christian fellowship under the care of a class leader or into sections approved by the leaders' meeting such sections to be*

under the oversight of a person who shall have the name and status of a class leader.[214]

At Zoar, this arrangement seems to have faltered, as in 1908 the Leaders agreed that *'the two society classes be reformed'*: one for males and one for females. Evidently nothing happened as in 1912 it was decided to hold a members' social *'with a view to reforming the classes.'*

In 1911 concern was expressed *'over the present indifference in attendance at church.'* A special committee was set up to examine the matter further, one of many that would meet in succeeding years. These concerns prompted the Leaders to plan for a fortnight's mission conducted by a member of the UMC's Deaconess Institute in London.[215] At one Leaders' Meeting, with the mission in mind, it was decided to purchase *'a few streamers'*. The idea, it may be assumed, was to brighten up the front of the church. A four-day mission was arranged for November 1915, with the only other recorded detail being that *'Sankey Hymns'* [216] should be used at the services.

In 1917 the Leaders and Teachers met jointly *'to discuss the matter of engaging some outside assistance for deepening the spiritual life of the church and Sunday School.'* Another Deaconess mission was planned, but in the end the Deaconess Institute was unable to provide one of its number because of a sudden illness.

The agenda of the Leaders' Meeting included an annual review of the spiritual welfare of the membership. When in 1917 the UMC Conference issued a questionnaire on this subject, at Zoar a committee was appointed to suggest what responses might be submitted.

QUESTIONS	ANSWERS
1. Decline of Membership - *What are the chief causes of decline in church membership in your District?*	We do not report any decrease.
2. Fellowship -	
a) What proportion of your membership meets in class?	Ten per cent.
b) What other meetings have you which are held distinctly for spiritual fellowship?	Senior Christian Endeavour Society Meeting weekly. Attendance 15-20. Mid-week preaching service.

c) How many churches hold regularly a Sunday evening Prayer Meeting? Is there a week evening Prayer Meeting? How are these attended?	Sunday evening Prayer Meeting held – Fair attendance. No week evening Prayer Meeting held.
3. Membership – *Are the conditions of Membership laid down in the Foundation Deed Poll (Minutes 1907, p41, clause 7) namely:- repentance and faith, a life in harmony, attendance at the Lord's Supper, and week night fellowship, adhered to in the admission of new members?*	The answer is in the affirmative.
4. Shepherding - *a) To what extent is pastoral visitation systematically carried out?*	We have no regular system of Pastoral visitation.
b) Is every member of your Church under the shepherding care of some leader as provided in the Foundation Deed Poll (Minutes 1907, p41, Clause 5)	We have no system of allocation of members for visitation as prescribed by the Deed Poll.
c) To what extent is house to house, visitation carried out in the immediate neighbourhood of your churches?	None, other than that done by the Free Church Council.
5. Is divine Worship regularly brought before our Leaders' Meeting for consideration with a view to greater reverence and more reality in all parts of the service?	We frequently review the conduct of the services with a view to improving the devotion.
6. Preparation of Members - *Are your young people definitely prepared for Membership?*	The answer is in the negative.
7. Loss of Scholars - *What are the chief causes of decline in the numbers of Scholars in your District?*	a) Primarily Sunday Labour b) Lack of desire to attend c) Lack of Sunday School Teachers owing to claims of the war

Membership

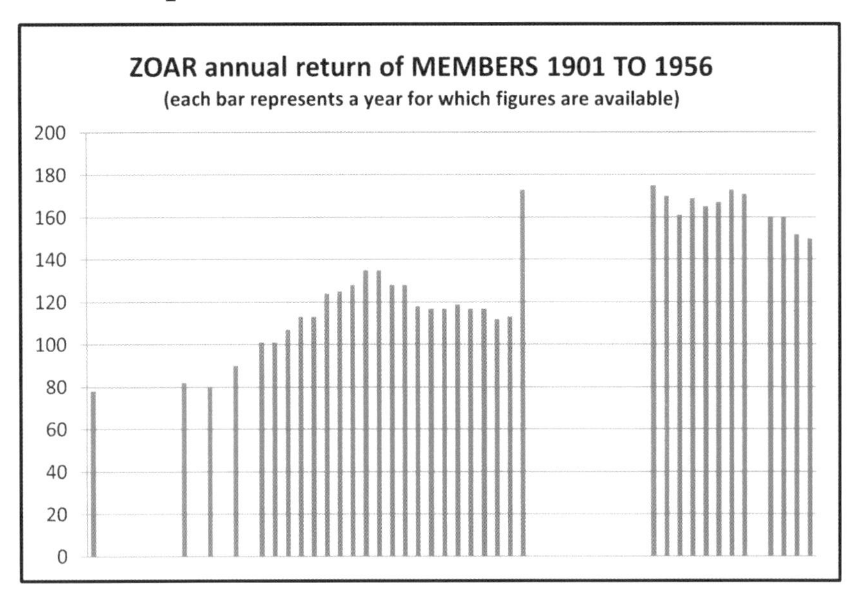

Figure 77 – Membership Statistics

One of the annual tasks of the Leaders was to review the membership list, so that a return could be reported[217] to the Circuit Meeting. Those who were Class Leaders undertook this task. In 1917, when reporting the updated figures to the Leaders' Meeting, they suggested there was a need *'to find means whereby a more accurate list of members can be provided.'* This was an odd suggestion, given that Class Leaders were supposed to maintain a record of their Class members and keep in touch with them. It is instructive of the relationship of the ministers to the life of the local church that their help was evidently neither expected nor sought. A while later there was agreement *'that all who are made members shall only become members by their own full consent.'* All this suggests individuals were added to the list without their knowledge and that some were not aware of the personal commitment expected.

Through the Twenties and Thirties, the Leaders sought ways in which they might promote greater awareness of what membership involved. In 1926 there was mention of a preparation class for potential members.[218] Various ideas were suggested and tried in order to ensure the active involvement of members in the life of the church. In 1930 it was agreed *'that in future each proposed member should be given a statement of the conditions of membership, such a statement to have a detachable form for signing and to be drawn up by Mr. J T Tennant and the minister.'* Then in 1933 it was decided *'that the young members be asked to attend a "recognition" meeting for the purpose of being formally received into church membership.'* There is no record of the outcome.

Membership tickets were issued quarterly and there was a suggestion in 1935 that members should pay 1/- for their tickets. The outcome was a decision 'to defer same until a greater necessity arises.' The suggestion was not repeated.

In 1946 a recognition service took place when some 21 young people were received as members. However, this does not seem to have been the usual practice as in the following years records imply people were again simply added to the list. It is not evident if their consent was sought. By the early years of the twenty-first century the membership was recorded in the eighties, matching the total recorded a century earlier.

The women of the church

The membership of the first Leaders' Meeting, following the formation of the United Methodist Church, was totally male. Acknowledging this deficiency and perhaps influenced by the suffragette movement of the time,[219] in 1911 the Leaders agreed a Church Meeting be called *'to solicit the co-operation of women in church work.'* The Minute books point to 1913 being the first year when a female was nominated to join the Leaders' Meeting, while in 1916 Miss Annie Hale and Miss E Hickman were the first women included among the representatives to the Circuit Meeting. In the 1920s when special events were being planned the ladies would be asked to look after the catering and on one occasion the suggestion was made that a Ladies' Committee be formed *'in order [to encourage the ladies] to take a deeper interest in the work of our church.'* While the trust body continued to lack female members, women gradually became part of the Leaders' Meeting and by 1930 of the eight representatives sent to the Circuit Meeting, five were women.[220]

It was sometime in the early 1930s that a **WOMEN'S OWN** meeting was established at Zoar, part of a nationwide movement within Methodism. The 1935 Centenary celebrations helped bring about a more significant position in the life of the church for Zoar's Women's Own. The Trustees' minutes only record *'that the Ladies of the Church be called together at an early date to make arrangements for a sale of work in the spring of 1935.'* However, when the centenary celebration committee was set up, of its substantial 51-strong membership, 26 were from the Women's Own and in the publicity cards for the celebrations the officers of the Women's Own were listed in their own right. If the leadership of the church - Trustees and Leaders – was primarily male, the inclusion of the officers of the Women's Own on the centenary invitation marked a symbolic recognition of their increasing influence.

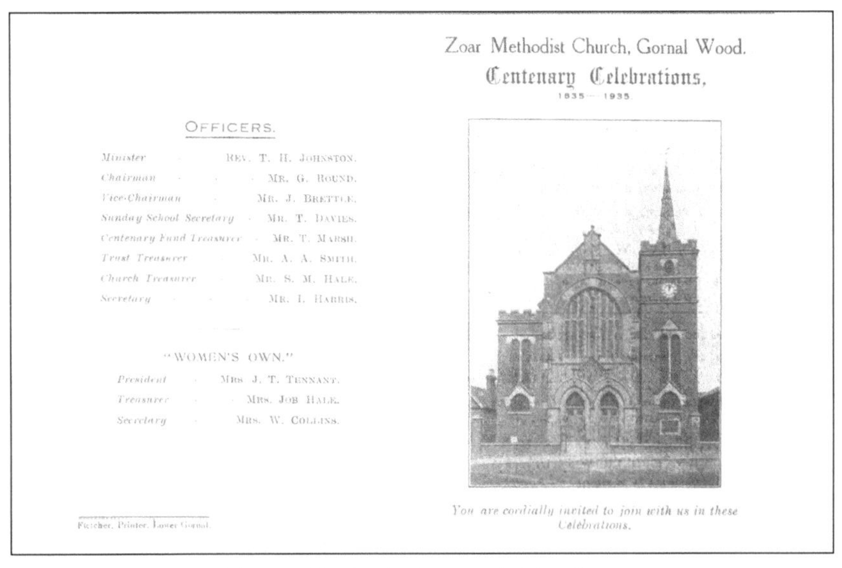

Zoar Methodist Church, Gornal Wood.

Centenary Celebrations,

1835 — 1935.

OFFICERS.

Minister	REV. T. H. JOHNSTON.
Chairman	MR. G. ROUND.
Vice-Chairman	MR. J. BRETTLE.
Sunday School Secretary	MR. T. DAVIES.
Centenary Fund Treasurer	MR. T. MARSH.
Trust Treasurer	MR. A. A. SMITH.
Church Treasurer	MR. S. M. HALE.
Secretary	MR. I. HARRIS.

"WOMEN'S OWN."

President	MRS J. T. TENNANT.
Treasurer	MRS. JOB HALE.
Secretary	MRS. W. COLLINS.

You are cordially invited to join with us in these Celebrations.

Fletcher, Printer, Lower Gornal.

Figure 78: The Centenary Celebrations

From 1945 on, the Women's Own was made responsible for appointing a list of its members to take up the collection at the afternoon service of the Sunday School Anniversary.

The first recorded occurrence of a female being invited to be responsible for leading worship on one of the 'special' Sundays came a year later with an invitation to Mrs Mumford (wife of the then resident minister) to conduct the Sunday School Anniversary Repetition afternoon service.

It was not until 1993 that the first female Church Stewards[221] were appointed: Gwen Marsh (née Browne - the long serving choir mistress, who, late in life, also trained as a Local Preacher – see figure 75) and Betty Mills (née Jones).

Figure 79: Betty Mills

Mid-Week Services and Activities

The Pleasant Thursday Evening meeting continued, having its own committee with two presidents, a secretary, treasurer and two registrars. Despite its well-organized structure, it was a struggling format. In 1914 it became *'an ordinary preaching service'* and the *'weekly penny collection'* was stopped.[222] Its survival was evidently in the balance in the next few years when debates about its future would lead to temporary increases in numbers attending. 1934 led to a one-off change in the starting time for an interesting and unlikely reason,

> ***Nov 25th 1934.*** *Resolved that in view of the Royal Wedding on Thursday next between His Royal highness the Duke of Kent and Princess Marina of Greece and the close proximity of the time of our Thursday service to that when the royal couple are due to pass through our village on their way to Himley Hall (where they are spending their honeymoon) our service be held at 8 o'clock instead of 7.*[223]

In 1908 there were Christian Endeavour[224] and Band of Hope[225] meetings taking place. Records do not indicate for how long they continued at Zoar. Nationally, during the early years of the United Methodist Church's existence the annual Conference was advised year on year of declining numbers in both organisations. Zoar's Christian Endeavour meeting must have ceased sometime before 1937, because in that year a Leaders' Meeting minute notes a new Christian Endeavour society being set up specifically for the young people, following their request for a fellowship meeting. Then in 1939 the Leaders *'resolved that a Sportsmans* [*sic.*] *Service be held on the Sunday afternoon April 2nd at 2.30 and all arrangements be made by the Christian Endeavour Society.'* In July 1942 the Leaders contacted the Christian Endeavour Headquarters to ask if it would be acceptable to merge the CE meeting with the church's Thursday preaching service for the duration of the war. Thursday services, which replicated the format of Sunday Worship, continued to be held weekly until 1982, after which they took place on an occasional basis.

Special Sundays

Three main celebrations occurred annually, the Sunday School Anniversary, the Trust Sermons or Church Anniversary and the Harvest Festival, along with other special Sundays, some annually, others occasionally or to mark one-off events.

• A Sunday in February was usually observed as Hospital Sunday (See Chapter Eight and the heading *Help in the Community*).

• In 1910 a service was held to mark the funeral of the late King, Edward VII.
• There is mention in the Leaders' Meeting minutes for 1913 of a Choir Sunday and this celebration was still taking place in the 1950s and 1960s.
• There are infrequent references to Missionary meetings, sometimes on a Sunday afternoon, more often in mid-week. In the UMC the practice was to hold an annual missionary meeting, when proceeds would then be split, two thirds to Overseas Missions and one third for Home Missions.[226]
• Zoar enjoyed the kudos of hosting the Sedgley Urban District Council's annual Civic Service in the 1920s, 30s and 40s and on numerous subsequent occasions. For the 1925 service 400 orders of service were printed.

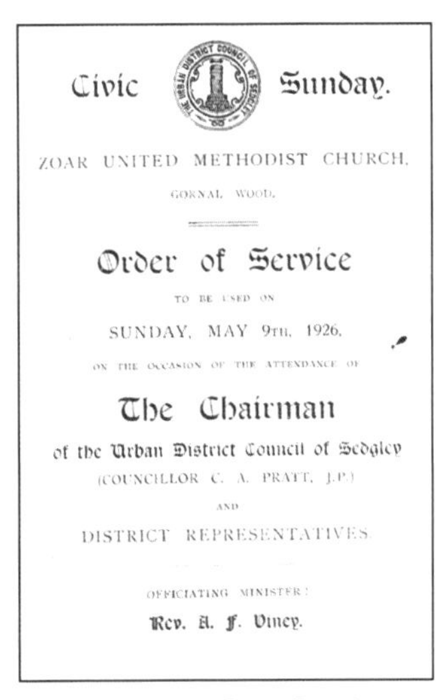

Civic Sunday.

ZOAR UNITED METHODIST CHURCH,
GORNAL WOOD.

Order of Service
TO BE USED ON
SUNDAY, MAY 9TH, 1926,
ON THE OCCASION OF THE ATTENDANCE OF
The Chairman
of the Urban District Council of Sedgley
(COUNCILLOR C. A. PRATT, J.P.)
AND
DISTRICT REPRESENTATIVES.

OFFICIATING MINISTER:
Rev. A. F. Vincy.

Figure 80: Civic Service front cover

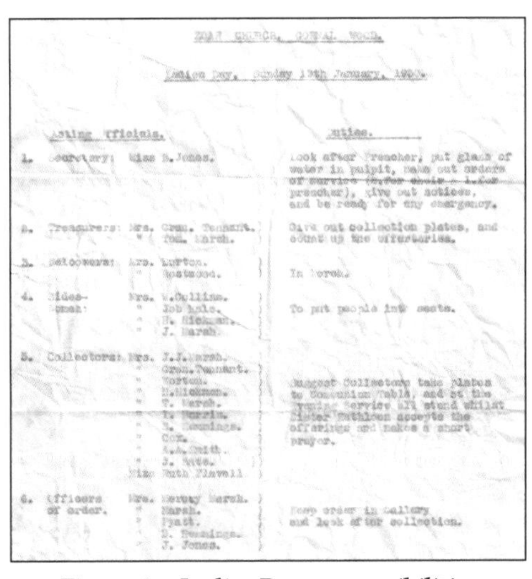

ZOAR CHURCH, GORNAL WOOD.

Ladies Day, Sunday 19th January, 1930.

Acting Officials.			Duties.
1. Secretary:	Miss	B. Jones.	Look after Preacher, put glass of water in pulpit, make out orders of service [illegible], give out notices, and be ready for any emergency.
2. Treasurers:	Mrs.	Gran. Tennant.	Give out collection plates, and count up the offertories.
	"	Tom. Marsh.	
3. Doorkeepers:	Mrs.	Lurton.	In Porch.
	"	Bostwood.	
4. Sides-women:	Mrs.	W. Collins.	To put people into seats.
	"	Job Hale.	
	"	H. Hickman.	
	"	J. Marsh.	
5. Collectors:	Mrs.	J. J. Marsh.	[illegible] Collectors take plates to Communion Table, and at the [illegible] Service all stand whilst Sister [illegible] accepts the offerings and makes a short prayer.
	"	Gran. Tennant.	
	"	Horton.	
	"	H. Hickman.	
	"	T. Marsh.	
	"	T. [illegible]	
	"	[illegible]	
	"	Cox.	
	"	A. A. Smith.	
	"	J. [illegible]	
	Miss	Ruth Flavell	
6. Officers of order.	Mrs.	[illegible] Marsh.	Keep order in Gallery and look after collection.
	"	Marsh.	
	"	Pyatt.	
	"	D. [illegible]	
	"	J. Jones.	

Figure 81: Ladies Day responsibilities

• Sunday 19 January 1930 was the occasion of the first Ladies' Day. However, two male Stewards were designated to make the arrangements and detailed instructions were prepared for those ladies who were invited to take responsibility for various roles on the day.[227]
• Two years later a Men's Day was held for the first time.
• 1935 was the first year in which a Carol Service is specifically mentioned, planned for the afternoon of 22 December.
• At the end of 1936 plans were made for a New Year Party. All

organisations in the church and the Sunday School were *'to be invited to co-operate to make the party a success.'* Evidently it was a success as another one was arranged for the following year.

The Wake Tea

The Wake Tea continued to be held on the Monday after the Church Anniversary, with the charge remaining at 1/- per person for many years. In 1914 catering was prepared for 200, with trays of food provided by members. Having noted, in April 1917, the Government's guidance on voluntary food rationing, the Leaders called a meeting to discuss how it might apply to their activities. Already in the previous autumn it had been decided to remove sandwiches from the Wake Tea menu. In 1920 a local coal strike led to a decision to postpone the Tea if the strike was still in progress on the planned Monday and delay it until the men were back at work.

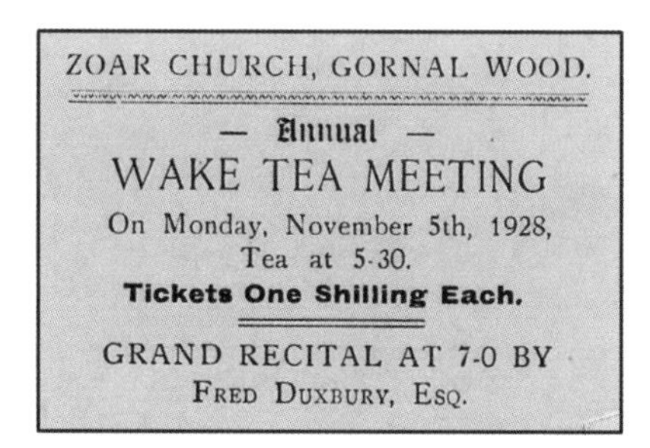

ZOAR CHURCH, GORNAL WOOD.

— Annual —

WAKE TEA MEETING

On Monday, November 5th, 1928,
Tea at 5-30.

Tickets One Shilling Each.

GRAND RECITAL AT 7-0 BY
FRED DUXBURY, ESQ.

Figure 82: Wake Tea ticket

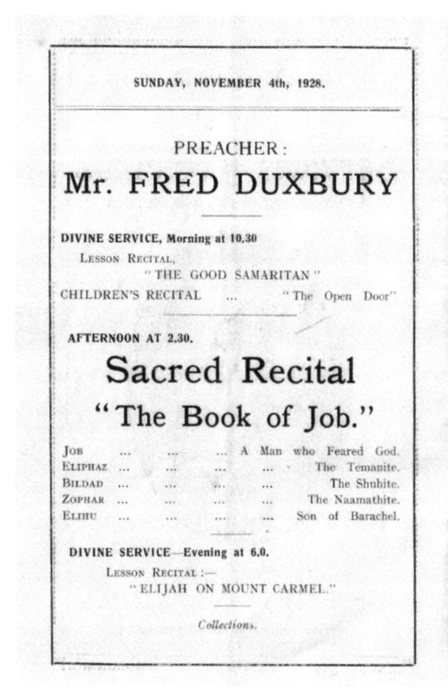

SUNDAY, NOVEMBER 4th, 1928.

PREACHER:

Mr. FRED DUXBURY

DIVINE SERVICE, Morning at 10.30

LESSON RECITAL,
"THE GOOD SAMARITAN"

CHILDREN'S RECITAL ... "The Open Door"

AFTERNOON AT 2.30.

Sacred Recital

"The Book of Job."

JOB	A Man who Feared God.
ELIPHAZ	The Temanite.
BILDAD	The Shuhite.
ZOPHAR	The Naamathite.
ELIHU	Son of Barachel.

DIVINE SERVICE—Evening at 6.0.

LESSON RECITAL :—
"ELIJAH ON MOUNT CARMEL."

Collections.

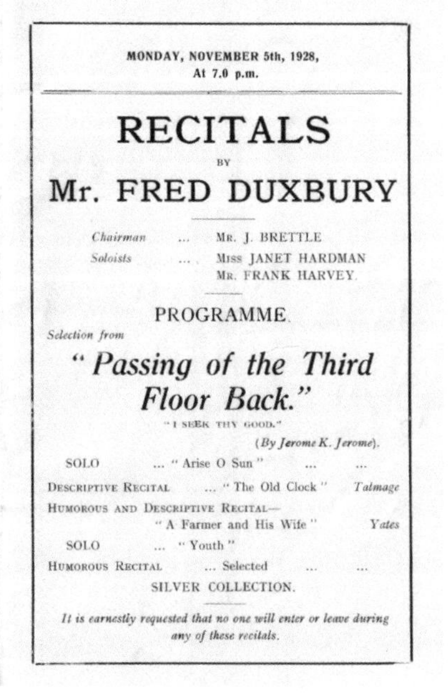

MONDAY, NOVEMBER 5th, 1928,
At 7.0 p.m.

RECITALS

BY

Mr. FRED DUXBURY

Chairman ... MR. J. BRETTLE
Soloists ... MISS JANET HARDMAN
MR. FRANK HARVEY.

PROGRAMME.

Selection from

"Passing of the Third Floor Back."

"I SEEK THY GOOD."

(By Jerome K. Jerome).

SOLO ... "Arise O Sun" ... ...

DESCRIPTIVE RECITAL ... "The Old Clock" *Talmage*

HUMOROUS AND DESCRIPTIVE RECITAL—
"A Farmer and His Wife" *Yates*

SOLO ... "Youth"

HUMOROUS RECITAL ... Selected ... ...

SILVER COLLECTION.

It is earnestly requested that no one will enter or leave during any of these recitals.

Figure 83: Duxbury's Programme

An important matter to be decided concerned the nature of the post-tea entertainment, with the choir frequently asked to make arrangements. For 1916 it was resolved that it be *'a speaking meeting with glees'* (a glee being a particular type of song[228]). Lest it be felt the members were being too frivolous during wartime it was decided in 1917 to hold a lecture instead of a concert. In the 1920s lectures were given on a wide range of topics, including *The evolution of Women, The Stories and Legends of Cornwall*, a *Dickens Recital* and a lecture on Shakespeare. 1928 witnessed the first of a number of visits by Mr Fred Duxbury, a professional elocutionist who travelled the country delivering religious and secular recitals.

In 1930 it was proposed to replace the Wake Tea with a concert provided by the choir, while in 1933 entertainment was provided by the *Handsworth College Concert Party*. This was a group of student ministers from the ministerial training college in Birmingham, whose students Zoar regularly received to lead worship. Responsibility for arranging the Wake Tea was subsequently handed over by the trustees to the Leaders' Meeting, who kept the charge at a shilling (5p) in 1931, when the evening's activities included addresses from the two circuit ministers and a performance by the *'Sedgley Primitive Methodist Concert Party'*. The Tea was not held in 1935 because of all the other activities taking place to mark Zoar's centenary year and it was replaced in the following year by a special celebration to welcome the first minister to be resident in the Gornals. In 1937 a rally for Gornal Methodists led to a further delay in reintroducing the Wake Tea, but it was back in 1938 with a decision to cut the price from the long-standing 1/- per head to 9d. The ongoing status of the event is perhaps signified by the fact that the invited speaker was Ian Hannah, well respected academic, writer and member of Parliament for the nearby Bilston constituency.[229]

CHAPTER SEVEN
Young people's work

The rapid social changes of the twentieth century meant that Zoar had to face the universal challenge of sustaining and growing its work with children and young people. For some sixty or so years the work was primarily focused on the regular weekly activities of the Sunday School and celebrated in the annual Sunday School Anniversary.

The Sunday School Anniversary[230]
This event had become the main celebration of the church year by the end of the nineteenth century, taking place on the first Sunday in June. The choir supported the singing, surrendering the choir stalls to the children and moving to seats in the side gallery. The choir master/mistress was responsible for preparing the children (with a minute thanking them for their efforts always recorded at the next Leaders' Meeting). For several weeks before the day, practices were held following the afternoon Sunday School and mid-week.

In the first half of the twentieth century Zoar welcomed many of Methodism's leading figures, including UMC Presidents, such as William Treffry, along with other leading figures, including the church historian George Eayrs, to preach at the event. As the second half of the twentieth century unfolded, so the net was not cast so widely and by the 1980s and 90s local ministers and local preachers were usually requested to lead worship: one for the morning and evening services and one for the afternoon. The format remained unchanged over decades: songs by the children, supported by the choir, an address aimed at the children, prayers and a sermon lasting at least 20 minutes. The afternoon service was a little more relaxed and included recitations by some of the youngsters.

Each year the trustees agreed a financial target for the collection taken at the three services, with the sum for 1910 being set at £100; £150 in 1913; back to £100 in 1914; then £150 in 1917. With a £150 target set in 1918, there must have been much rejoicing when the sum achieved was £220. In 1920 a special appeal was made to raise £200, in anticipation of a redecoration project planned by the trustees, and the invited preacher was the President of that year's national Conference, the Revd. John Moore. The target then reverted to £150 through to the early 1940s. The one exception was 1926, when the Leaders' Minutes record that *'in view of the general stoppage* [it was] *agreed not to set a financial target.'* By 1950 the goal was £450.

The practice developed of nominating some twenty or so men to act as *'sidesmen'* or collectors of the offering on the day. The role was deemed an honour and to be seen collecting, especially at the evening service, was something much coveted. Oral history suggests the practice was intended to encourage them to give extra generously. The evening collection was taken before the final hymn and the trustees would retreat to the minister's vestry to calculate the day's income. Someone would know how much had been raised at those anniversaries already held elsewhere and the expectation was that individual trustees would add to Zoar's total until it exceeded the rest. The result would be announced before the blessing was given. Well into the 1960s the church would fill up for each service, with extra seats brought in and placed in the aisles in the evening: hardly in keeping with today's Health and Safety requirements.

Figure 84: Anniversary hand bill

Support for the Anniversary was solicited via visitation, along with the distribution of posters, window and hand bills. The minutes of 1914 report the print order being placed with local printing company Burrows, who would still be printing these items over 50 years later, interrupted for a few years when one of the church's own members fulfilled the order. The publicity order in 1917 was 50 posters, 100 window bills, 1,000 hand bills, along with 2,000 hymn sheets (in succeeding years this latter number would be anywhere between 1,100 and 1,500, with 500 for the Repetition services). Early in the century it was the teachers who were expected to

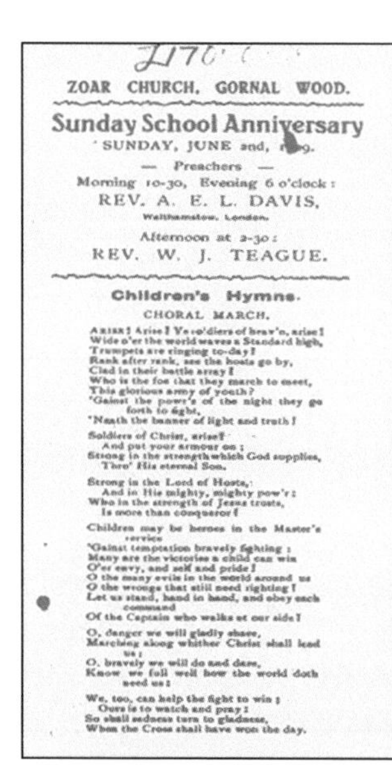
ZOAR CHURCH, GORNAL WOOD.

Sunday School Anniversary

SUNDAY, JUNE 2nd, [illegible]9.

— Preachers —

Morning 10-30, Evening 6 o'clock:
REV. A. E. L. DAVIS,
Walthamstow, London.

Afternoon at 2-30:
REV. W. J. TEAGUE.

Children's Hymns.

CHORAL MARCH.

Arise! Arise! Ye soldiers of heav'n, arise!
Wide o'er the world waves a Standard high,
Trumpets are ringing to-day!
Rank after rank, see the hosts go by,
Clad in their battle array!
Who is the foe that they march to meet,
This glorious army of youth?
'Gainst the pow'rs of the night they go forth to fight,
'Neath the banner of light and truth!

Soldiers of Christ, arise!
And put your armour on;
Strong in the strength which God supplies,
Thro' His eternal Son.

Strong in the Lord of Hosts,
And in His mighty, mighty pow'r:
Who in the strength of Jesus trusts,
Is more than conqueror!

Children may be heroes in the Master's service
'Gainst temptation bravely fighting:
Many are the victories a child can win
O'er envy, and self and pride!
O the many evils in the world around us
O the wrongs that still need righting!
Let us stand, hand in hand, and obey each command
Of the Captain who walks at our side!

O, danger we will gladly share,
Marching along whither Christ shall lead us;
O, bravely we will do and dare,
Know we full well how the world doth need us:

We, too, can help the fight to win;
Ours is to watch and pray:
So shall sadness turn to gladness,
When the Cross shall have won the day.

Figure 85: Typical Anniversary hymn sheet

both address and deliver the hand bills, but gradually the responsibility shifted to a team of *'helpers'*.

On the occasion of the 1918 Anniversary the names of all those associated with the Sunday School and who had been involved in the Forces were added to the handbills being delivered around the village. *Our Roll of Honour* indicates just how many young men this involved.

The first significant change from the traditional format came in 1976, when it was decided to stop holding an afternoon service for the Repetition, although the Anniversary Day retained three services until the mid-1990s. In 1987 the teachers first discussed a possible change in the content of the services, with substantial

Our Roll of Honour.

KILLED IN ACTION.

Frank Bowyer
Samuel Bradley 1
Arthur Bradley 1
David Bradley
William Burrows
Henry Clarke, M.M.
Walter Cox
Samuel Cox
Alfred Collins
Arthur Clarke
Joseph Hyde
William A. Jones
Daniel Parkes
Bernard Smith

REPORTED MISSING.

Benjamin Bennett
Leonard Bradley
Benj. Baker
(Prisoner of War.)
John Williams

WITH H.M. FORCES.

John Burrows
*Joseph Bowyer
*Joseph Baker
William Baker
Arthur Beddard
Isaac Bradley
Joseph Beddard
*Samuel Bradley 2
Ben Bradley
William Bayliss
Arthur Bradley 2
*Thomas Cartwright
*Joseph Cartwright
John Collins
*Joseph Cox
*Edward Cox
*William Cox
Leonard Cox
Leonard Cooper
John Cox
William Collins
Thomas Cooper
Wilfred Davies
Daniel Davies
William Davies
Bert Elderton
Albert Evans
*Benj. Flavell
Arthur Flavell 1
Enoch Flavell
Thos. Flavell
Arthur Flavell 2
Job Flavell
*Albert Greenway
**Ernest Greenway
**John Greenway
Enoch Greenway
**Joseph Gilbert
George Greenway
Fred Guest
William Guest
**J. E. Hemmings
Richard Hemmings 1
Richard Hemmings 2
B. A. Hemmings
*Joseph Hale
*Ernest Hale 1
*Harry Humphries
Sydney Hale
*Isaac Harper
*Edward Harris 1
*Joseph Harris
Leonard Harris
Thos. Harris
Joshua Harris
Ernest Hale 2
*Edward Hale
*John Hale
George Hale
Edward Harris 2
Ernest Hickman
Enoch Hartill
James Hickman
*John Jones
Samuel Jones
*Joseph Kennedy
Arthur Lord
Arthur Massey
*Joseph Marsh
*Isaac Marsh 1
William Massey
*Wilfred Moss
Leonard Marsh
**John T. Massey
Jos B. Marsh
William Minton
Peter Mason
Isaac Marsh 2
Richard Marsh
Sydney Marsh
Thomas Marsh
Granville Marsh
Walter Massey
William Parfitt
Joseph Powers
*David Powers
*Edward Parkes
George T. Pugh
George Southall
Wilfred Southall
Enoch Smart
Joseph Smart
Benj O. Smith
David Smith
William Simmons
Charles Timmins
Ben Timmins
*Isaac Timmins
Isaac Tomlinson
John Witton
*Joseph Witton
*Joseph Wakelam
Sam Wakelam
*Benj. Williams
Sydney Wood

* Wounded.
** Wounded twice.

Figure 86: The Roll of Honour

change through the 1990s. After many years of faithfully preparing the children for the anniversary, in 1991 Gwen Browne stood down and handed over her role to Janet Ferris and the title Sunday School Anniversary was changed to Children's Anniversary Services, marking a more informal approach. In 1996 the children were provided with t-shirts to wear on the day. Further change came in 1998 when repetition services ceased and an Anniversary Weekend was introduced, continuing for a number of years and including a tea and evening service on the Saturday.

Figure 87: Typical Anniversary junior choir

This photograph of the anniversary singers is from the 1950s. Girls were expected to wear white dresses and boys white shirts and maroon-coloured ties. The youngest children in front of the pulpit are standing on a temporary platform which was first acquired by the trustees early in the twentieth century. The organist, William Timmins, can be seen at the back and the choir mistress, Gwen Browne, is in the pulpit, alongside the preacher for the day.

Once the year's anniversary services were finished, the young people who had performed were given '*a treat*'. In 1917 the treat was cancelled in the light of the Government's guidance on voluntary food rationing, but the monies to pay for it were reserved for a post-war treat. The treat in its earliest days usually involved a parade from the church to a local farmer's field with fun, games and a tea, as recorded in 1938,

> *Our Sunday School Parade and Treat took place on Tuesday, August 7th, in good weather, the evening being spent on the field at Coopers Bank Farm, kindly let by Mr. J. Edwards.*[231]

The 'treat' subsequently became a coach outing to seaside locations such as Rhyl, Blackpool, Weston-Super Mare and Southport or to leisure parks, including Trentham Gardens, Drayton Manor Park and Bewdley Safari Park. In the late 1950s it was quite a sight to see five or six coaches lined up outside the church, ready for the day's outing. In the 1980s the Sunday School teachers at Tipton Street Methodist Church in Sedgley asked if they could share in the outing and, given the smaller numbers who qualified to go on the trip, this was agreed.

The Sunday School

The earliest surviving records for the Sunday School commence in 1919.[232] The minutes of a meeting, held that December, noted some 38 teachers present. J T Tennant and William Smith, stalwarts of the Trust, had evidently served the Sunday School for several years as they were appointed life-long Superintendents on this occasion. George Round and Joseph Brettle were assistant Superintendents, Howard Smith, Treasurer, Noah Westwood, Missionary Treasurer, William Bradley, Secretary, Cyril Round, Stanley Brettle and Doris Round, registrars, and Thomas Hemmings was organist.

Events and actions of note:

- Book Prizes were distributed annually for attendance at Sunday School and, additionally, to those who collected for missionary funds. Two grades were set for attendance, with a first prize for more than 96 attendances (two attendances per Sunday being counted) and 84 for a second. In 1920 a third level prize was introduced (72 attendances). In 1922 it was resolved that *'prize winners be strongly urged to have Methodist Hymn Book or Sunday School Hymnal for their prize.'* In 1956 those opting for such a prize were allowed a larger maximum value.
- Regular support of missionary activity. Through 1921 regular collections were taken for the *'Starving children of Europe fund'*. A Ladies Committee was appointed to help with mission fund raising. In 1925 the teachers were asked to contribute a minimum of 1/- (5p) to the missionary effort for that year. In 1927 it was proposed that the Sunday School Missionary Committee should work with the Women's

Missionary Auxiliary Committee of the church. In 1929 £7/15/0d was raised and in 1956 £48. In 1957 there is a first reference to JMA ('Junior Missionary Association') and £55 was collected. This involved scholars having a collecting card onto which they sought to add as many names as possible, along with a promise of so much per week. They would then seek out their sponsors weekly, passing on their monies to the JMA secretary, and at the end of the year receiving a certificate and medal.

• In 1920 it was decided to re-introduce *Sankey's Hymnal* for use in the afternoon school, a decision reversed in 1936. Clearly this was a controversial issue, as in 1938 it was agreed *'that a meeting of the adult portion of the school be called to decide on same.'*

• Minutes regularly appear in the inter-war years recording the appointment of senior officers to meet with teachers who were irregular in their attendance. Six received such attention in 1921 and nine in 1931.

• In 1925 the first of a number of similar subsequent entries mentioned visiting any young people who were absent from the Sunday School for more than two Sundays in succession and the appointment, in the senior classes of *'scholar visitors'* who were the peers of the absent *'scholars'* (as the young people were still described).

• In 1934 the trustees decided to take out insurance cover for scholars and teachers in case of accident on or off the premises when involved in Sunday School activities. Maximum indemnity was £500 and the premiums 1/6d (7½p) per 100 scholars per annum, with a minimum premium of 10/- (50p). This was something the UMC nationally had been encouraging churches to do since 1913.[233]

• It was decided in 1945 to buy copies of the *Methodist Sunday School Hymnbook*, which was still in use at the start of the 1970s.

• The 1950 Minutes record the first reference to a Sunday School Christmas Party, which was held shortly after Christmas, with tea at 4.30 pm and games at 6.00 pm. 30/- (£1.50p) was allocated for prizes.

• In 1951 the registrars were asked to take responsibility for sending cards to scholars who did not attend on two successive Sundays.

• In 1956 some 94 scholars (excluding the Primary Department which looked after the under-fives) qualified for attendance prizes and classes were divided as follows:

Boys 7-8 years, 8-10, 10-12 and 12-17 years

'Young Ladies' 7-10 years, 11-12 and 15-16 years

'Ladies Class' (mainly older ladies)

• Six medals were purchased in 1957 to be awarded to the scholars who achieved an '*outstanding*' attendance record. This may have been a 'one-off' action, as none was awarded the following year.
• It was decided in 1958 to hold a Sunday School Teachers' Dedication Service. This became an annual event.
• A coach was provided in the 60s and 70s to transport children from the nearby Straits Estate to the afternoon Sunday School. It was driven by the Sunday School Secretary, John Marsh.

Figure 88: the Outstanding award medal

Attendance

The table below give a picture of the relative strength of the Sunday School. [234]

Year	Number on Register	Morning Attendance	Afternoon Attendance
1923		267	418
1924		278	444
1928	689	230	384
1931	593	140	320
1934	531	166	290
1938	349		200
1942	275	60	142
1975	156		
1978	60		
1988	43		
1990	31		
1991	25		
1997		12	12
1998		24	8

These figures do not include the Primary Department, which catered for under five-year children. In 1968 it recorded attendances varying between 45 and 60.

Although Zoar's figures for the 1920s were encouraging, signs of decline were beginning to emerge. Across the Church as a whole, there was increasing acceptance of the challenges threatening ministry among the young. This was highlighted in 1926 when the Chairman of the Birmingham and Dudley District, Price Lewis,[235] sent out a circular to be read in all the churches.[236] It encouraged attention be given to two major issues,[237] one of which was young people. The key paragraphs devoted to the latter were,

> *[the recognition of an] urgent need for the Churches and Schools to review and revise their methods of work amongst the young people already associated with us, in order that they may be well trained in Christian knowledge and brought to enjoy the blessings of early decision for Christ and His Church.*
>
> *Our numerical returns for the year [across the whole of the District] present few conspicuous cases either of failure or success. Our adult membership is slightly increased, in spite of the removal, through various causes, of 290 names from our Church Rolls. Our Sunday schools, however, show a decrease of 203 scholars, and there is a decline in attendance. The large decrease in the number of enrolled abstainers is presumably a matter of tabulation, and need not alarm us. But training in temperance principles, is an essential part of our duty towards the young.*
>
> *The most disquieting feature of our returns is the decrease of 136 Junior Members, following on a decrease last year of 211. The hope expressed in the Resolution of last year, that proper vigilance and pastoral care in the Sunday Schools would make good the decline has not been fulfilled. We would earnestly urge our Churches and Schools not to neglect the effort to bring our boys and girls to personal decision for Christ, and to train them in the right use of religious observances.*

Nationally, the belief existed that if methods could be improved then the decline could be turned around. Churches were encouraged to look carefully at the methods used in the conduct of classes. Back in 1909 the UMC Conference had published a report '*Principles and Methods on which it is suggested United Methodist Sunday Schools should be conducted*'.[238] At the 1925 Conference the report from its Young People's and Temperance Committee included the following observation and expectation,[239]

> *... our scholars are still leaving our Sunday Schools ... and drifting away from the church in tragically large numbers. But a new outlook is capturing the thought of our workers, a new leaven is spreading, and we can now ground our hope for the future in solid achievement. As the leaven spreads, richer and more lasting results are obtained. The forces against us have been intensified*

by post-war conditions, but the growth of new ideas will outstrip the advance of materialism and enable us in time to win through. Educational processes lack the spectacular, but they are steady and sure.

From the early 1920s the UMC employed two Sunday School Demonstrators, firstly Miss Blumer and Miss Hope Giles, to encourage this more professional approach to teaching in Sunday School. Following the 1932 Union an additional staff member was recruited.[240] Their task was to travel around the country lecturing and demonstrating 'the best methods',[241] which included encouraging teachers to meet in preparation classes. Nationally, in 1926 there were 610 such classes and by 1930 this had increased to 892 (among a total of 2,059 Sunday Schools nationally).[242]

As far as Zoar was concerned, 1929 was the first year when any reference was made to the idea of holding a preparation class. It was to meet every fortnight on a Friday and one of the ministers was to be asked to lead it. Clearly it struggled, as in 1930 *'it was resolved that a fresh effort be made to revive the preparation class'* and, on this occasion, that the minister *'be invited to the first meeting.'* 1936 witnessed a third attempt at getting the idea going and this time the minister was to be asked to take charge of it. The next mention was in 1948, *'resolved that a teachers' preparation class be organized and Rev. N Mumford be asked to take charge of same.'* On this occasion it was also decided to purchase 12 copies of notes for Sunday School lessons.[243] In 1953 there is mention of Mr Tom Davies, who at the time was the Sunday School Secretary, being asked *'to be responsible for the instruction of the new teachers training class and that instruction be based on the Primary lessons.'* This earnest desire to improve the quality and therefore, it was hoped, the effectiveness of Sunday Schools in maintaining and increasing numbers was highlighted at the 1932 UMC Conference, when it was pointed out, *'... that eighty per cent of the membership of the church is recruited from the Sunday School.'*[244]

The pattern of the afternoon Sunday School, which by the 1950s was the main gathering, consisted of opening worship, led by the Superintendent for 15 minutes; classes for 30-40 minutes; and a final coming together when someone from outside the Sunday School was sometimes invited to offer a brief word before closing prayers and a hymn.[245]

As signs of declining numbers became a yet more obvious concern in the 1960s, there would be regular discussions in Teachers' Meetings about how to reverse the trend. Suggested solutions included cards saying *'We missed you'* to be delivered to absent youngsters, writing to all parents whose children had been baptised inviting them to join the Sunday School, visiting the homes of absent children, changing the more formal, traditional approach to include quizzes and choruses instead of hymns. Several times it was suggested that teachers might benefit from training opportunities, but there does not seem to have been much enthusiasm to take up the idea. The attendance statistics indicate all this was a losing battle, not helped by the ways in which society at large underwent massive changes in the second half of the century: the days when Sunday School was one of the few Sunday activities were fast disappearing. In 1984 and again in 1991 conversation took place about the closing down of afternoon school. Closure came in December 1999, when it was decided to concentrate on morning school.

Weekday and other activities for young people

Concern about holding the interest of young people manifested itself in different ways throughout the twentieth century. Over the years, various practical steps were introduced to provide for and hold onto the young people.

• In 1919 evidently there was a Sunday School tennis club. The trustees' minutes include a request from the club to acquire land at the rear of the premises in order to build a tennis court there. While the trustees agreed to this request no subsequent minute exists to record what, if anything, happened.

• In its 1922 annual review of the spiritual life of the church the Leaders' Meeting gave particular attention to the older young people. It was decided to set up a Guild meeting with them particularly, but not exclusively, in mind. The national Guild Movement had its origins in Wesleyan Methodism at the very end of the nineteenth century, with weekly or periodic meetings for devotional, literary, social and musical purposes and Christian service.

• There was a particular concern about the involvement of the young men in the life of the church by 1930. A joint meeting of Leaders and Teachers conceived the idea of a social for the *'Senior Male classes [in the Sunday School] with the object of enlisting their sympathy and devising the best means of obtaining more active participation in the work of the church.'*

• That the Guild proved effective as an activity for young people seems unlikely, because in 1936 the young people told the Leaders they would like to hold a Young People's Fellowship. This was agreed on the understanding that, *'it takes the form of a Christian Endeavour Society … that*

Mr Harold Fletcher be asked to take charge of same … that a Junior Class also be formed and Mrs J H Harvey be asked to take charge.'

- 1954 marked the first occasion of planning for a Youth Sunday.
- A mid-week early evening meeting for younger children was started in 1957. Called Sunshine Corner, it ran for many years under the sterling leadership of Mina Bennett. In 1966 it recorded an average attendance of 45. It had a theme song *'Sunshine Corner that's the place to be'*.
- That was also the year in which a Boys Brigade[246] began for boys aged over twelve.

ZOAR GUILD

GORNAL WOOD.

Session:

October 1927—April 1928.

Meetings Alternate Wednesdays,

7-30 P.M.

OFFICERS:

President: Mr. J. T. TENNANT, J.P.

Vice-President: Mr. G. ROUND

Treasurer: Mr. J. PHILLIPS

Pianist: Miss N. HAYWARD

Hon. Secretary: Mr. I. HARRIS, Tipton Street, Sedgley.

W. [illegible]. Lower Gornal. Phone, Sedgley 35.

Figure 90: Guild programme cover

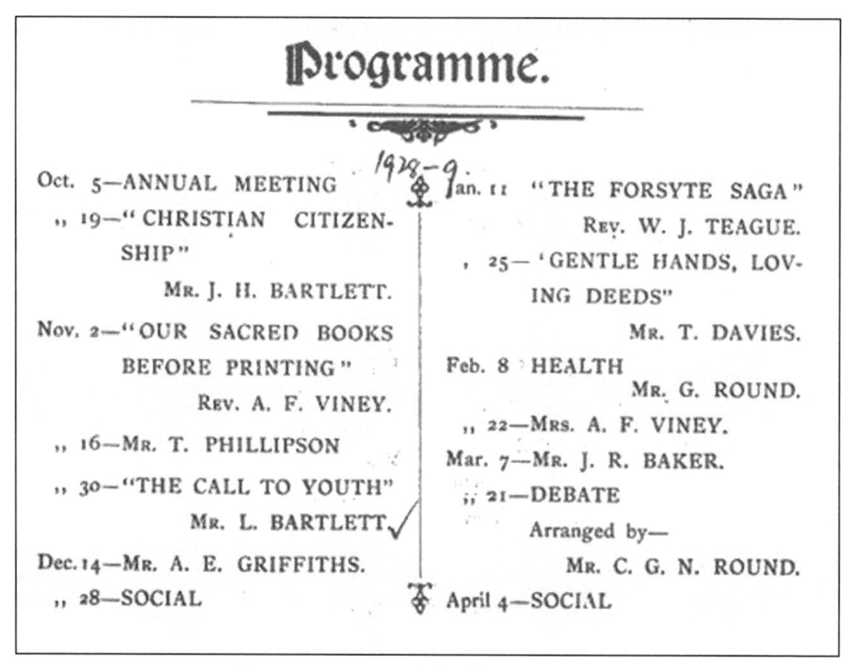

Programme.

1928–9.

Oct. 5—ANNUAL MEETING

" 19—"CHRISTIAN CITIZENSHIP" Mr. J. H. BARTLETT.

Nov. 2—"OUR SACRED BOOKS BEFORE PRINTING" Rev. A. F. VINEY.

" 16—Mr. T. PHILLIPSON

" 30—"THE CALL TO YOUTH" Mr. L. BARTLETT.

Dec. 14—Mr. A. E. GRIFFITHS.

" 28—SOCIAL

Jan. 11 "THE FORSYTE SAGA" Rev. W. J. TEAGUE.

" 25—"GENTLE HANDS, LOVING DEEDS" Mr. T. DAVIES.

Feb. 8 HEALTH Mr. G. ROUND.

" 22—Mrs. A. F. VINEY.

Mar. 7—Mr. J. R. BAKER.

" 21—DEBATE Arranged by—Mr. C. G. N. ROUND.

April 4—SOCIAL

Figure 90: Typical Guild programme

Figure 91: Senior guiders with Sylvia Harris, far right

• A Girl Guides troop was led by Sylvia Harris and Jean Jones led a Brownie troop.

• During the 1950s and 60s various meetings were introduced for the teenagers, some held in the church vestry (suggesting this was a small group, as the vestry was small!) and some at the minister's manse.

- In the late 1950s a bible study group for teenagers and young adults was being held, led by the then minister, Revd Perry Smith.
- A young people's mid-week house fellowship was begun by John and Jennifer Evans in the 1960s, ending when they moved to Bristol, where John trained for the Baptist ministry.
- 1968 witnessed a proposed youth event organised at Zoar by the Circuit Youth Council. Called *the Glory Hole*, it involved the transformation of the Sunday School interior with all manner of decorations and lively music. The trustees were not all in favour of the event, but it was agreed it could take place.

• 1972 was marked by the establishment of a Youth Club, started by David Webb.

• Provision was made in the early 1970s to take the young people away for a weekend at a residential centre. This was begun by Bryan Cottrell and John Evans.

• Starting in the 1980s and running for around three decades, Holiday Bible Clubs, were held in school holidays and were well attended.

Reports presented at the Annual General Church Meeting minutes of 2003 typically illustrate activities relating to children and young people in the early years of the twenty-first century. These included Brownies and Guides, Playgroup (34 children and a waiting list), Youth Group (Meeting at the home of Mark and Wendy Raybould and with an attendance of up to 14), and a Mothers' and Toddlers' Group (up to 39 children and 40 adults).

Figure 92: A Holiday Bible Club poster from 2015

Sunday School staff after 1950
Superintendents / Leaders
Harold Fletcher and Ben Smith
Bryan Cottrell and George Thompson
Brian Cotterill
Vic Collins
Team: Vic Collins, John Collins, Robert Ferris, Liz Wright
Liz Wright
John Collins.

Secretary
Tom Davies, Harold Jones, John Marsh, Jean Marsh, Mrs J Wyman, Vic Collins.

Organist / Pianist
Cliff Collins
Julie Ball and Lindsay Newton
A rota: Geoff Marsh, Lindsay Newton, Brian Jones, Mina Bennett, Nick Holmes and Craig Nicholls.

Treasurer
Cliff Collins,
Bryan Cotterill.

Teaching Staff

This list includes all who are recorded as attending teachers' meetings, some of whom, for example, helped the teachers or linked to the youth groups. Some made brief contributions, others served for many years.

Muriel Abbis, Vera and Bob Aston, David Aston, Mina Bennett, Paula and Michael Beardsmore, Rachel Bird, Mrs D Brockhouse, Peter Carter, John and Carol Cockerill, Vic and Margaret Collins, Carol Corbett, Joyce Darby, Peter and Lorna Fellows, Robert Ferris, Janet Hadlington, Margaret Hale, Sylvia Harris, C. Heathcock, Sally Ann Hickman, Jean Hinett, Mary Holmes, Marion Hyde, Ward Jones, Wendy Jones, Stephanie Keyes, Janet Malpass, Jean Marsh, Reg Marsh, Linda Morris, Sylvia Needham, Arthur and Mollie Nock, Graham Pick, John Powell, Mary Roadway, Jane Roper, Mark and Wendy Raybould, Julie Slater, Kath Smith, Geoff and Olive Sproson, David Webb.

Chapter Eight

Relating to others

Illustrating how the members of Zoar related to the Methodist Church nationally, to other Christian denominations and the community within and beyond Gornal Wood village during the twentieth century.

Zoar and its Methodist links:

The national perspective

The final years of the nineteenth century witnessed significant conversations taking place between representatives from the various branches of Methodism. In 1907 a scheme for the union of three of the smaller ones led to the Methodist New Connexion (with 37,009 members, including Zoar) joining with the United Methodist Free Church (79,948) and the Bible Christians (32,202) to establish the United Methodist Church (UMC).[247]

For Zoar, the event seems to have passed off with little notable consequence. This was perhaps not surprising, given that neither the UMFC nor the Bible Christians were active in the locality. The Trustees acknowledged the name change at their meeting in October 1907, with a minute which declared *'we therefore take the name United Methodist Church.'*

While the two largest branches of Methodism, the Wesleyans and the Primitive Methodists, had felt unable to join the 1907 scheme, in 1932 they and the UMC became one Methodist Church. Zoar Leaders and Trustees were now in a formal relationship with their Wesleyan Methodist neighbours in Himley Road for the first time since the expulsions of 1835. The Zoar trustees made enquiries as to the cost of receiving the coverage of the uniting ceremony, which was to be broadcast live from London by the BBC on 20 September 1932. The report back gave rise to the following minute,

> *... it was decided to receive the broadcast in our church, invitations to be present to be sent to the vicar of Lower Gornal and the secretary of St Paul's Protestant Mission, in addition to the Wesleyan, Primitive and United Methodist churches.*

There is then a note appended, *'The Vicar of Lower Gornal and his curate attended.'*

Supporting national Methodist activities

The Trust and Leaders' Meeting minutes record numerous examples of financial support being offered to Methodist projects and appeals. Examples included:

- In 1910 the choir gave a rendition of 'The Messiah' with the proceeds, totalling £1/3/2d, being given to the United Methodist Church's *'Thanksgiving Fund.'*[248] This appeal aimed to raise £100,000 to *'strengthen'* the funds of the denomination, as an expression of thankfulness for the achievement of union.
- 1912 saw a collection taken for the Local Preachers' Mutual Aid Society, a fund established for local preachers who needed financial support. Initially there was a Sunday retiring collection, but this subsequently changed to an annual donation from Church funds. In 1924 the Leaders agreed that *'we voluntarily assess ourselves to pay £2/10/od per year to the local Preachers' Mutual Aid Society in consequence of the very large amounts paid to recipients in this Circuit.'* Similar sums were contributed over succeeding years.
- £1/0/od was sent to the *Women's Auxiliary Missionary Fund* in 1913, typifying the response offered to various missionary enterprises for work both overseas and at home. A special response was made in the same year to raise £30 for *'the Conference missionary debt'*.
- 1920 marked the establishment of a connexional Ministers' Superannuation Fund to which Zoar responded.
- In 1931 a connexional appeal for the *'Young People's Section'* was taken up.

Regional Methodism

In the days of the MNC, Zoar was a constituent church in the Dudley Circuit which linked regionally with neighbouring circuits to form the Dudley District. With the establishment of the United Methodist Church (UMC) in 1907, Zoar continued to be part of an unchanged Dudley Circuit, now in the Birmingham and Dudley District. This larger District consisted of eleven former MNC Circuits, nine United Methodist Free Church Circuits and one Bible Christian Circuit and a total of 6,248 members.[249] JT Tennant was elected as vice-chairman (1927) and then chairman (1928) of the District, a rare honour for a layman. Consequent to the 1932 Union scheme the District relationships turned away from Birmingham and towards Wolverhampton, and Zoar and the Dudley Circuit found themselves on the eastern fringes of the Wolverhampton and Shrewsbury District.

Local Methodism

Through the years of its membership of the Dudley MNC Circuit (1836-1907) Zoar remained the second strongest church numerically after Wesley church in Dudley. The creation of the UMC made no difference to the make-up of the Dudley Circuit, but the 1932 Union scheme brought substantial change. Initially there were three Dudley Circuits, one from each of the three constituent branches of Methodism. Zoar was involved in negotiations which led to them coming together by 1934, so that five Methodist churches in the Gornals were together in the same Circuit for the first time, viz. Five Ways, Mount Zion and Zoar (all formerly United Methodist and before that MNC) along with the former Wesleyan churches of Himley Road and Kent Street. The former Primitive Methodist congregation at Lake Street continued its association with the Brierley Hill group of churches until 1962 when the Gornal and Sedgley Circuit was established, a move which meant that for the first time since their formation the three former MNC churches were separated from their Dudley links.

From the earliest days of Methodism one of the guiding principles of the Circuits was for the stronger churches to help the smaller or struggling causes. This unity was evidenced in a variety of ways, not least in the creation of the quarterly Circuit Preaching Plan. In the days of the MNC and UMC this was prepared by a committee appointed by the Circuit Meeting and included lay representatives from the individual churches and chapels. The number of times a minister visited a particular church to lead worship influenced the amount of money that church contributed to Circuit funds, so every ministerial visit carried a financial cost. Occasionally churches would appeal to the Circuit Meeting that they could not afford so many appointments, which meant another church had to agree to take up the spare capacity and pay extra. Zoar supported some of the smaller churches, either paying part of their contribution or accepting extra ministerial appointments. Harts Hill, Kates Hill and Woodside were helped in this way.

Despite struggling with its own finances in the years following the first World War, Zoar agreed to help out Wesley church in Dudley who at the time were responsible for some 51% of the Circuit's income. The Leaders agreed to up their contribution from £15/7/8d to £20 each Quarter and not to ask Wesley to surrender any ministerial appointments to them.

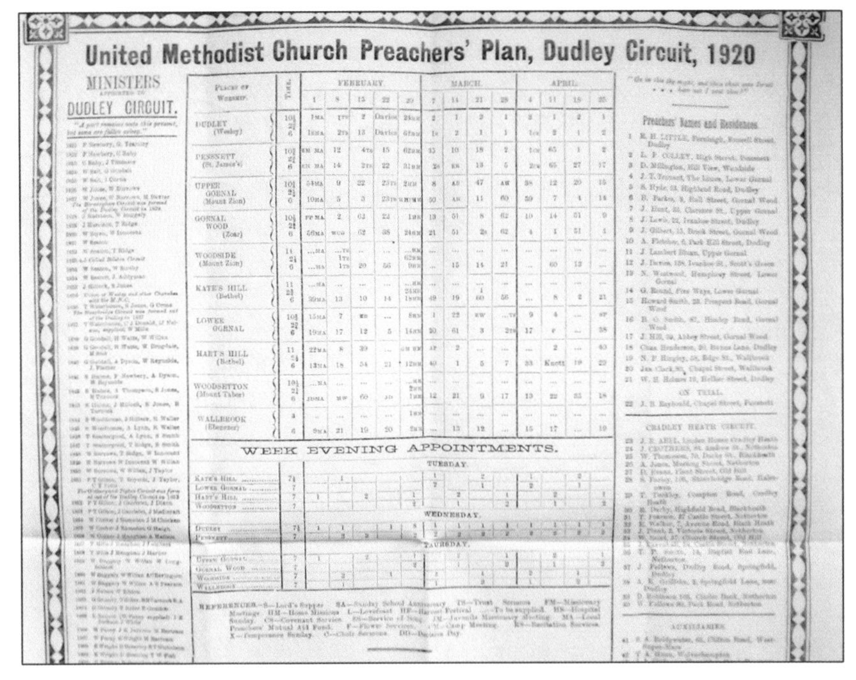

United Methodist Church Preachers' Plan, Dudley Circuit, 1920

MINISTERS APPOINTED TO DUDLEY CIRCUIT.

Places of Worship	Time
DUDLEY (Wesley)	10½ 2¾ 6
PENSNETT (St. James's)	10½ 2¼ 6
UPPER GORNAL (Mount Zion)	10½ 2½ 6
GORNAL WOOD (Zoar)	10½ 2½ 6
WOODSIDE (Mount Zion)	11 2¼ 6
KATE'S HILL (Bethel)	11 2½ 6
LOWER GORNAL	10½ 2½ 6
HART'S HILL (Bethel)	11 2¼ 6
WOODSETTON (Mount Tabor)	10½ 2½ 6
WALLBROOK (Ebenezer)	3 6

WEEK EVENING APPOINTMENTS.

TUESDAY.

WEDNESDAY.

THURSDAY.

Preachers' Names and Residences.

ON TRIAL.

CRADLEY HEATH CIRCUIT.

AUXILIARIES.

Figure 93: 1920 Circuit Preaching Plan

Joint Methodist activities in the Gornals

In 1913 it was agreed to share a mission with the Wesleyans from Himley Road, something repeated in 1922 and again in 1924, when, in advance of the mission, a week of prayer was planned and Zoar Leaders determined that all weekday activities apart from the Guild were to be cancelled so that attention could be concentrated on the mission. During the 1913 mission, over one hundred 'Decision' cards were signed by those who responded to the appeals to commit themselves to following Jesus.[250]

Such shared initiatives were being encouraged across the three main branches of Methodism (the UMC, the Wesleyans and the Primitive Methodists) which, following the creation of the UMC, had set up a Joint Concerted Action Committee aimed

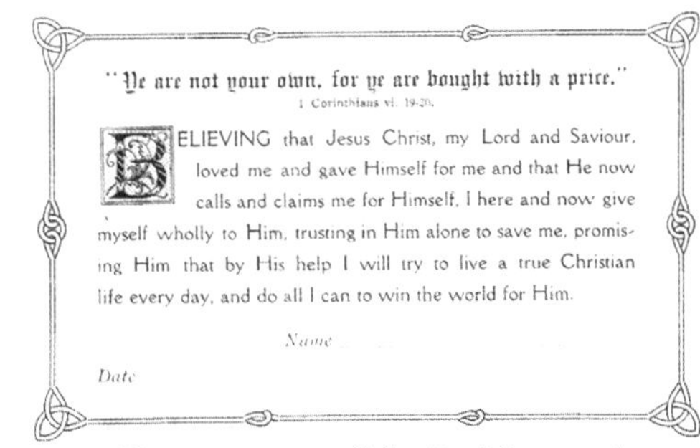

"Ye are not your own, for ye are bought with a price."
1 Corinthians vi. 19-20.

BELIEVING that Jesus Christ, my Lord and Saviour, loved me and gave Himself for me and that He now calls and claims me for Himself, I here and now give myself wholly to Him, trusting in Him alone to save me, promising Him that by His help I will try to live a true Christian life every day, and do all I can to win the world for Him.

Name

Date

Figure 94: one of the Decision cards issued at the 1913 mission services

at encouraging the sharing of mission and other activities.[251]

The First World War led to further ecumenical activity. The Himley Road Wesleyans joined Zoar for prayer meetings alternately at each church in January and April 1915.

In the 1920s, the Leaders allowed the Five Ways UMC and Lake Street Primitive Methodists to hold a mission in the village, using the Zoar Sunday School as its base, when *'Mr. Penfold the missioner [would] give his life story.'* What involvement Zoar members played is not noted, but subsequently it was agreed by the Leaders that *'[a] special sacramental service be arranged for the converts during Mr. Penfold's first mission and Mr. Tennant and Mr. Brettle ask them to attend and be received into fellowship.'*

In 1932, the *Lower Gornal and Gornal Wood Methodist Rally* took place, involving all four local churches, along with their Sunday Schools.[252] They gathered outside Zoar at 2.00pm, sang a hymn, walked to Five Ways, sang another hymn and then processed to the Lower Gornal Athletic Football Field for a rally with four hymns and four addresses by the ministers involved. The leader's penned notes included detailed timing for all contributions, with each minister given seven minutes

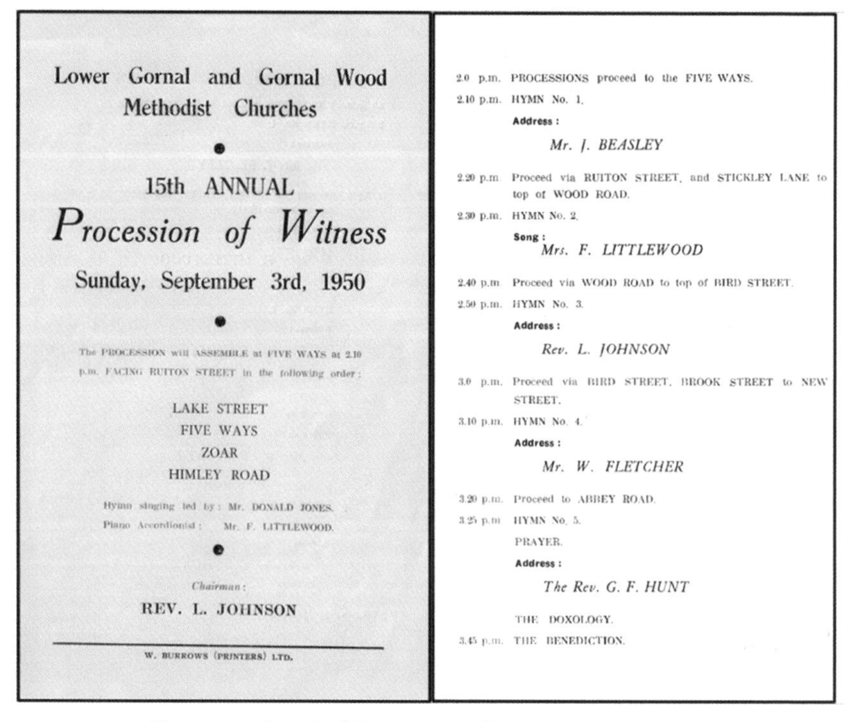

Lower Gornal and Gornal Wood
Methodist Churches

15th ANNUAL
Procession of Witness
Sunday, September 3rd, 1950

The PROCESSION will ASSEMBLE at FIVE WAYS at 2.10 p.m. FACING RUITON STREET in the following order:

LAKE STREET
FIVE WAYS
ZOAR
HIMLEY ROAD

Hymn singing led by: Mr. DONALD JONES.
Piano Accordionist: Mr. F. LITTLEWOOD.

Chairman:
REV. L. JOHNSON

W. BURROWS (PRINTERS) LTD.

2.0 p.m. PROCESSIONS proceed to the FIVE WAYS.
2.10 p.m. HYMN No. 1.
Address:
Mr. J. BEASLEY

2.20 p.m. Proceed via RUITON STREET, and STICKLEY LANE to top of WOOD ROAD.
2.30 p.m. HYMN No. 2.
Song:
Mrs. F. LITTLEWOOD

2.40 p.m. Proceed via WOOD ROAD to top of BIRD STREET.
2.50 p.m. HYMN No. 3.
Address:
Rev. L. JOHNSON

3.0 p.m. Proceed via BIRD STREET, BROOK STREET to NEW STREET.
3.10 p.m. HYMN No. 4.
Address:
Mr. W. FLETCHER

3.20 p.m. Proceed to ABBEY ROAD.
3.25 p.m. HYMN No. 5.
PRAYER.
Address:
The Rev. G. F. HUNT

THE DOXOLOGY.
3.45 p.m. THE BENEDICTION.

Figure 95: A typical Procession of Witness programme

for their address. In 1935, the rally was renamed the *Procession of Witness*, becoming an annual event, usually taking place on the first Sunday afternoon in September and following a longer route with hymns and short addresses at five different locations. The format was unchanged for decades. In 1994 it was renamed *March for Jesus*.

After the Second World War, if not before, in the week before Easter, services were held in each of the churches in turn, as shown in Figure 95.

PALM SUNDAY, April 2nd.

Services for Palm Sunday will be held in all the Churches.

HOLY WEEK SERVICES.

Each evening from Monday to Thursday there will be a United Service for all our Methodist Churches in Gornal.

The Services will begin at 7.30 p.m. and will be held in a different Church each evening.

MONDAY, April 3rd, at ZOAR.

"All ye that pass by."

Speaker: The Rev. Dr. WILBERT F. HOWARD, M.A., F.B.A., (The Principal of Handsworth College.

Zoar Choir will sing from "Messiah," the chorus, 'Behold the Lamb of God that taketh away the sin of the world.'

TUESDAY, April 4th, at FIVE WAYS.

The Wounded Face.

Speaker: The Rev. HAROLD S. DARBY, M.A., (The Resident Tutor at Handsworth College).

Five Ways Choir will sing the chorale, 'O Sacred Head once wounded.'

WEDNESDAY, April 5th, at MOUNT ZION.

The Cross and the Soul.

Speaker: The Rev. Dr. HENRY BETT.

Mount Zion Choir will sing from "Messiah" the air, 'He was despised and rejected of men,' and the chorus, 'Behold the Lamb of God that taketh away the sin of the world.'

THURSDAY, April 6th, at LAKE STREET.

The Cross and the Church.

Speaker: The Rev. AARON SMITH (The Chairman of the District).

The Lake Street Male Voice Choir will sing, 'Were you there when they crucified my Lord.'

GOOD FRIDAY, April 7th.

The Cross.

There will be services at Himley Road, Kent Street and Mount Zion at 7.30 p.m.

HIMLEY ROAD: "The Crucifixion" (Stainer) will be given by the Choir preceded by a short service conducted by the Rev. NORMAN W. MUMFORD.

KENT STREET: The service will be conducted by the Rev. PHILIP S. WATSON, M.A., (Tutor at Handsworth College, and will include excerpts from 'Gethsemane to Calvary' (Witty) by the Choir.

MOUNT ZION: Stainer's "The Crucifixion" will be given by the Choir.

Figure 96: Holy Week Shared Services 1950

One very different example of joint activity was the formation of the Gornal Methodist Cricket Club in the mid-1960s. Its first captain was Roy Picken (Himley Road), with Ward Jones (Zoar) as Vice-Captain. The team joined the Kidderminster and District Cricket League, being placed in the bottom division. Their somewhat embarrassing claim to fame was their inability, for many years, to win a cricket match. Despite this, there was a great spirit and fellowship among the players. The team photograph was taken in 1968 when a single wicket competition, won by the minister, the Revd Alan Fisher, took place at Buffery Park in Dudley, where the team first played before relocating to the grounds of Himley Hall and later to a ground on the outskirts of Wolverhampton.

Figure 97: Gornal Methodists Cricket Team

Relationships with other Christian denominations

St James Anglican Church, Lower Gornal

Relations with the local Anglicans were limited, but cordial. When special events took place, each would send an invitation to the other. For example, in 1928 when the new vicar, Revd. G R Cooke, MA, MC, was due to be instituted, the Leaders were invited to send representatives to the service. And, as mentioned earlier, on the occasion of the broadcasting of the 1932 Act of Methodist Union celebration from London, both the vicar and his curate attended Zoar to listen to it.

Gornal and Sedgley Free Church Council (FCC)

For Zoar Methodists, at the start of the Twentieth Century, ecumenical co-operation was primarily about working with other branches of Methodism and other non-Conformist traditions. Together, they formed the Gornal and Sedgley Free Church Council (FCC). Zoar provided a number of its Presidents, including William Smith and J T Tennant, as well as Vice-Presidents. There was a certain practical intimacy in the relationships, so that, for example, when the Revd. E Hughes of Ruiton Congregational Church retired in 1915 after 37 years of service, £1/1/0d was sent to his testimonial fund. Representatives from the individual churches met on a monthly basis.

During the First World War, Zoar shared in an FCC open air service in July 1916 and in January 1918 shared in an FCC week of prayer, agreeing to cancel their own activities to support it. With the coming of the end of the war, the Leaders agreed to support an FCC thanksgiving service planned for the evening of the day after the signing of the peace treaty and to take place at Ruiton Congregational Church. Thanksgiving services were also planned at Zoar for the following Sunday.

The FCC had its own magazine *The Messenger* which was still being published in the 1960s. Each member church paid for so many copies at a discount and then sold them on. In 1918 to help with the increased cost of producing the monthly magazine, the Leaders agreed to forego their commission and pay the cover cost of 1½d per copy. At the end of every year the young girls who distributed the magazine were given prizes for their efforts. Examples of the monthly circulation figures were 1928 – 608; 1936 – 685; 1946 – 675.

The Gornal & Sedgley Free Church Messenger.

THE ORGAN OF THE FREE CHURCH COUNCIL.

Vol. XXIII No. 12. December, 1928. PRICE 1½d.

Mr. J. T. TENNANT, J.P.

Mr. E. WILLIAMS.

Mr. ISAAC MARSH,

Where are you going to, my Pretty Maid?
I'm going in Bus to

MARSH'S

Sir, she said. They keep all the latest styles in Boots and Shoes.

BUS TERMINUS, GORNAL WOOD.

AND OF COURSE THEY DO REPAIRS.

William H. Hartill,

Architectural and Monumental Mason,

Castle Street, SEDGLEY.

Estimates Free

For Woodwork and all kinds of Building Repairs try

A. HYDE, Carpenter, Joiner and Undertaker.

82, Rock Street, UPPER GORNAL.

Estimates Free. Only best materials used.

RUSSELL BROS.,

Decorators and Builders' Merchants

LOWER GORNAL.

Figure 98: The Messenger

In 1923 Zoar agreed to join a FCC scheme to help raise money for Wolverhampton General Hospital, pledging a sum of £25. In the late 1920s the FCC itself was struggling with declining support for its bi-monthly meetings being reported to Zoar's Leaders as a cause for concern. In 1936 the FCC organised a mission in the locality which was to be led by students from Cliff College in Derbyshire.[253] Zoar agreed to support the mission and not only hosted half of the team (11 of the 22 'trekkers') but also took on responsibility for distributing publicity material.

Salvation Army

From 1910, if not before, and through to the 1950s the Salvation Army were allowed to make an annual collection at Zoar, usually in February, as part of their 'Self Denial Fund' appeal. In the earliest years this actually involved SA officers standing at the door at the end of worship. Occasionally, for example in 1932, when the Leaders felt the congregation had been asked for a large number of financial calls, they declined to support a collection.

Other Ecumenical Links

In 1933 a *Dudley Christian Social Council* was being established and Zoar was invited to send representatives, which they did. However, on reflection it was decided that as they were outside the Dudley borough they would not pursue membership, but as a gesture of support and goodwill a donation of 5/- (25p) was forwarded to the organization.

Community Activity and support

Mission and outreach

In addition to shared mission events, from time to time the Zoar leaders organised their own outreach activities. One example was that held in 1915 when they conducted a four-day mission in the village.

During the 1920s, across wider Methodism there was growing awareness of the challenges and opportunities offered as major housing projects were begun across the country. The Stickley Estate,[254] between Gornal Wood and Lower Gornal, was one such project. In 1922, when people were starting to move into the estate, discussions took place at Zoar, *'to see what can be done with regard to inviting people now coming onto the housing scheme to our services'*. What action followed the discussion, if any, is not recorded. However, when the Circuit made plans for a church building on the new Priory Estate, a similar project, in Dudley, the Zoar Leaders agreed to offer financial backing. In 1926, a meeting of the Birmingham and Dudley District addressed this issue, encouraging local churches to do the same in cooperation with other denominations,

> *Amid the many and varied matters of business which received our careful considerations, [one of two which received greatest attention was the] need for all our Churches to be alert and watchful for promising openings in the new districts now offering better conditions for the housing of the people, so that we may share with other Churches in providing for the spiritual needs of the new centres of the population.*[255]

This appeal failed to produce any shared or individual response among the local churches as far as the Stickley Estate was concerned.

In 1948 there was a surge of evangelistic outreach. Zoar hosted a rally in February inspired by the international Youth for Christ movement, promoted by the American Evangelist Billy Graham during the 1950s. Rallies like this were to become a regular monthly activity among the Methodists of Lower Gornal and Gornal Wood, continuing well into the 1970s. In April a Cliff College Mission took place. Established in the twentieth century by the Wesleyan Methodist Church, Cliff College was a lay training centre, whose students, as part of their training programmes, would visit local Methodist churches for a week or fortnight and conduct services, indoors and out in the community, as well as visiting schools and homes.

Helping those needing support

Serving a mining community and with many miners among their membership, the Leaders sought to offer practical help when various national mining disputes were taking place. At the time of the 1912 strike over a national minimum wage, Sedgley Urban District Council sent out an appeal to all local churches asking for collections to be taken and contributed to a fund to help distressed families, of whom there were said to be 468. The aim was to add £100 to the fund. In response to the national coal miners' strike of 1921[256] it was agreed to send the collection from an evening service in November to the Lower Gornal Soup Kitchen Committee *'to assist in the providing and maintaining of a soup kitchen for feeding hungry children'* and if less than £5 was collected it should be made up to that figure. In the event £6/6/od was raised. The committee's appeal reported that they were feeding 225 children twice weekly.

The Leaders were concerned to try and help disadvantaged members of their own church community as well, charging themselves with responsibility to make enquiries regarding *'any necessitous cases owing to the prevailing distress.'* On one occasion officers were asked to *'devise some means of raising subscriptions'* to help out a member who had been out of work for a long time owing to serious illness. During one of the miners' strikes of the 1920s, a request was made to consider a collection *'at an early date for the unemployed members of the church and Sunday School.'* A rummage sale was held in 1925. This apparently inconsequential event had some greater significance in that it was quite clearly aimed at helping the poor: the 2d admission charge *'to be returned on purchase of goods.'* In that year the trustees, reminded of the fact that one of their number had suffered a serious accident, asked Noah Westwood to *'interview trustees and friends'* in order to collect aid.

Like most Methodist churches Zoar maintained a Poor Fund. It was regularly boosted by the collection taken at the Christmas Day service or one of the Sundays around Christmas. In 1919 it was suggested that those who were unable to attend the service should send a voluntary subscription. The fund was boosted in other ways, for example, from selling the harvest produce, while in January 1931 the choir were asked to perform the operetta 'Gipsy Queen' with proceeds to the fund.

As well as occasional one-off gifts, at Christmas a number of needy people would be given sums of money. For example, in 1915 four grants of 2/6 (12½p) and one of 10/- (50p) were agreed. In 1922 eleven people were given 5/- (25p) and one 10/-. In 1932 it was proposed *'Grants to various needy people [should be] raised from 6/- to 7/6'*. Also, it was reported that Mr. G Round had offered 60 loaves for the poor and that *'the ladies be asked to arrange for distributing same.'* The Leaders' Minutes of December 1945 refer to the *Christmas Gift Fund* instead of the *Poor Fund*, although the people responsible for handling the monies involved were still termed the *Poor Stewards*. In 1947 the fund stood at £9/3/1d after the distribution of several Christmas gifts, mainly of 10/-, but with 2 or 3 receiving more. Interestingly, by way of comparison, while these 10/- gifts were being distributed the preacher conducting the morning and evening Sunday School Anniversary services received £4/4/0d, Supernumerary (Retired) ministers were being paid 15/- per service, and student ministers who came each Quarter from the Ministerial Training college in Handsworth, Birmingham were receiving £1/1/0d plus expenses.

The Leaders were not oblivious to needs further afield, both at home and abroad. In 1920 and 1921 collections were taken for *'starving children in the famine stricken areas of Europe'* (a consequential effect of the

First World War in some parts of Europe) and in 1922 for the *'Wenchow Distress fund'*. Wenchow in China was a part of one of the UMC's overseas Districts. In December 1938 a retiring collection was taken on behalf of *'distressed areas of South Wales.'* And in 1941 support was offered to the Lord Mayor of London's Air Raid Appeal.

Hospital Sunday

One annual event through which the needs of the wider local community were met was the observation of *Hospital Sunday*,[257] with local hospitals benefiting from collections taken up on a specified Sunday. The idea of churches offering regular financial support for local hospitals developed in the second half of the nineteenth century.[258] As the event gained momentum, so, in the weeks preceding Hospital Sunday, churches were provided with posters and booklets to be placed in pews. Zoar had to pass over taking up a collection in 1922 due to pressure on finances.

In the years prior to the formation of the NHS many people were unable to afford the cost of medical services and often it was thanks to subscription schemes and/or the support of philanthropists that hospitals were established.[259] Such was the case with the Dudley Guest[260] and the Wolverhampton Royal[261] hospitals. In 1944 the Wolverhampton Eye Hospital was added to the list and in that year Zoar donated two guineas each to the Guest and the Royal and one guinea to the Eye hospital.

In pre-NHS days, these financial donations were acknowledged with

1948 The Royal Hospital, Wolverhampton
(INCORPORATED UNDER ROYAL CHARTER.)
AMALGAMATING GENERAL HOSPITAL, WOMEN'S HOSPITAL, DISTRICT NURSING ASSOCIATION

SERMON COLLECTION (Available to Lady Day, 1949)

No. 250

The Patient will be treated as out- or in-patient at the discretion of the Honorary Medical or Surgical Officer.

Patient's Name in full..

Age........................ Married, Single, or Widowed........................

Full Postal Address..

Occupation........................ Employer........................

Approved Society........................ Panel Doctor........................

Subscriber's Name..

Address..

Date........................

Tickets will not be accepted unless bearing the name of the Subscriber and the particulars required above duly filled in

Patients must attend punctually at the time made for the appointment.
The number of this Ticket is registered at the Hospital.
Tickets of Recommendation are issued to Annual Subscribers, at the rate of two for each guinea so subscribed.
The person presenting this Ticket will be interviewed by the Almoner, and free treatment will NOT be given if patient or the person on whom the patient is dependent is in a position to join the Contributory Association.

If patient is called upon to pay maintenance charge, this Ticket will be taken into consideration.

Figure 99: Hospital Treatment Ticket

Tickets of Recommendation to be given to people needing, but unable to afford, treatment. In 1940 £2/2/0d was raised and the church was given five outpatient and five dispensary tickets to pass on.

Asked by the Council in 1923 to support the local District Nursing Association fund, at first the Leaders declined. However, when asked to host the local Civic Service two years later, the occasion provided an opportunity to donate the offertory to this project.

Occasionally the afternoon SSA Repetition service was marked with a flower service, with the flowers being sent to one of the local hospitals.

The Two World Wars

War had an impact on regular Sunday worship and mid-week activities, with the starting times for all evening gatherings being moved forward in February 1916, because of a fear of air raids. Joshua Jones was asked to make arrangements for darkening the windows, with the upstairs windows masked and blinds fitted downstairs. The Sunday evening service was moved into the school building, but the earlier start time was soon abandoned. The Christmas Day service that year was cancelled.

During the years of the First World War a number of special fund-raising activities were organized for the benefit of those serving in the armed forces. In 1915 it was decided to sell the harvest Festival produce and spend the proceeds *'on the soldiers on active service.'* Greetings cards were sent to all those associated with the Sunday School. In 1916 the Leaders *'resolved that Christmas cards and packets of cigarettes be sent to the scholars "on service" with the colours'* and Harvest Festival gifts were passed onto Wordsley Hospital *'[for the benefit of] wounded soldiers and sailors'*.

On three occasions, gifts of fruit, flowers, eggs, vegetables, chocolates, toffee, biscuits, cigarettes and tobacco were sent on behalf of the Sunday School to the First Southern General Hospital which was located at nearby Stourbridge. In 1918 they sent 305 eggs, 100 cigarettes and a bag of tomatoes. Also, during this war, vegetables from the Harvest Festival were sent to the Royal Navy in response to a national scheme, administered by the *Vegetable Products Committee for Naval Supply*, which had an active branch in Sedgley.

Blinds were back on the agenda in September 1939 when a Leaders Meeting was held on the first Sunday of the month, the day war was declared. Amazingly the first two items were accepting the Treasurer's report and agreeing to buy tickets for the Circuit Rally! Only then was the declaration of war addressed,

> *A discussion took place as to how we should be affected by the war which was declared on Germany this morning by the Prime Minister at 11.00am and it was resolved that blinds be ordered for darkening the church windows and it be left in the hands of the secretary to make necessary arrangements.*

However, the redoubtable members were not going to have their lives unnecessarily disturbed. A decision the following week to continue with evening services *'as long as daylight would permit their being concluded by 7.00pm – afterwards services to be held in the afternoon from 3pm to 4.15pm'* was rescinded only a week later by a Church Meeting. The members *'viewed with disfavour the prospect of afternoon services and it was unanimously resolved to continue the evening service at 6 o'clock.'*

In November, the Zoar folk responded to a connexional appeal aimed at raising £5,000 *'to provide comforts for the Soldiers, Sailors and Airmen'*. In December they contributed to a similar appeal by the local newspaper, the *Express and Star*. More special collections were made during the course of the war, for example, in August 1941 £2/4/0d was sent to the local Air Raid Distress Fund. In October 1943 there were collections for *'the "Boys" Christmas Fund'* and in October 1944 the British Legion were allowed to take up a retiring collection for Earl Haig's fund. When the Circuit passed on an appeal on behalf of the *Blitzed Churches and Circuits Needs* in 1945, the Leaders accepted the challenge of raising 3d per member per week for three years, appointing a committee to implement the scheme. In 1949 it was reported that a total of £141 had been raised.

The impact of the war was felt in other ways. In December 1940 it was decided that the annual Sunday School outing should be cancelled. In 1941 the Church Meeting made plans for fire watching of the church premises. One of the problems faced was that of a fuel supply to heat the church. An *'Application for a license* [sic] *to acquire coal'* was submitted, it being stated that this was only for the winter months. A Civic Service was held in September 1943 to mark Battle of Britain Sunday.

One of the more intriguing war-time happenings occurred in 1943, the trustees succeeding in saving the iron railings at the front of the site. Part of the national 'War Effort' involved the collection of scrap metal – gates, fences, pots and pans, old prams etc. with the intention of recycling it in the production of munitions and other equipment.[262] When correspondence with the Ministry of Works and Planning gave rise to a decision that *'both the railings on the boundary wall and the gates are to be retained for safety', the trustees deemed themselves 'very fortunate'.*

A respected role in the local community

That the church had a respected role to play was evidenced by an invitation to provide three representatives to the local *Food Control Committee* in May 1917 and then an invitation from the Sedgley Urban District Council to participate in discussions about how the war dead of the locality might be commemorated.

Two representatives were sent, in 1925, to the *League of Nations Union*[263] group being established in Sedgley. In 1930 the Leaders agreed to a letting for the local branch to meet in Gornal Wood. Then in 1935 when the Union planned a national 'peace ballot'[264] Zoar was invited to send five representatives to a meeting to discuss the matter.

When the Sedgley UDC were planning local celebrations to mark the Silver Jubilee of King George V, Zoar was invited to send representatives to help with the project. With the coronation of George VI in 1937 Zoar chose to hold its own special service, publicising it with a poster and printing 300 special orders of service.

In 1944 members were encouraged to attend a FCC meeting arranged to oppose plans for opening cinemas in the district on Sundays.

Lettings

Although Zoar was built primarily for religious purposes, its usefulness as a community asset cannot be overstated, particularly, as the following list shows, for working people in the years before World War II, who, for the first time, had the opportunity to rent well-appointed, conveniently located and, most importantly, affordable premises to discuss politics, transact Friendly Society business, improve public health or just do things that made life more enjoyable. In 1911, the Gornal Wood band moved in on Friday evenings. In 1912 the Red Hall Adult School held classes for rent of 25/- a year to cover lighting and heating and made their own arrangement with the caretaker for his services. Another early letting was to the Labourers' Union, whilst in 1914 it was agreed that the Lower Gornal Liberal Women could meet for their AGM and committee meetings, at 10/6d a year, and also public meetings, at 5/- a time. With a parliamentary election in prospect in 1918, it was decided the premises would be made available to "either" political party, meaning the Conservatives and the Liberals and although in 1919 it was agreed that in future the school would not be let for concerts or political meetings, the following year the local Labour Party was allowed to *'have the use of the crocks'*.

In the 1920s rooms were let on Saturdays for use as a pay station by the Dudley Union, part of a national scheme giving financial support to men disabled in the war and unable to work and the local Board of Guardians also hired the premises. In 1921, during the miners' strike, the Leaders agreed that the school could be used for the visit of Mr Frank Hodges, *'in view of the special circumstances and the undertakings of the [miners'] representatives that no damage shall be done'*. At the time, Hodges was the Permanent Secretary of the Miners' Federation of Great Britain and so this was a major event in the life of the village and the surrounding area. Lake Street Primitive Methodist Church were allowed the use of the Sunday School for their sale of work in 1924 and were congratulated by Zoar trustees for their effort. Not all lettings were so friendly. 1928 witnessed some sort of stand-off with the local football team who used rooms.

From 1930, the group formed in Sedgley in support of the League of Nations met at Zoar and in 1934, following a request from Miss Hickman, Divisional Superintendent, it became the local headquarters of the Girl Guide movement. They were allowed to use the premises for three months free of charge and afterwards for £3 per annum, of which the caretaker received £1 for the extra duties required. In 1936 Staffordshire County Council rented space for a school clinic. They were charged £1 a week, which included 4/- for gas, 6/- for coke, 2/6d for the caretaker and 7/6d for Trust funds, a substantial sum at the time, implying significant use of the facilities for an important community service. During the 1930s Friendly Societies the Rechabites and the Midland Counties Mutual Benefit Society continued to use Zoar for their meetings.

By the early 1940s, the church premises had become so popular with local groups that the church's own ladies' group, Women's Own, became concerned about the availability of their regular meeting room at the back of the church prompting the trustees to confirm that their usage took priority. At the same time the Minister's Vestry was reserved for church purposes, making sure that there was always room available for a church meeting if required.

Post-war, Zoar continued to play an important role in public health, from 1952 it hosted the County Council's Infant Clinic and Welfare Centre. At this time, when ration books were still being issued, the Ministry of Food's local Food Officer approached the church trustees about using the schoolroom for ration book distribution, but the request was turned down as there was not enough space available due to the clinic's presence.

Chapter Nine

Zoar and its ministers[265]

Before the split from the Himley Road Society, the first Methodists who began to meet in the village were served by Wesleyan Methodist itinerant preachers based in Dudley. They were stationed there usually for one or two years and their main task was to preach. The following names are recorded in *Hills Arrangement*,[266]

1795 **Jonathan Barker** and **John Woodrow**
1796 **John Simpson Snr.**
1797 **John Burdsall**
1801 **John Wood Snr.**
1803 **James Blacket**
1804 **Edward Gibbons**
1805 **David Deakin**
1806 **J Edmondson Snr.** (who was President of the Methodist Conference in 1818) and **John Simpson Jnr.**
1810 **James Etchells**
1811 **John Rigg**
1813 **Thomas Thompson Snr.**
1814 **John Hodgson**, **Samuel Sugden** and **Richard Waddy**
1816 **James Allen Snr.** and **John Walmsley**
1818 **Thomas Dowty** and **Josiah Goodwin**
1820 **Thomas Ashton**
1821 **Thomas Edwards Snr.**
1823 **John Rosser**
1824 **Joseph Hunt**, **Joseph Lysk** and **Joseph Sutcliffe**
1826 **John Simpson Jnr.**
1827 **Jacob Stanley Snr.**
1829 **William Pemberton**
1830 **Edward Oakes** and **John Waterhouse**
1831 **Samuel Sugden** and **James Topham**
1832 **William France**
1833 **John Rowe**, **Thomas Edwards Snr.** and **Benjamin Frankland**
1835 **John H Adams**, **John Henley** and **John Smedley**

A Dudley Circuit Quarterly Preaching plan, published shortly before the union scheme of 1932 which brought together the Wesleyan,

Ministers appointed to the Dudley Circuit.

"A part remains unto this present, but some are fallen asleep."

F Newbery, G Yearsley
1822 F Newbery, C Raby
1823 C Raby J Tittensor
1824 W Salt, G Goodall
1825 W Salt, J Curtis
1826 W Jones, W Burrows
1827 W Jones, W Burrows, M Baxter

The Birmingham Circuit was formed of the Dudley Circuit in 1828

1828 J Harrison, W Baggaly
1829 J Harrison, T Ridge
1830 W Styan, W Innocent
1831 W Seaton
1832 W Seaton, T Ridge
1833-4-5 *Called Bilston Circuit*
1833 W Seaton, W Sorsby
1834 W Seaton, J Addyman
1835 J Hillock, S Jones
1836 *Union of Wesley and other Churches with the M.N.C.*
1836 T Waterhouse, S Jones, G Orme

The Stourbridge Circuit was formed out of the Dudley in 1837.

1837 T Waterhouse, C J Donald, (J Nelson supplied) W Mills
1838 G Goodall, H Watts, W Willan
1839 G Goodall, H Watts, W Brogdale, M Salt
1840 G Goodall, A Dyson, W Reynolds, J Flather
1841 S Hulme, F Newbery, A Dyson, W Reynolds
1842 S Hulme, A Thompson, S Jones, B Turnock
1843 S Hulme, J Hillock, S Jones, B Turnock
1844 S Woodhouse, J Hillock, R Waller
1845 S Woodhouse, A Lynn, R Waller
1846 T Scattergood, A Lynn, S Smith
1847 T Scattergood, T Ridge, S Smith
1848 W Burrows, T Ridge, W Innocent
1849 W Burrows, W Innocent, W Willan
1850 W Burrows, W Willan, J Taylor
1851 P T Gilton, T Boycott, J Taylor, C Y Potts

The Oldbury and Tipton Circuit was formed out of the Dudley Circuit in 1852.

1852 P T Gilton, J Candelet, J Dixon
1853 P T Gilton, J Candelet, J Medicraft
1854 W Cocker, J Ramsden, J M Chicken
1855 W Cocker, J Ramsden, G Haigh
W Cocker, J Maughan, A Hallam
1857 T Mills, J Maughan, J Lambert
1858 T Mills, J Maughan, J Harker
1859 W Baggaly, W Willan, W Longbottom
1860 W Baggaly, W Willan, A C Bevington
1861 W Baggaly W Willan, A R Pearson
1862 J Nelson, W Eddon
1863 G Grundy, T Rider, B B Turnock B.A.

Ministers appointed to the Dudley Circuit (continued).

1864 G Grundy, T Rider, E Gratton
1865 L Saxton (W Pacey supplied) J K Jackson, J White
1866 W Pacey, J K Jackson, M Bartram
1867 W Pacey, E Wright, M Bartram
1868 E Wright, D Brearley, S T Nicholson
1869 E Wright, D Brearley T W Fish
1870 T Boycott, D Brearley, J E Walsh
1871 T Boycott, A Hilditch, T Stoneley (supply)
1872 T Boycott, A Hilditch, J L Fox
1873-4 D Round, A Hilditch, C Bamford
J Hillock, Sup., 1847-1874
1875 D Round, J R Welham, T Porteus
1876 J Graham, J R Welham, T Porteus
1877-8 J Graham, J R Welham
1879 J Robinson, T G Seymour
1880 J Robinson, T G Seymour, C T England
1881 J Robinson, C F Lea, W D Bainbridge
1882 J Robinson, C F Lea, G D Riley
1883 E J Hope, J Whitton, J W Walls, J R Welham (rests)
1884 E J Hope, G Parker, J Stephens
1885 E J Hope, G Parker, S E M'Quire
1886 E J Hope, G Parker, M Hodsman
1887 E J Hope, J Shaw, M Richardson
1888-9 W F Newsam, J Shaw, J A Robinson
1890-1-2 W F Newsam, J P Treloar
1893 T T Rushworth, G T Akester, M Langdale
1894 T T Rushworth, G T Akester, M Langdale A C Bevington, Sup.
1895 T T Rushworth, G T Akester, S O Rider
1896-7 T T Rushworth, W Usher, S O Rider
1898 W Bainbridge, C F Hill, S O Rider

The Cradley Heath Circuit was formed.

1899-1900 W Bainbridge, C F Hill
1901 E Fletcher Denton, W Gillis,
1902 E Fletcher Denton, W Gillis T T Rushworth
J Hughes, Sup.
1903 Enoch Hall, W Gillis, T T Rushworth, J Hughes, Sup.
1904-5 Enoch Hall, W Gillis, T T Rushworth, Sup.
1906-7-8 J L Hookins, M Langdale T T Rushworth, Sup.
1909-10-11-12 J L Hookins, F Rhodes, T T Rushworth, Sup.
1913 J L Hookins, Kaye Garthwaite T T Rushworth, Sup.
1914-15 R H Little, Kaye Garthwaite T T Rushworth, Sup.
1916-17-18 R H Little, Kaye Garthwaite
1919 R H Little, L P Colley
1920-21-22 J Hooley, L P Colley
1923 W H May, L P Colley
1924-5-6 W H May, A F Viney
1927-8-9 W J Teague, A F Viney
1930-1-2 W. J. Teague, N. Green.
1933 W. E. Walker, N. Green.

Figure 100: Ministers serving Zoar

Primitive and United Methodist branches of Methodism, records a list of those (now called ministers rather than preachers) who after the 'wedding' of 1836 served Zoar and those other churches who had left Wesleyan Methodism to join the MNC and subsequently the UMC.

Following the national union of 1932 the Zoar leaders agreed to a joint meeting with Five Ways, Himley Road and Lake Street (who were still in a separate circuit to the others) *'to see what advantage can be gained from Methodist Union.'* In 1934, one of the first decisions of the new Dudley Circuit that had been created post-union was to group together the churches in the Gornals under the oversight of one minister. This led to a proposal that, for the first time, a minister should be based there and a manse acquired somewhere in the locality, with the Gornal churches authorised to action the matter and asked to contribute a total of £100 towards the cost. Zoar agreed to offer £24. There was a suggestion raised about buying land in Summer Lane (a site mid-way between Lower Gornal and Gornal Wood) on which to build a new manse, but no immediate action was taken.[267] In 1936 the incoming minister for the Gornal chapels, the Revd. Dean Sherriff, became the first resident minister, living at *Valdore* on Himley Road.

Zoar took the lead in marking the occasion, hosting a joint welcome event and later in the autumn a joint rally.

Figure 101: Revd Dean Sherriff

GORNAL METHODIST CHURCHES.

Meeting at Zoar

THURSDAY, 15th OCTOBER, 1936,

TO WELCOME REV. G. DEAN SHERRIFF

(the first Methodist Minister to be stationed in Gornal).

Tea will be served at 6 o'clock.

TICKETS 9d. EACH.

Community Singing at 6-45. Public Meeting 7-15.

Figure 102: Welcome to the first resident minister

With a minister resident in Gornal Wood, discussions began with a view to splitting the Dudley Circuit, however in May 1939 Zoar's Leaders suggested the matter should be left until the anticipated hostilities had ended. It would be 1962 before anything finally happened, when the Gornal and Sedgley circuit came into being.

The ministers responsible for Zoar didn't always have an easy relationship with the trustees when it came to matters relating to the building. For example, in 1942 they *'granted'* the then minister *'permission'* to hold youth services *'as and when he may deem it necessary.'* The expectations concerning the leading of worship were something that would be alien to twenty-first century ministers: in the 1940s the minister was expected to conduct two of Zoar's Thursday mid-week services every month, with similar expectations from the other churches for which he was responsible. In 1946 Revd. Norman Mumford asked to be relieved of one of those services so that he could spend more time with the young people. The Leaders acceded to the request. The matter of transport for the minister was discussed in 1945,

> *The question of making an allowance to our minister towards the cost of a motorcycle (which is being chiefly used for the benefit of the five Gornal churches) was discussed and it was resolved to support the proposal at the next meeting of the five churches to the extent of paying £10 towards the cost of the cycle and an allowance for expenses of up to 10/- (50p) per Quarter.*

By 1950 the matter of giving a grant of £5 towards the Revd. Hunt's car was on the agenda.

Ministers associated with Zoar in the post Second World War era

(in alphabetical rather than date order)

Harold Anfield, Norman Burrows, Alan Fisher, John Hartley, Yvonne Haye, Roger Hides, Fred Hunt, Stephen Jackson, Kevin Jones, Henry Le Ruez, Stephen Levett, Harry Lister, John Lloyd, Norman Mumford, Suzanne Newton, George Nuttall, Keith Rowbottom, Perry Smith, Jemima Strain, John Webster.

Members of Zoar who entered the Methodist Ministry

Matthew Wilfred MARSH 1887 – 1967

Wilfred lived in Gornal Wood (in Coopers Bank and then Bull Street) in his early years. Known in the Dudley Circuit as 'the boy preacher', he was educated at the local council school and then at Dudley Grammar

School. He entered the United Methodist Ministry in 1914, training at Victoria Park College, Manchester. In 1917, he married Lilian Kerena Rodda, an Elementary and Sunday School teacher from Falmouth, Cornwall. He travelled widely during his ministry, serving in Worksop, Louth, Chester, Oldham, Salford, Hanley, Chatham, Plumstead, Exeter, Isle-of-Wight, Denby Dale and Sheffield. Having a passion for study, he read widely in theology, philosophy and general literature. A gifted musician, he sang and played the piano.[268]

Anthony Ward JONES b.1950

Ward lived in Gornal Wood in his early years, attending Red Hall Infants and Junior Schools and High Arcal Grammar School. Before moving away from Gornal, he served as a Sunday School teacher at Zoar and began training to become a Local Preacher. He studied for the ministry at Wesley House, Cambridge, serving in Circuit ministry in Clitheroe, Royal Wootton Bassett and Frome, before seventeen years as leader of the Methodist Church in the West of England.

Ian Michael JONES b.1950 (grew up with, but unrelated to Ward Jones)

Ian lived in Gornal Wood, being educated at Red Hall School and Tettenhall College. He studied for the ministry at Wesley House, Cambridge. After entering Circuit ministry, he later chose to move into the world of education.

Timothy FLOWERS

The most recent entry into full-time ministry. Tim grew up in Dudley. Following his training at the Queen's Foundation in Birmingham, he was stationed in the Tamworth and Lichfield Circuit. Very much involved in community work, Tim also took on an honorary chaplaincy with the Army Reserve, which eventually led to a full-time Army chaplaincy appointment.

Figure 103: Revd Tim Flowers

Chapter Ten
Lay Leaders

Church Stalwarts in the first half of the Twentieth Century

For many years, a collection of photographs was displayed on the walls of the minister's vestry. Many more could have been added, but these were the ones chosen by their successors, the one addition here being that of William Lees.

Figure 104: William Smith, JP,[269] whose obituary noted, *'Of humble parentage, he began life with little or no help, by sheer force of character and persistent effort he won for himself a position and honours which are possible only to a few.'* A parish overseer and District Councillor, he rose from *'ordinary worker'* to become General Manager of Gibbons' Dibdale Works, where equipment for the gas industry was manufactured. Connected with Zoar for some 40 years, he served as teacher and co-superintendent in the Sunday School. As chairman of the Trustees, he was much involved in the building of the 1906 Zoar. He helped to establish the Gornal and Sedgley Free Church Council.

Figure 105: John Thomas Tennant, JP, was perhaps the most influential figure in the Zoar Society in the last quarter of the nineteenth century and first quarter of the twentieth century. He grew up in the fellowship of Zoar, where his father, John, was choirmaster for some thirty years. Generally regarded as the 'father' of Zoar, JT served as Trust Secretary and Chairman, Sunday School Superintendent, Local Preacher, Circuit Steward, secretary of the Dudley Circuit and member of the

Birmingham and Dudley District Synod (which he was elected to chair in 1928).[270] He represented the District from time to time at the UMC Annual Conference.[271] His contribution to the local community was equally extensive. He served as a Justice of the Peace, as well as a County and District Councillor. In this latter role he was a member of the Sedgley Urban District Council for 27 years, being its chairman in 1904, 1905 and 1912.[272] In 1927, to mark his 70th birthday, the church and Sunday School held a social gathering at which he was presented with an illuminated address and a set of books. Individuals were invited to donate between one and ten shillings towards the cost.

J T Tennant had a brother George who was a completely different character. George was a gifted musician. In an era of silent films, he played the piano at the Alexandra Hall Theatre in Gornal. He was offered, but declined, the opportunity to take on the role of organist at Zoar, although he would willingly stand in if the regular organist was unavailable. On such occasions, he was known to slip out during the sermon for a drink at the neighbouring White Chimneys Inn and come back to strike up the congregational 'Amen' which followed when the preacher had finished. Apart, that is, from one occasion when he is reputed to have failed to return in time.[273] J T Tennant died in 1934 and his fellow trustees recorded their appreciation of him in their minutes,

> *We the trustees .... desire to place on record our high appreciation of his sterling character and the interest he showed for many years as a fellow trustee. His wide knowledge and sagacity were ever at our disposal and gave him a leadership in our counsels attained by few. We bless God upon every remembrance of him.*[274]

Figure 106: Isaac Harris

In 1933 special mention was made at the Leaders' Meeting of **Isaac Harris**'s 21 years' service as Secretary Steward, a role in which he served as secretary to the Leaders' Meeting and was, along with the Treasurer Steward, one of the two senior lay people in the life of the Society. He would continue in this role for almost as many years again, finally giving notice, in March 1953, that he was standing down. He and his son, Vincent, both served as trustees.

Figure 107: George Round

Born in Dudley in 1866, **George Round** was a grocer in Ruiton Street, Lower Gornal. Such was his contribution to Zoar that an Illuminated Address was presented to him when late in life he was due to move out of the village and felt it an appropriate time to give up his various responsibilities at Zoar. It was presented after the evening service on 28 April 1935, by his longtime friend Joseph Brettle. He was a Sunday school teacher, trust treasurer, and served the Dudley Circuit as Local Preacher and Circuit Secretary.

Figure 108: Joseph Brettle

Gornal Gas Works Manager, **Joseph Brettle** (1871-1963), served 60 years as a Sunday School teacher (27 as superintendent), 51 years as a Local Preacher and 50 years as a trustee. To mark his 80th birthday in 1949 and acknowledge his contribution to the life of Zoar, a celebratory event was held at the church.

Figure 109: Joseph Gilbert 1869-1962
He lived all his life in Gornal Wood, in Graveyard, Brook Street, Bull Street and Red Hall Road. He and his wife, Elizabeth, had nine children, one of whom died in childhood. A humbler background than most of his Zoar contemporaries, he spent virtually all of his working life, as his father before him, as a miner. He was assistant superintendent of the Sunday School and a Trustee, having joined the trustees in 1899 and serving on the reformed trust of 1949 until his death.

Figure 110: William Lees[275]
A local solicitor, his early church connections were with Ruiton Congregational Church. Following his marriage to Charlotte Marion Smith (daughter of fellow Zoar stalwarts William and Elizabeth Smith) he joined the congregation of Zoar, serving as a trustee and was regularly called upon to chair important social events. In his professional life, he served as clerk to the Coseley District Council and the South Staffordshire Joint Smallpox Hospital Board. A member of the Sedgley Urban District Council and the Dudley Board of Guardians, upon his death at the young age of 48, glowing tributes were paid to *'a devoted family man'* who in carrying out his responsibilities as a council clerk, was always considered to be approachable, giving advice readily and, as courteously, listening to suggestions.[276]

Church Stalwarts in more recent years

Recorded here are some of those who have served Zoar faithfully over the years. Their contributions are mentioned at various points in the chapters relating to the twentieth century. Of those who moved away from Gornal, John Powell has offered long service in the Cardiff Circuit, fulfilling various roles, including that of Circuit Steward. In the earliest years of his life, John and his parents lived in the caretakers' cottage. Bryan Cotterill, descended from the Hemmings family, who provided a number of trustees and organists, was made an honorary Alderman of Dudley Borough Council in 2021. The award was made in recognition of his twenty-two years as a ward councillor and, in his photograph, he can be seen holding his badge of office.

Mention must also be made of Bill Caldwell, who, over many years, has served both Zoar and the Circuit as 'Church and Community worker', which, in practice has seen him involved in preaching and pastoral work, conducting weddings, baptisms and funerals, serving as a school chaplain, taking assemblies and being involved in Christian radio.

Robert and Vera (nee Cox) Aston

Mina Bennett

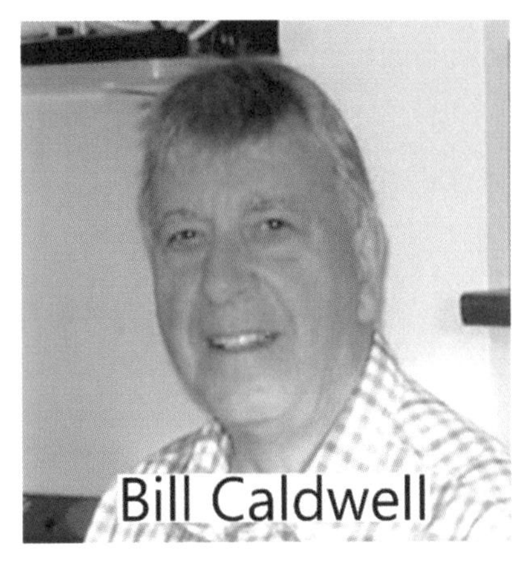

Bill Caldwell

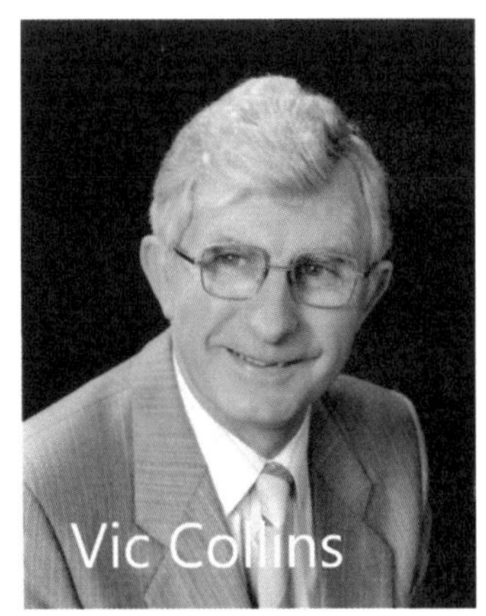

Vic Collins

Bryan
Cotterill

Harold Fletcher

William
(Bill)
Fletcher

Harold Jones

Jean & John
Jones

Geoff Marsh

Linda Morris

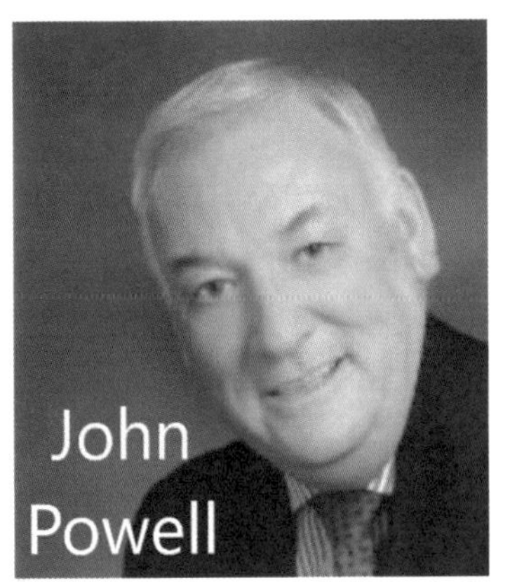
John
Powell

Gordon & Liz Wright

CHAPTER ELEVEN

Time to hand on the baton

What became ever more clear to me over the years of my own full-time work in the Methodist Church, which began in 1976, was that from the 1950s on, if not before, the Church needed to be open to radical change: not its message, but the style of presenting itself and its message to the world around, along with the form and nature of its worship, fellowship and spiritual nourishment. Put another way, the idea of what it means to 'be' Church had to be transformed: to find a way forward which could both excite Christians to want to go out and change the world and, at the same time, impinge on the lives of the wider community, intrigue them, whet their appetites to explore further and help them begin to make sense of what it is to be a Christian.

'Zoar, Gornal Wood - the life and times of a Methodist Church' tells the story of one church's practice of 'being' and 'doing' Church over nearly two centuries. There was a sense of vitality and determination evident in that small group expelled from the Himley Road Society in 1835. They and their immediate successors established a physical and spiritual presence at the heart of the village. Their efforts blossomed and flourished, leading to the opening of a new and more substantial suite of premises in 1906. Through into the Twenties and Thirties Zoar's members continued to make a substantial contribution to life in the village and across wider Methodism through activities that were unchanged over decades, their high point being the annual Sunday School Anniversary. Even in the late 1950s and early 1960s extra seating had to be brought into the church and the aisles filled with chairs in a way that would leave today's Health and Safety authorities in a state of apoplexy. Milestones in the timeline were marked by Wake teas, grand bazaars and days of celebration. The leading figures in the local community attended and the leading figures in Methodism came to join in the celebrations.

Maybe it was symbolic of an era coming to an end that in 1956 the 50th Anniversary of the present building was overlooked. All of which is not to be pessimistic. Far from it. These may be difficult times for the Christian Church in the West, but they are also exciting. Churches, individuals and denominations are having to experiment. Sometimes new ideas work. Sometimes they fail. The challenge is to keep trying: to find effective ways of sharing the unchanging heart of the Gospel message. But, sometimes, the right decision is to call a halt. Decisions taken by the national Methodist Conference led to the break-up of the numerically declining Zoar family and, for some, a move to join the Himley Road Methodist Church. As a small number had moved out in 1835, so in 2023 a similarly small group returned to the parent church, on both occasions, due to a decision of a national Conference. This history marks an ending of Methodist witness based at Zoar and, at the time of publication, the Springs Church has taken on responsibility for Christian ministry and mission from these premises. It is the earnest desire of the former members of the church, the Local Circuit and the District that this can become a permanent arrangement. History will record if central Methodism has the foresight to give the required permissions for that to happen.

This book records a particular and significant contribution to the wider history of Gornal Wood. It is offered to all who care about the village, to ensure there is a record of what has been. It is offered to the leaders of Springs Church, wherever they finally settle in the village, as a foundation document. May they achieve great things and touch the lives of Gornal Wood's residents as effectively as their Methodist forefathers and mothers did for nearly 200 years.

Endnotes

1 *The Bicentennial Edition of the Works of John Wesley*, (Abingdon Press: Nashville, Tennessee), vol.24, p.72. (Hereafter *Works Bicentennial Edition*)
2 The Minutes of Conference were and are published annually and record the meeting of the Church's national governing body, the Methodist Conference. From 1744, as Methodism expanded, John Wesley began to hold these annual gatherings, initially involving only senior itinerant ministers, to discuss the progress of their work and how it could be taken forward. Over time the various branches of Methodism all held an annual conference, albeit with different combinations of ministers and laypeople.
3 See *Works Bicentennial Edition*, vol.10, p.183.
4 Assistants were those approved by John Wesley to assist him in mission activity. As the work expanded, so their numbers multiplied. On Assistants see *Works Bicentennial Edition*, vol.10, pp.77-79; p.139, notes 167, 168; p.159, note 304; and p.177, note 427.
5 *Works Bicentennial Edition*, vol.10, pp.208-209. In these early days the itinerants were truly travelling preachers, moving every two months.
6 James Jones spent much of his ministry in the Staffordshire Circuit and indirectly played a part in the development of Methodism in Dudley: in 1750 he paid for the first purpose-built chapel in the Black Country at Tipton Green, mid-way between Wednesbury and Dudley.
7 An Itinerant was an individual serving Methodism full time and subject to the direction of the annual Conference as to where he would mission. A Half itinerant served part-time. See *Works Bicentennial Edition*, vol.10, p.273. In 1768, the Conference decided that half-itinerancy was to be 'forbidden' where such income involved a trade (*Works Bicentennial Edition* vol.10, pp.358-360).
8 H H Prince, *The Romance of Early Methodism in and around West Bromwich and Wednesbury, (West Bromwich*: Tomkins, 1925), p. 9. 'The Hollow' or 'The Holloway' was a natural amphitheatre located about a mile from the centre of Wednesbury and actually situated in the parish of West Bromwich. See also See also S Lees, 'Wednesbury and West Bromwich as Wesley knew them' in *Proceedings of the Wesley Historical Society* (hereafter *WHS Proceedings*), vol.4, no.6 (1904) p.154.
9 *Works Bicentennial Edition*, vol. 19, pp.310-311.
10 Around 1760 the first chapel was erected in Meeting Street, to be replaced by another building at Spring Head in 1812. See S Lees, op cit, pp.154-157.
11 S T Kimborough Jr. and K G C Newport, *The Manuscript Journal of the Revd. Charles Wesley MA*, vol.2, (Nashville Tennessee: Abingdon Press, 2007), p.342.
12 See J M Fletcher 'The Beginnings of Methodism in Wednesbury' in *The Blackcountryman*, vol.7, no.1 (the Black Country Society, 1974) pp.10-11.
13 *Works Bicentennial Edition*, vol.19, pp.343-349.
14 These included Justices William Persehouse and John Wood. See further *Works Bicentennial Edition*, vol.19, p.349 and vol. 20, p12.
15 *Works Bicentennial Edition*, vol.19, pp.322-323.
16 *Works Bicentennial Edition*, vol. 20, pp.10-14.
17 *Works Bicentennial Edition*, vol. 9, pp.132-158.
18 Kimborough and Newport vol.2, p.374.
19 Ibid. p.400.
20 Ibid. p.402.
21 The hymn is reproduced in T Jackson, (Ed.) *The Journal of the Revd. Charles Wesley MA* – to which are appended selections of his correspondence and poetry, vol.2, (London 1849), pp.458-459. The hymn was included in Wesley's *Hymns and Sacred Poems*, 1749.
22 S Lees, 'Wednesbury Methodist Traditions' in *WHS Proceedings*, vol.4, no.7 p.199.
23 Kimborough and Newport, vol.2, p.382.
24 See 2 Samuel. 16.5-6. Shimei, son of Gera, cursed King David and his officials at Bahurim and attacked them with stones. This is one example of the way in which the Wesleys often referred to biblical incidents in relation to what happened in their own lives.
25 See *Works Bicentennial Edition*, 1751 vol. 20, p.381; 1757 vol. 21, p.92; 1761 vol. 21, p.311;1764 vol. 21, p.445-6; 1770 vol. 22, p.219; 1773 vol. 22, p.383; 1774 vol. 22, p.400; 1776 vol.23, p.7; 1779 vol. 23, p.120; 1781 vol. 23, p.195; 1784 vol. 23, p.481; 1788 vol.24, p.72.
26 *Works Bicentennial Edition*, vol.20, p.311.
27 *Works Bicentennial Edition*, vol.20, p.381.
28 Kimborough and Newport, vol.2, p.613.
29 *Works Bicentennial Edition*, vol.21. p.245.
30 In its early years it reached far beyond the borders of Staffordshire, embracing Derby, Warwick, Worcester, Salop and part of Gloucester. See A C Pratt, *Black Country Methodism*, p.118.
31 A Mather, 'The Life of Mr Alexander Mather', in T Jackson (Ed.), *The Lives of the Early Methodist Preachers*, vol.2, (London: Wesleyan Conference Office, 1871), pp.178-179.
32 Ibid pp.179-183.
33 The Southall family were originally Presbyterians. However, they began to travel to the Tipton Green chapel built with money provided by the local half-itinerant James Jones.
34 Rev J Aikenhead, 'Memoir of Mr William Southall of Dudley', in *The Methodist Magazine for the Year 1823*, vol.XLVI (London), pp.568-575.
35 In 1852 the high death rate and poor state of public health in Dudley led central government to send William Lees to prepare a report on conditions in the town. It included the following entry, '*The Mambles King Street:- Fifty to sixty houses, no water. All dirty pallid, diseased, and some idiots. The people complain even in the midst of their filth, of want of water. All so bad as to be indescribable, a man almost dying, a woman with half a face, children devoured with filth, prostitutes and thieves. The physical and moral condition of this place is indescribable.*' See https://uptheossroad.wordpress.com/2015/10/12/slums-of-the-black-country-the-mambles-dudley/ (Accessed August 2024). Also W H Cross, *King Street Methodist Church Dudley 150th Anniversary Souvenir*, (Dudley: Phoenix Printers, 1938), p.11.
36 A C Pratt, *Black Country Methodism*, p.120. Pratt's list is incomplete here. He does not include Darlaston. However, on the previous page he quotes from Alexander Mather concerning the anti-Methodist agitation in the Black Country in the early 1740s where there is mention of a preaching house in Darlaston. This building was licensed for worship in 1762. See http://www.historywebsite.co.uk/articles/Darlaston/ChurchesChapels.htm (Accessed August 2024). Mather's reference to the Dudley preaching house implies it was open in 1763.
37 *Works Bicentennial Edition*, vol.21, p.445.
38 A A Rollason, *The Old Non-Parochial Registers of Dudley*, (Dudley: Herald Press, 1899), p.43.
39 *Works Bicentennial Edition*, vol.24, p.171.
40 A A Rollason, p.43.
41 R Davies, A R George and G Rupp (Eds.) *A History of the Methodist Church in Great Britain*, (London: Epworth Press, 1988), vol. 4 p.246. See also, W H Cross, *King Street Methodist Church Dudley*, pp.11-13 for a brief description of Dudley town in the Eighteenth Century.
42 W Davies, *Early Methodism at Gornal Wood*, (1939) offers the only known account of how Methodism arrived in the village. Davies' dates relating to Wesley's visits and the birth of Gornal Methodism are not consistent with the related details in Wesley's Journal. The March 1790 visit to Dudley by Wesley is the most

likely occasion on which the Gornal miners heard him preach. This would then allow for the commencement of cottage services in 1791 (see Davies, p.17). If Davies is recording oral history, as was most likely the case, rather than working from written records, then it is understandable that dates may have been confused.
43 See Davies, pp.1, 2 and 17.
44 'brutal sports' refers to the practice of betting on cock fights.
45 Davies, p17.
46 'Coal, anchors and nails Dudley manufacturing in the 19th century', the *Black Country Bugle*, (Cradley Heath: 10th September 2009).
47 Davies p.18.
48 A Barnett, 'Yesterday, to-day and tomorrow' in *Forward – Souvenir Brochure*, (Gornal and Sedgley Circuit: 1962).
49 The Society was recognized as a member of the Dudley Circuit in 1803. See A chronological history of the people called Methodists [electronic resource], of the connexion of the late Rev. John Wesley; from their rise, in the year 1729, to their last conference, in 1812. (d2chuymlzmhuro.cloudfront.net) (Accessed September 2024).
50 *Chapel Account Book 1827-1869*. This account book appears to have begun life as that of the first Wesleyan Society, becoming the account book of the breakaway New Connexion Methodists. Entries for 1827–1835 clearly relate to the original Wesleyan Society, whereas those from 1836 relate to the subsequent MNC Society. Someone among the 'exiles' evidently took the account book with them and continued to use it for the new Society.
51 Davies pp.19-22.
52 *Chapel account book for 1827-1869*. The building was eventually replaced by the present-day Himley Road chapel on the same site, in 1895.
53 *The Wesleyan Methodist Magazine for the Year 1827*, vol. VI, Third Series, (Vol. 50 from the commencement), (London: 1827), p.132. This magazine was a national publication and its first editions were issued as a defence of Methodist principles and doctrine, to counter falsehoods put about by opponents of the Methodist cause. By the time of its 1827 Jubilee edition it was available monthly and had become a means by which the Societies across the country were kept in touch with what was taking place elsewhere and also informed about missionary work overseas. See also pp. iii, iv of the same volume.
54 Ibid.
55 *Minutes of the Wesleyan Methodist Conference* (Hereafter *Wesleyan Minutes*), 1826 p.125. The District Chairman was a senior minister elected to chair District meetings. At the time the role was an occasional responsibility as the major part of their work was focused on the Circuit in which they were stationed by the Conference.
56 W R Ward, *Early Victorian Methodism: the correspondence of Jabez Bunting 1830-1858*, (Oxford: OUP, 1976), p.171. It is somewhat ironic that the land had been donated by Lord Dudley, chief mine owner in the locality and the foundations then dug mainly by miners during a miners' strike.
57 *Wesleyan Minutes*, 1826 p.145.
58 Ibid. pp.143-147.
59 Rollason, *The Old Non-Parochial Registers of Dudley*, p.44 See also R Leese, *The Impact of Methodism on Black Country Society, 1745-1860*, (Manchester: unpublished DPhil. thesis submitted to the University of Manchester, 1972), p.133. Leese suggests that the 1836 Trust membership was drawn from across the circuit, with individuals of some substance asked to serve as trustees in order to give strength and credibility to the King Street cause after the fractures which had just taken place across the chapels of the Dudley Wesleyan Circuit.
60 *Chapel Account Book 1827-1869*. Unreferenced facts in this chapter are taken from this source.
61 E A Rose 'The Methodist New Connexion' in *Wesley Historical Society (West Midlands Branch) Bulletin*, vol.3, no.4, (Autumn 1979), pp.40-42. The MNC's own interpretation of what happened is recounted in its Jubilee record. See T Allin, W Cooke, S Wright and P James, *The Jubilee of the Methodist New Connexion*, (London: John Bakewell, 1848). (Hereafter, Allin, et. al., *Jubilee*). Also, J Blackwell, *Life of the Rev, Alexander Kilham*, (London: MNC Bookroom, 1838).
62 'Society' was the term used in the early days of Methodism and applied to any group meeting regularly to hear the preaching of the Word. Societies might not, in the early days, have had a chapel building available to them. Instead they would meet in homes or rented accommodation.
63 In 1817, the Birmingham Circuit had only 2 chapels, 4 Societies and 101 members.
64 See W Baggaly, *A Digest of the Minutes, Institutions, Policy, Doctrines, Ordinances and Literature of the Methodist New Connexion*, (London: 1862) pp.157-164. (Hereafter, 'Baggaly, *Digest*') The initial Home Mission project began in 1816, '*... for the extension of [the MNC's] borders, and for the promotion of the Redeemer's kingdom.*' It did not receive the financial support required in order to remain viable. The MNC Conference chose instead to concentrate outreach work in Ireland (from 1825) and, in due course, overseas in Canada (1837) and China (1859). A revised Home Mission scheme was introduced in 1859.
65 *Minutes of the Methodist New Connexion Conference* (Hereafter *MNC Minutes*), (1821), p.5.
66 The information has been taken from *MNC Minutes* for the relevant years.
67 A Circuit Plan was and still is prepared locally and published information about which preachers were to conduct services in the chapels or societies around the Circuit for the following Quarter.
68 W Baggaly, 'Rise and Progress of the Methodist New Connexion in Dudley' in *MNC Magazine*, (1862), pp.22-29.
69 The sketch of Ebenezer is taken from S G Davies, *Wesley Chapel, Dudley* – A Centenary Souvenir 1829 – 1929, (Dudley: 1929), p.31.
70 Ibid., p.13. Davies indicates that Ebenezer was eventually disposed of in 1845.
71 W Baggaly, *Rise and Progress*, pp.23, 24.
72 See *Methodist New Connexion Wolverhampton Circuit Minutes* for 1835-36 deposited in the Wolverhampton Archives and Local Studies Centre, Wolverhampton. The Dudley Society is not recorded among those listed in the Circuit Minutes. In that particular year the Circuit was actually designated as the Bilston Circuit. As has already been shown, the name of the circuit changed a number of times in the 1820s and 30s.
73 See *Methodist New Connexion Wolverhampton Circuit Minutes*, April 1836. While Dudley is absent, these other four places are listed.
74 'Five Ways, Lower Gornal' should be distinguished from the 'Five Ways' chapel listed in the Dudley MNC Circuit of 1836. This latter was a different Society, located at Coseley. For a brief account of the origins of 'Five Ways, Lower Gornal' see E A Underhill, *The Story of the Ancient Manor of Sedgley*, (1942), pp.415-417.
75 'The Gornals' was a shorthand title collectively including Upper and Lower Gornal and Gornal Wood.
76 W Baggaly, *Rise and Progress*, p.26.
77 See, for example, A Briggs, *The Age of Improvement 1783-1867*, (Harlow: Longman, 1979) pp.236-260; 286-312; 344-367.
78 See G J Barnsby, *The Dudley Working Class Movement 1750-1860*, (Dudley: Dudley Leisure Services, 1986).
79 For further detail see D A Gowland, *Methodist Secessions: the Origins of Free Methodism in three LancashireTowns*, (Manchester: MUP, 1979), pp.31-40,

W R Ward, *Religion and Society in England 1790-1850*, (London: Batsford, 1972) pp.160-175 and R Currie, *Methodism Divided – a study in the sociology of Ecumenicalism*, (London: Faber and Faber, 1968), pp.217-236.
80 *Wesleyan Minutes*, (1835), pp.542-545 and p545ff. The Warren case dominated the agenda and gave rise to a major review of disciplinary procedures. See also *Wesleyan Minutes*,(1836), pp.87-89.
81 W R Ward, *Religion and Society in England 1790-1850*, (London: Batsford, 1972), p.161.
82 R Currie, *Methodism Divided*, p.219.
83 G Robson, *Dark Satanic Mills? Religion and Irreligion in Birmingham and the Black Country*, (Milton Keynes: Paternoster Press, 2002), p.56.
84 ibid
85 W Baggaly, 'Reception of the Wesleyan Seceders of the Dudley and Stourbridge Circuits into the MNC,' in *MNC Magazine*, (1836), pp.394-398.
86 O A Beckerlegge, *United Methodist ministers and their Circuits*, (London: Epworth Press, 1968), p.91.
87 *Our Circuit Chronicle - The Organ of the Dudley Methodist New Connexion Circuit*, New Series vol. VI no. 11, (November 1904).
88 'The birth of a Gornalwood church - in the club room of a local boozer!' in the *Black Country Bugle*, 14th April, 2005, p.12
89 A Barnett, unpublished *Notes on the History of Lower Gornal*, available at Gornal Wood Library).
90 The building had been erected in 1828-29, at a cost of £4,100, to function alongside the King Street chapel due to the expanding work of the Dudley Wesleyans. It had been opened by the Revd. Jabez Bunting on 16th August 1829. (See A A Rollason, *Old Non-Parochial Registers of Dudley*). It was ironic that Bunting should be involved in the chapel opening as it was he, above all others within the Wesleyan Methodist leadership, who had resisted the Warrenites so forcefully. In the MNC's Jubilee souvenir publication Wesley church was described as *'a commodious and very beautiful structure, which having been legally conveyed to our friends by the Wesleyan Conference, and settled on trust, according to our Model Deed'* (See Allin, et. al., Jubilee, p.365.)
91 Baggaly, *Digest*, p.42. The Dudley Circuit reappears in the circuit lists for the 1836 MNC Conference.
92 Allin, et. al., *Jubilee* p.354.
93 E A Rose, 'The Methodist New Connexion 1797-1907. Portrait of a Church', in *WHS Proceedings* vol.47, (October 1990), pp.247.
94 Census research indicates that the surname *'Wosdell'* was actually *'Wasdell'* and *'Endor Guest'* should be *'Eder Guest'*. *'Eder'* is a name found in the Old Testament and given to one of the three sons of Mushi. See 1 Chronicles 23.23 and 24.30.
95 *Our Circuit Chronicle*, (November 1904).
96 *Black Country Bugle*, op. cit.
97 A Barnett, op. cit.
98 *Our Circuit Chronicle*, (November 1904).
99 *Our Circuit Chronicle*, (November 1904), incorrectly records this date as being the opening of the brick-built Tabernacle. As the following paragraph clarifies, this latter event did not take place until one year later.
100 *MNC Minutes*, (1838), p.6.
101 Entries in the chapel's account book establish quite clearly two separate opening services: one in 1836 for the wooden Tabernacle and one in 1837 for the brick Tabernacle.
102 *Our Circuit Chronicle*, (November 1904) and Beckerlegge, op. cit. p132
103 T Genge, *Sedgley and District*, (Stroud: Sutton Publishing, 1995), p.33.
104 *Chapel Account Book 1827-1869*.
105 A Briggs, *The Age of Improvement 1783-1867*, (London: Longman, 1979), p69.
106 Information gathered from national Census returns for 1841, 1851 and 1861. The newspaper quotation is taken from *Walsall Observer*, (3rd January 1891), p5.
107 Document reference DGS/II/5/8/13 held at Dudley Archives.
108 *Electoral Register for Seisdon North*, 1838.
109 *Electoral Register for Sedgley Polling District*, 1861.
110 Information relating to his death taken from the death certificate registered 28th March 1848.
111 *Register of Deaths for Morrison, Muskota in the province of Ontario*, entry 009154.
112 William Bradley became a farmer and along with his bother Richard (who subsequently joined the renewed trust in 1854) farmed the neighbouring Abbey Farm in the 1850s.
113 A C Pratt, *Black Country Methodism*, (London: Charles H Kelly, 1891), pp.31-32.
114 Hugh Bourne and William Clowes, founders of the Primitive Methodist Church, were thrown out of the Wesleyan Methodist Church for holding such meetings early in the nineteenth century. The 'Prims' or 'Ranters' as they were known colloquially, by those who considered their worship to be over-enthusiastic.
115 The Church Army was an evangelistic organisation and mission community in association with the Church of England. For further information see https://en.wikipedia.org/wiki/Church_Army (Accessed July 2024)
116 See https://dmbi.online/index.php?do=app.entry&id=3682 and https://www.methodistheritage.org.uk/visit/gospelcar/ (Accessed June 2024).
117 *Our Circuit Chronicle*, November 1904.
118 See further J Kent, *Holding the fort: Studies in Victorian Revivalism*, (London: 1978), pp.9-37.
119 G Packer (ed.) *The Centenary of the Methodist New Connexion 1797-1897*, (London: Burroughs, 1897), p.120.
120 O A Beckerlegge *United Methodist ministers and their Circuits*, p.36.
121 *Chapel Account Book 1827-1869* See entries for 1851.
122 *Our Circuit Chronicle*, November 1904.
123 A C Pratt, pp.42-43.
124 *Chapel Account Book 1827-1869*. The names of the trustees were written alongside the entries for 1851. The same individuals are later noted as trustees of the new chapel. In this chapter all factual details which are not specifically referenced have been taken from one of three original records: the *Chapel Account Book 1827-1869*; the *Trustees' Minute Book 1876-1898*; or the *Trustees' Minute Book 1898-1923*.
125 G Savage, *Methodist New Connexion. Souvenir of the Dudley Conference*, (Pensnett: Savage and Harris, 1903), p.18.
126 'Gilbert Claughton's birthday honour 100 years ago' in the *Black Country Bugle*, (Cradley Heath, 14th June 2011), p.6.
127 *Our Circuit Chronicle*, November 1904.
128 *MNC Magazine*, 1855, Vol. 58, p.155.
129 By 1854 the growth of the MNC in the Black Country meant that the original Dudley Circuit had been divided into two, 'West' and 'East'.
130 O A Beckerlegge, p.50
131 A C Pratt, op. cit., pp.54-55.
132 Ibid. p.163.
133 *MNC Magazine*, 1855, Vol. 58, p.155
134 Bible, *New Revised Standard Version* (Hereafter *NRSV*)
135 *NRSV*, Genesis 19.22,23.
136 *NRSV*, Isaiah 15.5.
137 *NRSV*, Deuteronomy 34.3.
138 Leaders' Meetings were a feature of Methodist organisation from as early as 1739. See Davies and Rupp (ed.), *History of the Methodist Church in Great Britain*, (London: Epworth Press, 1965), Vol. 1, p.226. The Leaders' Meeting remained a key part of Methodist polity until major changes in organisation were introduced in 1974. Its membership and agenda

were subject to various changes over time, while its fundamental role as responsible for the pastoral wellbeing of the local church or chapel remained its prime responsibility. For further reflection on the Leaders' Meeting see Chapter 6.
139 Lay members who received some training and led worship. Nationally they made an essential contribution to the regular leading of Sunday services as there were far more Methodist churches and chapels than there were ministers.
140 Chapel or, later, Church Stewards were the senior lay people responsible for any activity not relating to the property.
141 This would appear to be a lay pastor, employed in addition to the Circuit ministers. There is a reference in the Trust Minutes for 1901 to a Pastor J Grady attending the meeting. It is unusual to come across such an appointment in the MNC.
142 To become known in later years as the *"Chapel or Church Anniversary"*.
143 The trustees evidently did not insist on the date being linked to that of the original opening ceremony.
144 Special harvest thanksgiving services became increasingly popular during the second half of the nineteenth century. The practice first emerged in Cornwall in the 1840s. The first mention of income from a Harvest Festival at Zoar is in July 1882, when it produced collections totalling £7/15/6d, compared to £4/10/0d at the Chapel Anniversary.
145 Sunday School Anniversaries became a significant feature of the Sunday School Movement, as its influence continued to flourish through the nineteenth century.
146 This information was included on the front page of the chapel's *Balance Sheets for the year 1897*.
147 See, further, Davies, George and Rupp (ed.), *History of the Methodist Church in Great Britain*, (London: Epworth Press, 1965), Vol. 4, pp.572-575.
148 A Bennett, *Anna of the Five Towns*, Penguin Modern Classics, 1969. See Chapter 13,'The Bazaar' pp.224-233.
149 Letter dated 21st July 1898 from the Superintendent Registrar, James Jones.
150 References to *'Minutes'* relate to detail recorded in the various trustees' minute books.
151 The author's experience, as a member of the church.
152 On the significance and importance of these tickets, see Sarah Lloyd, *The religious and social significance of Methodist tickets, and associated practices of collecting and recollecting, 1741-2017*, (unpublished paper for the University of Hertfordshire). Also, https://biblicalstudies.org.uk/pdf/whs/01-5.pdf (Accessed August 2024)
153 A calculation based on the population figures given at the beginning of this chapter and an assumption that the population of Gornal Wood was no larger than that of Lower Gornal.
154 A D Gilbert, *Religion and Society in Industrial England - Church, Chapel and Social Change 1740-1914*, (Longman: London, 1976), p.194.
155 A Bennett, *Anna of the Five Towns*, (Harmondsworth: Penguin Books, 1969), p.54. Although set in the Potteries it offers descriptive insights into various common aspects of Victorian Methodism. These meetings were similar in style and activity to camp meetings, but were more often held in the church building.
156 ibid, p. 69.
157 ibid, chapters four and five, pp.54-72
158 http://www.mkheritage.co.uk/bfhng/docs/Jul10%20The%20Victorian%20Funeral.htm (Accessed March 2018). Account no longer accessible.
159 See further, https://en.wikipedia.org/wiki/Temperance_movement_in_the_United_Kingdom (Accessed August 2024). In places like the Black Country many churches supported the Temperance movement because of the suffering experienced in many working class families related to drunkenness.
160 On the Order, see https://en.wikipedia.org/wiki/Order_of_Free_Gardeners and https://www.culturenlmuseums.co.uk/story/friendly-societies-free-gardeners/ (Accessed December 2023)
161 T Genge, *Sedgley and District - a second collection (of photographs)*, Alan Sutton, 1997, p.116.
162 *Birmingham Daily Gazette*, Friday 20 April 1877, p1.
163 https://en.wikipedia.org/wiki/Sunday_school (Accessed August 2024)
164 This is a reasonable assumption based on the fact that the benches in use when the author attended the Sunday school in the 1950s and 60s were of the type illustrated in Figure 34 which is Victorian.
165 A Bennett, *Clayhanger*, Penguin, 1976, pp. 123-129
166 Smith, M. K. (2004) 'Adult schools and the making of adult education', the encyclopaedia of informal education, www.infed.org/lifelonglearning/adult_schools.htm (Accessed August 2024). For more information about the adult Sunday School movement see J W Rowntree and H B Binns,. *A History of the Adult School Movement*, (London: Headley Brothers, 1903) and M G Currie, *The Adult School Movement. Its origin and development*, (London: National Adult School Union, 1924).
167 See, for example, A Briggs, *The Age of Improvement 1783-1867*, (London: Longman, 1988), pp. 336-338.
168 C Girdlestone, *Seven sermons preached during the prevalence of cholera in the Parish of Sedgley*, (Reprint. Milton Keynes: Lightning Source UK, 2012)
169 Quoted in E Pritchard, 'Board Schools and their appearance in Lye and Wollescote' in *The Blackcountryman*, Black Country Society, Vol. 50, No. 4 (Autumn 2017), p.74.
170 Quoted from 'Reports of the Assistant Commissioners appointed to enquire into the state of population in England, 1861, Vol. II.' in an undated Newman College of Education, Birmingham, document entitled, *'Resources for Teaching: Birmingham and the Black Country'*. As well as offering commentary, the resource document quotes extensively from the report itself. George Coode was one of the assistant commissioners sent out by the Government to assess the state of education around the country. His area included the Black Country. The information gathered nationwide helped give rise to the 1870 Education Act which, while making education neither free nor compulsory, was a major step forward in providing wider opportunities for educational provision.
171 *Slater's Classified directory of the extensive and important manufacturing district 15 miles around Birmingham*, (Isaac Slater: Manchester, 1851), p.119. Slater's Directory records that as well as the school held on the Zoar premises and the National School attached to the Parish Church, there was also a day school at the Wesleyan Methodist Church with Sarah Langford as the mistress. Miss Wasdell's school fee was recorded in the chapel account books.
172 Barnsby, *Social Conditions in the Black Country 1800-1900*, pp.150-160.
173 Ibid., p.151.
174 *MNC Minutes*, 1851, pp. 47-48.
175 See further, E Royle, pp.350-365. His act was the first really effective attempt to offer educational opportunity to the majority of children
176 *Kelly's Directory of Staffordshire*, (London: Kelly and Co., 1896), p.305.
177 For more information on poor relief see https://en.wikipedia.org/wiki/Rates_in_the_United_Kingdom (Accessed December 2023). The poor rate was absorbed into 'general rate' local taxation in the 1920s, the forerunner of today's Council Tax.
178 A B Erickson, 'The Cattle Plague in England, 1865-1867' in *Agricultural History*, Agricultural History Society,

Vol. 35, No. 2 (Apr., 1961), pp. 94-103
179 S A Hall, 'The Cattle Plague of 1865' in *Proceedings of the Royal Society of Medicine*, Vol. 58.10 (Oct 1965), pp. 799–801. The prayer read, *Lord God Almighty, whose are the cattle on a thousand hills, and in whose hand is the breath of every living thing, look down, we pray Thee, in compassion upon us, Thy servants, whom Thou hast visited with a grievous murrain among our herds and flocks. We acknowledge our transgressions, which worthily deserve Thy chastisement, and our sin is ever before us; and in humble penitence we come to seek Thy aid. In the midst of judgment, do Thou, O Lord, remember mercy - stay, we pray Thee, this plague by Thy word of power, and save that provision which Thou hast in Thy goodness granted for our sustenance. Defend us, also, gracious Lord, from the pestilence with which many foreign lands have been smitten; keep it, we beseech Thee, far away from our borders, and shield our homes from its ravages; so shall we ever offer unto Thee our sacrifice of praise and thanksgiving, for these Thy acts of providence over us, through Jesus Christ our Lord. Amen.*
180 The SSWW company had been formed in 1853 and gradually expanded its area of responsibility. By 1893 an average of 7 million gallons was being supplied daily. In that year it built its first reservoir at nearby Sedgley. See further http:// www.south-staffs-water.co.uk/about_us/ history.asp (Accessed August 2024)
181 A retort worker worked in a gas works, operating a large oven in which coal was baked to manufacture coal gas.
182 All the facts quoted without specific reference in this chapter are taken from one of the following sources: the *Trustee Minute Book 1898-1923* and *Trustee Minute Book 1923 -1948*. In seeking to appreciate relevant payments and charges mentioned in the text it may be helpful to know that when in the UMC after 1913 its ordained ministers were paid £110 per annum with a furnished house free of rent and rates. See *UMC Minutes* (1913) p.43.
183 This 'home' was a training centre for lay evangelists, opened in 1886 and closed in 1905. At the Primitive Methodist Conference of 1899 Odell was commended for his work there. After its closure, he was appointed as a connexional evangelist. See H B Kendall, *History of the Primitive Methodist Church*, London, Primitive Methodist Publishing House, 1919 pp150-151
184 *Our Circuit Chronicle*, New Series Vol. VI No. 11 November 1904.
185 Norman was a Liberal Member of Parliament for Wolverhampton South from 1900 to 1910, losing his seat in the first general election of that year. In the second election of 1910 he became MP for Blackburn, representing the constituency until 1923. Created Baron Honeyhanger in the Parish of Shottermill in the County of Surrey, in 1915, in 1918 he was admitted to the Privy Council. He served as chairman of several important government committees ranging from the Imperial Wireless Telegraphy Committee to committees on Patent Medicines and Rent Restrictions, Betting Duty and Industrial Paints. Norman was also appointed a Justice of the Peace for Surrey.
186 In 1923 Homer would serve as High Sheriff of Staffordshire. See E. A. Underhill, *The Story of the Ancient Manor of Sedgley*, 1942
187 This detail is pasted into the Trust Minutes for October 10th 1906. It is a cutting from the text of the *UMC Minutes*.
188 These bricks were made from Staffordshire red clay in Pensnett. The Ketley Brick Company was founded in 1805 and in 2024 was still in business, manufacturing the same bricks among its current range. Ketley Brick - Staffordshire Red Bricks (ketley-brick.co.uk) (Accessed August 2024)
189 The order of service for the day spoke of the "dear old Zoar" and the "New Zoar".
190 Fithern was a member of Mount Zion MNC chapel in Upper Gornal. A prominent local politician, he was one of the lay stalwarts of the Dudley MNC Circuit.
191 It was not until 1935 that marriages could be registered without the attendance of the local Registrar for Births, Marriages and Deaths. The Revd. T Hooper Johnson was the first minister able to register marriages.
192 The Workmen's Compensation Act 1906 dealt with the right of working people for compensation for personal injury.
193 The Women's Own was a mid-week afternoon meeting attended by mainly older ladies. See Chapter Six for more information.
194 This being the only carpeted area of the floor space.
195 At the time Gornal Wood was in the Bilston constituency. John Baker held various jobs in iron foundries, steelworks, brickyards and engineering works prior to becoming a locomotive driver. In 1898 he became national organiser of the National Amalgamated Union of Enginemen and Cranemen, later rising to be general secretary in 1907. From 1906–1910 he was a member of Stockton-On-Tees Borough Council. During the First World War he served on munition tribunals and a number of government committees. An early member of the Labour Party, Baker was subsequently selected to contest parliamentary elections on behalf of the party. In 1918 he stood unsuccessfully at Kidderminster, and also failed to be elected at Bilston in 1922 and 1923. He was finally elected as Bilston's MP at his third attempt in the 1924 general election. By this time he was an assistant secretary at the Iron and Steel Trades Confederation. He held the seat at the 1929 election, but was unseated in 1931 following a split in the Labour Party and the formation of a National Government.
196 See footnote 50 and the note about the use of this account book.
197 Crown size posters (15 x 20 inch), like the one in Figure 60, were used annually to promote the Sunday School Anniversary, Harvest Festival and Church Anniversary, along with special services such as the Centenary celebrations. Members were asked to display them in front windows. This practice continued well into the second half of the twentieth century.
198 Figure 62 shows the location of the outbuildings and farmhouse alongside the chapel. The farmhouse is the shaded building above the 'A' in Gornal.
199 J J Baker was a lifelong member of Zoar, serving as a Sunday School teacher, trustee and Treasurer Steward (In which capacity he was treasurer of the accounts which were the responsibility of the Leaders' Meeting). He worked in the mining industry from the age of twelve, spending most of his working life as a Chartermaster – engaging people to work in the local mines. In 1946 he was awarded a British Empire Medal for his services to the mining industry. *The Messenger -the organ of the Gornal and Sedgley Free Church Council*, Vol.XLII, No.5, May 1948.
200 While the caretaker's cottage belonged to the trustees, the neighbouring terrace properties were owned by trustee John Jones and purchased from him for £300 prior to the redevelopment of the site.
201 Suffice to say these photos come from a somewhat later date in their four lives.
202 While no records of the Leaders' Meetings from the nineteenth century are known to exist, a complete set for the period from 1908 on have survived. They consist of three volumes: 1908-1928; 1928-1956; and 1956-74. All facts which are not specifically referenced have been taken from these Minutes.
203 H Smith, J E Swallow and W Treffry *The Story of the United Methodist Church* (London: Henry Hooks,1932), p.14.

204 The Church Meeting was open to all who were members of the church.
205 These blanks were being used in the 1930s, if not before and were still available in the 1970s.
206 In 1912 the UMC Conference '[urged] *that earnest and increased attention be given to the presence of children, youths and maidens at Divine Worship and a distinct portion of each service be devoted to them.*'
207 Family Worship, eventually renamed All-Age Worship, involved a much more relaxed and child-orientated approach to worship.
208 While the post of caretaker was usually advertised in the Sunday notices and in the church porch, the organist's appointment was advertised in the local press, both the *Express and Star* and the *Dudley Herald*, presumably because of the need to search in a wider area to find a suitably qualified person.
209 Possibly the son of Tom Hemmings, who had served temporarily as organist, after the resignation of Arthur Tomlinson. In support of this connection is the fact that John was required to take some training. Did musical ability run in the family?
210 After Joseph Hale's resignation from the joint post in 1911, the role of choirmaster was subsequently given to Arthur Tomlinson who himself resigned in 1919.
211 'Close 'armony at the Zoar' in *Dudley Herald*, 19 May 1978, p.14.
212 There is no indication of why this was felt to be necessary or against what concerns they were to be insured.
213 Information from notes written by Miss Florence Hale.
214 *UMC Minutes*, 1908, p.41
215 The Institute, originally founded in 1891, had some 40 sisters, some working permanently in circuits, others engaged on missions, during which they would engage *'in visitation of the sick, poor and neglected in towns and villages.'*
216 Ira D Sankey and Dwight L Moody were American evangelists who visited the United Kingdom on a number of occasions. Sankey was a singer and song writer and Moody a preacher. Originating in the United States, Sankey's *Sacred Songs and Solos* was widely published and first used in the UK in the 1890s.
217 This was done following historical precedence: the Wesleys had regularly reviewed the membership lists of the Societies they visited, not hesitating to determine those who should be removed from the list. The Circuit Meeting continued to monitor the numbers for each Society, but the Leaders' Meeting of each local church was responsible for maintaining an accurate up to date list. The size of the membership was used as one of the factors in determining the allocation of the assessment paid quarterly by each church to the Circuit, this money being used for the payment of the ministers, the operation of the Circuit and an assessment levied by the District and Connexion.
218 It was the 1919 UMC Conference which first proposed the establishment of Membership Preparation classes, with young people particularly in mind (*UMC Minutes*, 1919, p.306). A booklet 'Joining the Church' was prepared by Revd. J A Watts as a resource for such groups (*UMC Minutes*, 1920, p.221).
219 See http://www.historylearningsite.co.uk/suffragettes.htm (Accessed June 2024)
220 From the mid-1920s through to the mid-19300s the number of female representatives varied between three and six.
221 After the Methodist Church Act of 1975, radical changes were made to the governance of local churches. Church Stewards replaced Society Stewards, taking on the latter's role, along with added responsibilities.
222 What this was used for is not explained. Probably to cover any costs related to its activities.
223 Himley Hall was the home of the Earl of Dudley who owned the local coal mines and was the chief local landowner.
224 The first Christian Endeavour society in the British Isles was formed in 1887 by the Rev. A W Potts at Hightown Congregational Church in Crewe, Cheshire. An engineer, George Charnock, had emigrated to America and as a result of his contact with the society at Portland, Maine he had written enthusiastically to his former minister about Christian Endeavour and its aims to promote an earnest Christian life among its members, to increase their mutual acquaintance, and to make them more useful in the service of God. Its initial focus was very much on young people. The Methodist New Connexion Conference of 1892 agreed to establish a Christian Endeavour Movement based on the American model. For the MNC the hope was that Christian Endeavour groups would create a bridge between Sunday School and church (See *MNC Minutes*, 1892 p.25). The organisation is still operating as an independent movement today, see http://www.ce-online.org/ (Accessed August 2024). In 1933 the Zoar Sunday School Teachers discussed the idea of a Junior Christian Endeavour meeting.
225 The Band of Hope was the idea of two people who shared a common concern. Ann Jane Carlile, an Irish Presbyterian lady, was convinced that children suffered because of the ready availability of 'strong drink' and regularly addressed groups about the subject. She met a young Baptist minister called Jabez Tunnicliffe, who had been shaken to the core by his experience of a dying alcoholic. Just before he died, the man had clutched at Tunnicliffe and made him promise to warn children about the dangers of drink. Having discovered their common interest, these two decided to start a regular children's meeting. It isn't clear who thought of the name first, but Ann is supposed to have said *"What a happy band these children make, they are the hope for the future."* The UK Band of Hope was born In London in 1855. Fifty years later, the Band of Hope numbered 3.5 million children and adults. Queen Victoria was its Jubilee patron and it was part of the fabric of Victorian society and the Church. See http://www.hopeuk.org/about-us/band-of-hope/ (Accessed August 2024)
226 *UMC Minutes* 1932, p.141
227 In compiling the history, I was surprised to discover that my late aunt, Betty Mills (née Jones) was designated as secretary to the appointed team.
228 For an explanation of glee singing see https://www.britannica.com/art/glee-music (Accessed September 2024).
229 Dr Ian Campbell Hannah (16 December 1874 – 7 July 1944) was a British academic, writer and Conservative Party politician. Born in Chichester, he was president of the University of King's College, in Windsor, Nova Scotia, from 1904-1906. In 1904 Campbell married American artist Edith Brand. After a spell in England, Hannah returned to America in 1915 to become professor of church history at the Oberlin Theological Seminary, Oberlin, Ohio. He returned to the UK again in 1925, to live on his family estate near Edinburgh. He was elected as Member of Parliament (MP) for the Bilston constituency at the 1935 general election and held the seat until he died in office in 1944. Hannah published several books, many with illustrations by his wife, including Sussex (1912), Berwick and the Lothians (1913), The Heart of East Anglia, and Capitals of the Northlands (1914), and The Story of Scotland in Stone (1934).
230 Information concerning the Sunday School in the later years of the twentieth century is taken from *Zoar Church Minute Book of Sunday School meetings Sept. 1966 to Sept. 2001*.

231 *The Messenger*, Vol. XXXIII No 9, September 1938.
232 *Sunday School Teachers' Meeting Minute Book 1919-1966*. Facts quoted in this chapter derive from this source, unless reference is made to the Trustees or Leaders, when the source will be the corresponding minute book.
233 The UMC had been encouraging its churches to take out insurance cover for some considerable time prior to this. See *UMC Minutes* (1913) p.393.
234 The Zoar statistics are incomplete because of gaps in the relevant minute books.
235 Mr Price Lewis, JP of Wolverhampton was one of a small number of lay members nationally who were appointed to serve as Chairman of a District in the UMC. He was regularly sought after by the Zoar trustees to conduct their Sunday School Anniversary Repetition services during the 1920s and 1930s.
236 The leaflet, dated June 1926, reported on the May District Meeting and reproduced a list of District Officers along with the detail of a *'Resolution on the Spiritual State of the District'*. Incidentally, the leaflet refers to the fact that the meeting took place during the General Strike with the consequence that travel was severely restricted.
237 The second was the issue of new housing. This was of interest to the Zoar Leaders with the building of the Stickley council housing estate on what was then the north western edge of the village. (See endnote 254 concerning the Stickley Estate).
238 *UMC Minutes* (1909) pp. 370-373. At the final UMC Conference of 1932 a report prepared by the UMC with its Wesleyan and Primitive Methodist counterparts followed the same lines. It was entitled *'A joint Commission of enquiry to formulate a constructive policy with regard to Sunday School work'*. (See *UMC Minutes* (1932) pp.374-382)
239 *UMC Minutes* (1925) p.307
240 *UMC Minutes* (1932) p.360
241 *UMC Minutes* (1925) p308
242 For comparison locally, within the Birmingham and Dudley District 46 of the 89 Sunday Schools reported the existence of training classes.
243 The UMC had begun publishing its own *Sunday School Lesson Magazine* in 1914. See UMC Minutes (1914) p.322.
244 *UMC Minutes* (1932) p.357.
245 A personal recollection of the author.
246 The Boys' Brigade, the first voluntary uniformed youth movement in the world, was founded in 1883. For information about its history, see, https://boys-brigade.org.uk/our-history/ (Accessed September 2024).
247 H. Smith, J. E. Swallow and W. Treffry, p.228. This book offers a comprehensive factual word picture of how the UMC came into being and its history through to the second union scheme of 1932 when the UMC joined with the Wesleyan and Primitive Methodist Churches.
248 See *UMC Minutes* (1907) pp.106-107 and (1908) p.305.
249 *UMC Minutes* (1908) p.110
250 The cards were retained in the Circuit safe.
251 There was a shared co-operation, '1. *In mutual defence; 2. In Christian, Moral, and Social Work, independent of all party associations and political creeds; 3. In the prevention of the unnecessary Multiplication of chapels, especially in small places; In the fraternal Development of Methodism in thousands of villages and small towns where it has at present no existence.'* See *Minutes of the First Annual Conference of the UMC*, London, 1908, p.353f.
252 Lake Street at this time was in the Brierley Hill Circuit, while the other three were in the Dudley Circuit.
253 Cliff College (still serving Methodism in the 21st Century) was a Methodist lay training centre for evangelism. Every summer it sent out mission trek teams for what were usually a fortnight of mission, led by a staff member.
254 This estate was built in response to the Government's post- First World War *'Homes for Heroes'* promise, which anticipated some 500,000 new houses being built and was enshrined in the 1919 'Housing and Town Planning Act' (Also known as 'the Addison Act' after Christopher Addison who was responsible for it). See 'Council Housing 1918-1939' in J Burnett *A Social History of Housing 1815-1970*, David and Charles, 1978, p215ff. Further information about the Stickley estate can be found in C. Lloyd, *A Home of their Own*, (Redwing Publishing, 2003) and A. Aitcheson, *Working Class Housing in Sedgley 1900 - 1923*, (2000).
255 *Resolution on the Spiritual State of the District* published in a leaflet reporting on the Birmingham and Dudley District Meeting, June 1926. The leaflet was distributed to members and churches along with a request that the text beread to congregations.
256 On the strike itself in the Black Country, see H J Haden 'The 1921 Coal Strike' in the *Blackcountryman*, vol. 4.4 (1971), pp.20-28 and L Rowbottom, 'The 1921 Coal Strike' in the *Blackcountryman*, vol. 5.1 (1972), pp.59-60.
257 M Higgs, *Life in the Victorian hospital*, (Stroud: the History Press, 2009), p.15.
258 Nationally £27,000 was raised in 1873 and in 1889 £41,000.
259 These included G B Thorneycroft, a local Methodist and ironmaster who gave the first £100 which launched the fund to build the Wolverhampton Royal. Thorneycroft one of the prominent Methodists invited to join the Trust body of the Wesleyan Methodist King Street chapel in Dudley following the MNC breakaway of 1835. See F Squires,'£100 launched the General Hospital, Wolverhampton' in the *Blackcountryman*, vol.3 no.2, (1970), pp.5-7. Also, A A Rollason, *Old Non-Parochial Registers of Dudley*', p.44.
260 This local hospital was brought into service in 1871 after buildings already in existence were purchased by local chain maker and philanthropist Joseph Guest. The buildings had been erected 22 years earlier by Lord Dudley and Ward with the intention of providing accommodation for miners blinded in colliery accidents. However the mining communities refused to have anything to do with the project. See http://en.wikipedia.org/wiki/Joseph_Guest#cite_note-3 (Accessed August 2024)
261 The hospital opened its doors in January 1st 1849 to 'patients who are such unable to pay for medicine and advice and are destitute of funds to make provision for them'. It was run by a non-stipendary Board of Governors and was totally reliant for its complete running costs on charity. See http://www.localhistory.scit.wlv.ac.uk/articles/RoyalHospital2/RoyalHospital.htm (Accessed September 2012. No longer active)
262 Some historians insist there was secrecy over how much was collected because there was too much. See, for example, J Farr, 'Who Stole our Gates' in *Picture Postcard Monthly*, (Nottingham, March 2010) No 371.
263 The LNU was a UK organization promoting peace and international justice, based on the ideals of the post First World War League of Nations.
264 In 1935 it organised a national peace ballot, when voters were asked to decide on questions relating to international disarmament and collective security. The ballot was not an official referendum but more than eleven million people participated in it, representing strong support for the aims and objectives of the League of Nations. The results were publicised worldwide. The results were not completely anti-war as those voting in favour of military action against international aggressors as a matter of last resort was almost three-to-one. See Peace Ballot - Wikipedia (Accessed August 2024).

265 The title 'preacher' was gradually replaced by the use of 'minister' and later 'presbyter'.
266 W Hill, *An Alphabetical Arrangement of all the Wesleyan Methodist Preachers*, (London: John Mason, 1838).
267 Land was eventually purchased in Summer Lane and a subsequent proposal to sell it rejected. However, it was not until the 1960s that a purpose built manse was erected on the site. It was sold some fifty years later.
268 *Minutes of the Methodist Conference*, 1968, p.178.
269 There were several photos displayed on the wall of the minister's vestry, all of which, except this one, were named on the back. It has been attributed to William Smith on the basis of the various roles and responsibilities he held, compared to others. Despite various enquiries, it has not been possible to achieve confirmation.
270 A F Viney, 'They are worthy' in *The United Methodist Magazine*, (London: United Methodist Publishing House, Nov 1927), p.335.
271 *Souvenir Handbook of the UMC Conference, 1932*, p.73.
272 A F Viney, op cit., p.336.
273 S A Williams, 'The Tennant Brothers' in the *Blackcountryman* vol.9 no.1, (1976), pp.59-60.
274 *Trust Minutes 1923-1949*.
275 It has not been possible to trace a photograph of William Lees. This is the splendid memorial headstone on his grave in All Saints Extension Cemetery, Sedgley. See https://www.findagrave.com/memorial/228733919/williamlees#source#view-photo=230350868 (Accessed June 2024).
276 *Dudley Chronicle*, 26th November 1925, p.5.